DIY: THE RISE OF LO-FI CULTURE

by

Amy Spencer

DIY: THE RISE OF LO-FI CULTURE

by

Amy Spencer

MARION BOYARS
LONDON • NEW YORK

First published in the United States and Great Britain in 2005 by
MARION BOYARS PUBLISHERS LTD
24 Lacy Road, London SW15 1NL

www.marionboyars.co.uk

Distributed in Australia and New Zealand by Peribo Pty Ltd
58 Beaumont Road, Kuring-gai, NSW 2080

Printed in 2005
10 9 8 7 6 5 4 3 2 1
© Amy Spencer 2005

A CIP catalogue record for this book is available from the British Library.
A CIP catalog record for this book is available from the Library of Congress.

ISBN 0-7145-3105-7
13 digit ISBN 9780-7145-3105-2
Set in Bembo 10/13
Printed by Bookmarque, London

With love to Kat and Dan and thanks to all the amazing people who answered my questions.

CONTENTS

INTRODUCTION

PART I: THE ZINE REVOLUTION

PART II: THE HISTORY OF DIY PUBLISHING

Punk
Punk Zine
Sniffin' Glue
Search and Destroy
The Impact of the Punk Zine
Post-punk
Maximumrocknroll

PART III: THE RISE OF LO-FI MUSIC

INTRODUCTION

I was fifteen years old when I first fell in love with the lo-fi ideals of do-it-yourself culture, with the idea of producing a zine or a recording for yourself and passing it on to others. I was excited by the thought that you could use the resources available to you – a piece of paper, a battered guitar, a cheap tape-recorder – to cross the boundary between who consumes and who creates. It was empowering to realize that anyone, however amateur, could produce something which would be valued as a finished product. In a society where the publishing and music industries are shaped by profit-margins, what is radical about the participants of this scene is that they simply want to exchange information about the bands, gigs, zines etc they have found exciting. The primary aim is to build unique idealized networks in which anyone can participate. Michal Cupid, an independent promoter from Bristol, explains that members of the DIY underground aren't, 'fixated with the promise of money, they are people who want to do something just to see it happen.'

When I first began to investigate the origins of the DIY ethic, I found that similar ways of working and familiar styles echo throughout different communities, repeating themselves over and over. The lo-fi approach appears in many forms: music, visual art, film, craft, writing, political activism, social protest. However, this book concentrates on underground movements where DIY and lo-fi ideals are translated into words and music: two fundamental areas where DIY culture has always had a long history and continues to flourish.

In the printed underground, zines are joined by independent magazines and newspapers, created with similar ideas and with the recurring ambition to simply put words into print. The 1930s sci-fi zine, the dada art zine, the chapbook created by beat writers in the 1950s, small-scale radical magazines of the 1960s, punk zines of the 1970s, the zine explosion of the 1990s, online blogs and guerilla newsreporting of today all started with individuals sharing a similar DIY ethos: the urge to create a new cultural form and transmit it to others on your own terms.

The DIY vision has become central to the underground music scene also, with the lo-fi ideals of skiffle groups in the 1950s, the punks of the 1970s, post-punk and the 80s indie scene enduring to the present day. Subverting the term 'hi-fi', 'lo-fi' music refers to a musical style in opposition to high production values. Encompassing an ideology that has been both championed and ridiculed over the decades, for some, this is the only way they are willing to make music, to others it represents an annoyingly shambolic, amateur style. It is, however, this celebration of the amateur that is at the heart of DIY scene in both music and literature – a celebration that continues today.

New technology has had a high impact on DIY culture, it is now easier to do-it-yourself than ever before. Though embracing the high-tech may seem in opposition to lo-fi creation, advancements like the internet enable a more far-reaching distribution of DIY publications than ever before. The independent ethos of the lo-fi approach has remained and the rise of the DIY movement continues. As Mark Perry infamously wrote in the punk zine Sniffin' Glue, 'Here's a picture of a chord and another one and another one – now go and form your own band!'. Whether your interest is music, literature or otherwise, it really is that simple to become involved. Well, why not?

Amy Spencer, 2005

PART I:
THE ZINE REVOLUTION

A Platform for the Individual

The Writer

Zines are non-commercial, small-circulation publications which are produced and distributed by their creators. Generally the zine writer is not a professional writer, nor are they being paid for their efforts, so who exactly is producing zines and why? The basic appeal of creating these home-made 'magazines' is easy to see – the opportunity to write whatever you want and tap into a willing audience, with no restrictions. The drawbacks are just as obvious – the time it takes to produce the zine as well as the costs involved. Many zine writers barely break even on their expenses.

Fredric Wertham, a New York psychiatrist, became interested in the fanzine phenomenon in the early 40s, while researching the links between psychology and literature. His work at first focused on the negative effects that popular culture could potentially have on an individual. He became well respected on the subject and was invited to give evidence before the Senate Subcommittee on Juvenile Delinquency in the 1950s. By the 1970s, he began to shift his attention to comic fandom subcultures. He tried to find out why people were publishing their own zines when they could instead be reading the mainstream commercial magazines. Instead of criticizing their work, he became intrigued by the fanzine founders – by their lack of commercial motivation and their celebration of the amateur writer. He later published these findings in his book *The World of Fanzines*[1] and is credited as one of the first people to be interested in the psychology of zine writing[2] – so the man who warned America of the dangers of popular culture became one of the first academics to be intrigued by underground publishing. In his book Wertham explains that: 'Zines give a voice to the everyday anonymous person. The basic idea is that someone sits down, writes, collects, draws or edits a bunch of stuff they are interested in or care deeply about, photocopies or prints up some copies of it and distributes it. The zine creating process is a direct one, remaining under the writer's control at all times. Perhaps its outstanding facet is that it exists without any outside interference, without any control from above, without any censorship, without any supervision or manipulation. This is no mere formal matter; it goes to the heart of what fanzines are.'

Zine writers are constantly asked why they write their zine. If they have something to say, why don't they submit their work to mainstream magazines and newspapers? The reasons are as varied as the zines they produce. Some aim to relieve a sense of boredom or loneliness. Some want to feel part of a wider community. Some want to discuss their personal obsessions. Others want to validate their lives and make people understand their way of thinking. There are also those who use zines as a means of distributing information and resources to others.

Money is rarely a motivation to start writing a zine, as they are frequently created on a small budget and sold for little or no profit. In reality, as many zine writers will not break even on their printing costs, it seems odd that they are willing to invest the time and money into these paper projects. However, after the initial idea to begin a zine, the process can become addictive. The writer has an outlet to express their ideas and experiences the enjoyment of physically designing the layout of the zine and putting together the finished product.

Since their beginnings in the sci-fi community of the 30s, zines have been traded amongst writers and it continues to be common practice for them to swap zines. This enables both parties involved to avoid commercial dealings and idealistically reverts the process back to a time when exchange of goods was more common than monetary exchange. A code of etiquette has therefore developed that involves sending trades, writing personal letters and reviewing each other's zines in your own. The zine is viewed differently from a commercial product. It resembles a gift more than a product, as it typically bypasses the profit motive. The flow of zines, and the personal network that has developed around them, resembles human contact. The zine is passed physically through the network connecting people together, sharing the sense of solidarity in their interest in the underground of independent culture.

Zine writing has thus become a culture in itself. Zine writers write about other zincs and often feature interviews with their writers. Writers such as Aaron Cometbus and Dishwasher Pete (see later) have become celebrities in the zine world.

As many zines document what is going on in a particular scene and with their origins as 'fanzines' being produced by self-proclaimed fans, the identity of the zine-maker can be problematic. Many may not want to be restricted to this role of fan. Particularly in the music scene, they may not want those who are producing the culture that they are writing about to view them simply as consumers who then rave about them in print. This is one of the problems of the zine experience, for writers to be taken seriously as producers in their own right.

Working away from a corporate culture, which divides the population into carefully researched demographics, zine writers form their own networks around their identities. Many writers create their zines as a conscious reaction against a consumerist society. They adopt the DIY principle that you should create your own cultural experience. It is this message that they pass on to their readers – that you can create your own space. Unlike the message of mass media, which is to encourage people to consume, the zine encourages people to take part and produce something for themselves.

The zine is run differently from a big commercial magazine, as the creators have the freedom of being able to produce what they what and when they want to without the pressure of deadlines. There is little censorship, and contributors make the most of this freedom. Zines come and go, they can appear for just one issue and then disappear. They are a temporal form of media, which isn't aimed at filling a commercially viable niche in the market but features whatever the writer feels like writing about. Sometimes, this can prove to be so popular that issue after issue is produced for decades.

As with many underground cultures there is a sense of possessiveness about zine culture. If a zine makes the transition into a mainstream magazine then it is often criticized, viewed with suspicion or seen as 'selling out.' Many feel that zines which do this are betraying the zine's amateur status, one of the things that is so celebrated in the zine world.

But is the ethos of the zine really concerned with producing an amateur form of media? It is interesting to look at the origins of the word 'amateur' which, although often carrying negative connotations, is derived from the

Latin word for 'lover'. These little known origins remind us that the amateur approach can be a more personal form of communication and does not have to be equated with sloppiness, an unprofessional production or a lack of talent.

Zine writers often write about their own personal take on the world and address social and political issues. It is also clear that earlier self-published newspapers and magazines of the 60s were indeed a very important form of journalism, one which contrasted the restrictive media of the time. But can the same be said of the zines which have been published since the emergence of punk at the end of the 70s, that mix serious journalism with the zine format? Many people have argued the valid point that zine writers cannot be said to be journalists because they are not professionals and are not being commissioned to produce their work. However, some zine writing is so articulate that it could easily stand alongside professional journalism. Not all zine contributors are happy to produce work in this style, there are those who work hard to set themselves apart from the mainstream. As the independent newspapers of the 60s worked hard to create an alternative to the established papers, many zines have attempted to provide a radically different alternative to mainstream magazines.

Though it is to an extent true that zines are open to everyone – anyone can publish their own work and anyone can read it – this is slightly over-idealistic. The thousands of zines currently available have content as diverse as sci-fi, music, personal confessions and political rants. However, the writers often fit a particular profile.

Many zine writers are employed in temporary or seemingly menial jobs where they feel little satisfaction. Some writers use this as material for their zine: writers like

Tyler Starr, who passes time at factory jobs by jotting down stories from his co-workers and sketching his surroundings for his zine, *The Buck in the Field*. He captures the lives of people working with no job satisfaction who are unable to leave due to financial constraints. Zine writers like Starr react against their experiences at work by writing zines – a creative outlet necessary to alleviate boredom.

There are countless exceptions but the zine tends to be written by a middle class, white population in their teens and early twenties. Many zine writers have challenged this assumption and produced radically different publications or have tackled the subject directly in print, but having the time and freedom to put together a zine is a privilege which many in this demographic do not question.

Zines can be criticized as being an elitist form of media. You can only have access to the information if you know exactly where to look, by talking to the right people or happening across a flyer or a zine being sold at a gig. Many people may miss out due to a complete lack of publicity and very small print runs. But the zine appears to be the perfect participatory cultural experience. Mainstream media can be, to some extent, bypassed and those involved in the scene can document their own history.

For many, the focus of zine writing is celebrating their position outside of the mainstream, having unusual interests, being a geek, rejecting the status quo. In his documentation of zine culture in *Notes from Underground Zines and The Politics of Alternative Culture,* Steve Duncombe claims: 'They [zine writers] celebrate the everyperson in a world of celebrity, losers in a society that rewards the best and brightest.'[3] It is this definition that best describes the position of the zine writers.

The Offbeat

That anyone can write about anything when producing a zine is both the blessing and the curse of the zine format. Some zines can be truly awful, scrappy illogical rants stapled together, others are brilliant and unique documents. As the historical development of the zine illustrates, the format can be used for any imaginable subject, and some of the most popular are those which defy classification. In some instances, before they begin writing the editors know nothing of the zine tradition and are simply inventing their own suitable format; thus creating almost by accident a publication that is recognized as a zine. These are often the best, these most cryptic and offbeat of zine offerings, giving an irreverent and truly individual perspective on the world from the writer's point of view. Amongst these zine-oddities is Mark Saltveit's zine *The Palindromist,* for people who write and read palindromes. Others focus on TV, such as *Geraldo Must Die!,* a rant against daytime TV talk shows, or the one-off issue in 1994 of *I Hate Brenda* by Darby Romeo, which was a zine devoted to attacking actress Shannon Doherty who played Brenda Walsh on the TV programme *Beverly Hills 90210.* Another quirky zine is *Convention Crasher,* where an anonymous writer sneaks into New York City's best trade shows using fake press passes and then writes about what he witnesses.

With zines being relatively easy to produce, it is evident that people will risk publishing almost anything. As they are radically different from the commercial magazine and don't face the same pressure to be commercially viable, and as there are no demographics, no markets, no profit and loss margins and no financial need to attract a large readership, writers don't feel they have to be too cautious in terms of what they print. Zines celebrate the idea that you can print anything and at least one other person will want to read it.

Murder Can Be Fun
Another zine that's certainly unique in terms of content is John Marr's *Murder Can Be Fun*. Where other zines may focus on music or community, this zine, named after a favourite Fredric Brown detective novel, is dedicated to the documenting of murders. Marr is a self-taught expert on the subject, spending his weekends doing extensive research in the library. He has written a historically accurate account of the Great Boston Molasses Flood of 1919 (in which 2.3 million gallons of molasses deluged city streets, knocking over buildings and killing twenty people); chronicled every death at Disneyland since it opened in 1955, every death to occur in a zoo and also written extensively about postal-worker killings (complete with graphs!).

The Duplex Planet
David Greenberger takes a different approach, and has the changed the way many people view the zine-writing genre. He fills the pages of his zine, *The Duplex Planet,* not with the reckless exploits of young punks, but with interviews with the residents of nursing homes with the aim of presenting the realities of the experiences of older people in America. The project first kicked off in 1979, when, after graduating with a fine arts degree, David Greenberger began working as activities director at a nursing home called *The Duplex,* in Boston. He assumed that he could include the residents in his passion for painting and help them to create their own work. What he found was unexpected and radically changed his assumptions about the elderly and ideas about art. Realizing that the

recreational facilities offered to the residents did little to challenge them, he connected with the residents by simply talking to them and asking, for example, what their fears were or what they thought about love. He began to produce a newsletter that encouraged the residents to write poems and answer unusual questions such as, 'What does it mean to sell out?', 'If *Gone with the Wind* didn't exist, what would be your favourite movie?', 'Would you swim in coffee if it wasn't too hot?', 'Who invented sitting down?' and 'Which do you prefer, coffee or meat?' These original questions, designed to provoke instantaneous answers, gave an insight into the minds of the residents. The answers were often surreal, almost visionary at times. Using humour to get to know the participants, and to encourage them to share their views, Greenberger used the newsletter as a form of emotional exchange, a means of connection. Although the questions were sometimes silly he never laughed at his subjects, instead trying genuinely to understand them.

He printed the answers to these questions in the newsletter. Originally intended to be just for the residents' entertainment, the readership of this newsletter soon grew. It was among his writer friends that Greenberger first discovered there was an interest in his project outside of the nursing home. Noticing that they were reading it as though it were literature, he realized that the writing had value and deserved to be published. The zine format was ideal for this project and he therefore began to produce little chapbook issues filled with writing, photos and illustrations, each with a theme, including subjects as diverse as coffee, gravity and broken hearts to Frankenstein.

The humour of the residents turned many of them into cult figures. They became characters that the reader could get to know through their responses. Greenberger was looking at them differently. He wasn't interested in compiling an oral history project, which concentrated on the memories of the residents' past while ignoring their present. Instead, he wanted to capture an essence of who they were.

It is human nature to try and connect with other people. But whereas most zine writers are typically trying to connect with others who are similar to themselves, Greenberger sought to communicate with people different from himself, believing that it was important to try and overcome the generation gap that may exist between young people and the elderly. In a culture where youth is so highly valued, and the ageing process so greatly feared, he uses the zine medium to explore the reality that people do not really change.

Although the Duplex nursing home closed in the mid-80s, Greenberger continued to work on his project and after moving to Upstate New York decided to interview residents in several nursing homes. His original idea has escalated, his zine has grown, and now his readers are able to understand what he first experienced when talking to the elderly residents and what they have to offer.

Although very different from any other zine printed before or since, *The Duplex Planet* has had a great following: achieving high numbers of readers and notoriety in the zine world. It has spawned a comic book series published by Fantagraphics, an anthology, entitled *Duplex Planet: Everybody's Asking Who I Was,* published by Faber and Faber, spoken word recordings, theatrical presentations and a series of concerts recorded for New York Public Radio. The residents themselves have become known outside of the nursing home. The often eccentric poetry of one resident,

Ernest Noyes Brookings, has been worked into the lyrics of many bands. Michael Stipe of REM was a subscriber and asked another resident, Ed Rogers, to design the lettering for one of their albums. Other residents have contributed to an exhibition of drawings and sculpture.

Dishwasher Pete

Dishwasher Pete's ambition is to wash dishes in every state in America and write about it. These written accounts have become his zine. Issue No. 7 finds Pete at a cafe in Boulder, No. 8 at an Alaskan fish cannery, No. 9 at a seafood restaurant in New Hampshire and No. 11 at restaurants in Montana, California and Ohio. He doesn't want the responsibility of a job he feels tied to and is happy to travel across the country working temporarily in each town. He loves the sense of freedom that it brings to his life, and relishes the addictive experience of walking out of jobs – as having few responsibilities he allows himself the freedom of spontaneous quitting.[4] He enjoys the drifting life, travelling across America in search of plates to wash. He is re-enacting the great American journey, glorified by the early pioneers, the hobo heritage, the beat generation and the hippies but coupling it with the sense of late 20th century malaise that seems so typical of young people's lives. Dishwasher Pete has discovered almost an underground workforce, high school drop-outs to college graduates working in backrooms washing dishes. He celebrates these characters and glorifies their work by documenting the history of dishwashing in his zine, from historical facts and literary references to dishwashing to the social attitudes the general public hold towards dishwashers today – attempting to give it the sense of seriousness that it lacks. He is a kind of guru among dishwashers. He enjoys this work and regularly finds others who are content with the job despite being surrounded by people telling them to find a proper career.

In many ways, he is typical of young zine writers. They often find themselves working in menial jobs, unwilling to 'sell themselves' to any employer and only prepared to work the minimum hours possible to get by, but wanting to do something different and, through the zine, having found a way of doing so. They can write down their thoughts and explore their everyday experiences and find an often-captivated audience. Dishwasher Pete is one of these zine writers. Through writing about the details of his life, the methods he has devised to pass time at work and the people he encounters, he has produced a zine that may at first appear trivial but in fact makes fascinating reading. Of course, though no one else writes a zine quite like this, there are countless other zines that chronicle an individual's life. Often people who feel that they have something to say, even if it is about themselves and they don't want to try and publish through conventional routes, become zine writers.

Dishwasher Pete's popularity, and the appeal of the offbeat zine, has transcended the underground world of the zine. Like many of the best zines, he has found an audience in the mainstream. In June 1996, he was invited to appear on American television on 'The Late Show' presented by David Letterman. Few watching the show would have realized that the man that was sitting chatting with the host was not in fact Dishwasher Pete, who was too shy to appear and had sent a fellow dishwashing substitute. He used the story as a feature for the next issue of his zine. Although he did not appear himself, Dishwasher Pete was the first zine editor to be invited on television.

The Personal Zine

As the zine moved quite rapidly away from being focused on one particular art movement, one specific music scene, just one band or one television programme, their writers became less interested in being fans and more interested in writing about their own lives. The zine moved away from being the 'fanzine' and became an important arena for writers to write about themselves and still find an audience. Many zines produced are of a very personal nature with those who often felt isolated due to their physical location or social pressures adopting the zine as a voice with which to explain their situation and a way to turn to others for support. Many similar zines formed a supportive network for their writers and these individuals gained a form of consideration rarely found elsewhere. The emotional punch of autobiographical writing made the personal zine a unique document.

Cometbus

Aaron Cometbus attracts a cult-like following. Viewed by many as a modern-day Jack Kerouac, he currently produces a zine called *Cometbus*; an autobiographical account of a punk kid growing up, of travels across America and life in punk houses. This zine succeeds in standing out as an original amongst the mass of zines in print by the virtue of the talent evident within Aaron's writing.

Cometbus was started by Aaron in 1983, when he was just thirteen years old. He has continued ever since, writing about his own life, his friends and the punk rock scene. Starting by printing five hundred copies at a friend's place of work, he could not have known what an impact his zine would have, how long it would run for, or the positive effect it would have on the zine scene. He just wanted to connect with the punk scene that was around him in Berkeley. As with many others, the zine seemed an ideal means by which to gain access to a music scene. By writing a zine you could be an insider, have direct access to bands and a means by which to communicate with others with the same interests. However, unlike other zines, *Cometbus* soon moved away from concentrating solely on music and started to include essays and travelogues as well as short stories. Aaron realized that the punk scene was not just about music, that the sense of community was also important. He saw that writing about people's lives and collecting their stories was an important contribution to the scene, and one which he was happy to make. He began to record the details of his own life within the punk community – the travelling across the country, the experience of living in squats, dumpster-diving for food and his adventures at punk shows. His zine soon began to bridge the gap between the punk zine and the personal zine. Like the best stories, he started to write about the major themes of life – falling in love, the strength of friendships and the struggle to live a life that is right for you. The zine has become a means for him to record his own life story, the photocopied hand-written pages feel like a letter to a close friend – one which his fans are eager to read.

Pathetic Life

Doug Holland's *Pathetic Life* is a different type of personal zine. Instead of celebrating his life within a community, it comments on his life apart from one. Living in San Francisco, Holland describes himself as 'unskilled, uneducated and unkempt, with missing teeth, a scraggly beard, old clothes and bad manners'. He chose the name for his zine from something an ex-girlfriend said to him, 'You've got no money, no friends, you live in a slum, you never do anything interesting and you're too damn fat to have sex. Your life is pathetic.'

In his zine, he records the details of his everyday life – how people treat him and how he feels as an outsider. He is the perfect example of someone who gave himself a (previously lacking) voice through his zine. In the everyday world away from zines, he is not paid much attention but through his zine he attracts readers who are hungry for more information. This zine predates the internet web journal but is very similar in terms of content.

Community Building

The Community

The impact of the small scale magazine, the self-published book or the zine lies not just in the act of producing the work but also in its distribution. For some writers, the zine experience ends with producing their zine and knowing it is being read. Chip Rowe, zine writer and author of *World Of Zines*,[5] believes that the zine is simply a magazine, not a cultural experience aimed at building a community: 'I don't think a zine is produced to build communities. It's produced to satisfy its creator. When it's made with anyone else in mind, it's a magazine.' Others disagree, believing that the fundamental purpose of zine-making is to reach out to others, finding a common bond and form alliances. For many writers it is this community-building that is the most important part of producing their zine. Networks are forged which serve to support not only the zine community but also artistic and activist activities.

Distribution is the biggest problem for the zine-maker. Once they have spend hours writing and putting their zine together they must find their readers. There are few places to sell them – only specialist record shops, in person at events or through a distribution company. It used to be that many zines were created almost in isolation, with little opportunity to circulate information about the zine beyond its founder's immediate circle. Many zines operated like this, just focusing on one local music scene because of the logistics involved in distributing it further afield.

Things began to change when a zine enthusiast called Mike Gunderloy, who was based in a small town in New York State, realized that there was a need for a publication that would review zines and list where you could buy copies. Having recently moved from the West Coast, where he had been active in sci-fi fanzine publishing, he stayed in touch with his friends through letter writing. He wanted to keep these friends up-to-date with recommendations of what he had been reading. After repeating himself in letter after letter, he realized that these lists could be mass-produced. In true DIY style, having identified the need, he decided that if anyone was going to produce this publication then it might as well be him. He named his review *Factsheet Five,* after a short story by English science fiction writer John Brunner. To begin with he reviewed sci-fi publications. Gunderloy saw similarities between different types of zines. Reading sci-fi zines in the early 80s, it became apparent to him that no matter what their subject, all of their creators evidently shared a similar sense of alienation from the mainstream press. When his research led him to a whole world of other types of zines, from the political to the humourous, he immediately realized that he enjoyed them too. He decided that in *Factsheet Five,* he would list all the zines he reviewed alphabetically so that zines with different subjects would be featured alongside one another and his readers would not be restricted by subject. Without Gunderloy's efforts, different types of zines would have remained in their subcultural ghettos and different genres of zine would never have merged.

The first issue of *Factsheet Five* appeared on May 4th 1982, with a print run of fifty copies, which he sent to friends. It was just two pages long and contained eight reviews. This quickly grew, however, as word began to reach zine writers that by simply sending their zine to Gunderloy, they would be reviewed and their readership would almost definitely increase. Before this point, most zines were sold by word of mouth. For the first time, zine writers became distinctly aware of each other on a much larger scale. Zines had previously been created almost in isolation. Zine writers from the same town may have known each other and zines were sometimes traded cross-country and overseas but no one really knew what was happening on a wider scale.

The popularity of *Factsheet Five* showed that there was certainly a need for such a publication, so Gunderloy began cataloguing the hundreds of zines that he received. He later referred to *Factsheet Five* as, 'the stupidest time-saving idea I ever had.' By the late 1980s, Cari Goldberg Janice joined *Factsheet Five*, first as art director and then as co-editor, and the newsletter was being produced bi-monthly with nearly a hundred and forty pages of reviews. The 1980s were the time when the number of zines in print surged. This was in part due to easy access by many to photocopiers, a relatively new form of technology, but also because now there was a strong network through which to sell your zine. It may also be that for the first time, through *Factsheet Five*, there was an indication of just how many zines were being produced, and many zine writers suddenly realized just how many others were producing zines.

Many zine writers can recall when they first discovered the medium of the zine. One such writer was Chip Rowe, who as well as producing the *Book of Zines* published the paper zines *This is the Spinal Tap Zine* and *Chip's Closet Cleaner*. He explains, 'My first influence, and for many zinesters, was *Factsheet Five* – I remember the moment I picked it up at the Guild Bookstore in Chicago – because that's how I discovered this community of people doing what I was doing. I didn't know it had a name.'

Gunderloy reviewed every zine that he received and sent free copies of the completed *Factsheet Five* to their creators in exchange. This method had its drawbacks as some readers thought that people were producing low-quality, unoriginal zines just to receive a free copy of *Factsheet Five*. Now zine writing became more accessible, it seemed easier, and hundreds of people were inspired to start their own zines. With so many people doing the same thing it was felt that there was strength in numbers and the zine community expanded rapidly. With the increase in zines, many critics believed that quality began to suffer as standards dropped. It was becoming so easy to produce a zine that people were not putting as much effort into their creations as earlier zine founders.

This increase in zines not only meant that zine readers had more choice, but that Gunderloy had much more work to do compiling *Factsheet Five*. After moving the operation to San Francisco, the job that he had set out to do became overwhelming and he quit in late 1991, after finishing his 44th issue. He confessed that by this point he was spending as much as fifteen hours a day reviewing all the zines he was receiving. 'I've reached the point where I can no longer invest my entire life in this project for the low [financial] returns it has been giving me lately.' As well as the time he spent on *Factsheet Five,* he also compiled his guide *How to Publish Fanzines* in 1988, which is now available in electronic format on the internet as a resource guide. Gunderloy and Goldberg Janice also co-authored *The World of Zines*[6], and began publishing books, such as Merritt Clifton's *The Samisdat Method,* about low cost off-set printing, as well as producing a compilation tape entitled 'Music for the Terminally Purplexed'.

Although Gunderloy realized that he needed to quit, he also knew that *Factsheet Five* was an invaluable resource for zine writers and fans and could not be lost. He sold it to Hudson Luce, an unemployed chemist from Kansas who claimed to be distantly related to the late magazine mogul Henry Luce. Luce's time working on the zine was brief and he completed just one issue. He found that the project was just too large and passed it on to former computer consultant R Seth Friedman in 1993. Friedman held ambitions to improve *Factsheet Five* and started by organizing it by subject and produced an index to each issue and continued running the magazine through the 90s.[7] In 2005, there are plans to revive the publication. It has found a new home in Arlington, VA and its new editors plan to produce a bi-monthly magazine with an estimated print run of ten thousand copies.

Not everyone believed that there was room for only one comprehensive zine directory. In 1993, John Labovitz launched his online E-Zine List with twenty-five entries. By 1999, it contained more than four thousand. Brent Ritzel began his bi-annual *Zine Guide* in late 1997 as an alternative. He did not know that *Factsheet Five* was struggling or that new editor, Seth Friedman, was finding the work-load overwhelming. Ritzel simply felt that *Factsheet Five* was becoming cynical and jaded. He found himself wanting to provide the alternative. He was not new to zines – he wrote a Chicago-based music zine called *Tail Spins* and during the process had been compiling his own database of zine information which he felt he ought to share. He took a different approach to *Factsheet Five*. Instead of simply listing or reviewing zines, he presented something more akin to a survey of the zines in print. Using the survey which he printed for readers at the front of *Zine Guide*, he produced a guide to his favourite zines.

Doug Holland, writer of *Pathetic Life*, began his own alternative called *The Reader's Guide to the Underground Press*, from his home in San Francisco. He was not aspiring to produce the next *Factsheet Five*. He wanted to review fewer zines and be completely honest about their quality. If a zine was bad, then he would say that it was bad. Most zines reviewed others well because of a sense of camaraderie, but Holland felt that this approach meant that there was a lack of quality control in the zine world.

Guides like *Factsheet Five* were vital in strengthening the zine world, making it much simpler for people to make contact one with one another and develop networks. Communication plays a key role in developing any form of community, in the zine world as much as anywhere.

Such resources have been of great importance in building the zine community. Stephen Duncombe recognizes that they are, 'absolutely critical. Without institutions like *Factsheet Five* that served as nodal points – or virtual community centres – there would have been either isolated publishers or scattered networks. By being able to see all these zines listed every month you not only had the ability to contact others outside your local network but you also had a much larger sense of being part of a real subculture – a zine world.'[8]

The networks that developed through zine distribution mirror in many ways the internet communities that exist today and can be viewed as one means that people found to spread information before the arrival of the internet. Within the zine world there are links from one publication to another, so the interested reader can follow a network, a trail much like the linked computer network. In zine distribution, the postal system is used as a mass means of communication and indeed the zine network has always been dependent on the postal system. This has developed from the mail art use of the postal network – the use of networks working through the postal system developed into other guises.

Not only do magazines like *Factsheet Five* attempt to tie the community together but zine distros have had an important part to play. The distro is a distribution centre for a number of zines, much like a little mail order shop. The distro became popular during the 90s riot grrrl era, when countless were run including collectively run Riot Grrrl Press and Ericka Bailie's Pander Zine Distro. The remarkable thing about the distros was that this wasn't just zine founders looking at ways to improve their own circulation figures, these centres were staffed by individuals who sometimes didn't even run zines, who simply wanted to 'help the cause' and work towards getting the information that they cared about out to the relevant audience.

Ericka Bailie's Pander Zine Distro, started in 1995, continues today. She explains that distros play an important role in the zine network. 'As anyone whose zines Pander carries can tell you, without the distro their readership wouldn't be what it is. Pander does all the hard work of making sure as many people as possible have access to your publication. I can often sell (around the world) more zines for one person than they've ever sold before.'9

She continues to explain that, although valuable, the distro does have its drawbacks. 'The major downside to this is the feedback factor: too many people think that because they've received a zine from a distro instead of the zinester this means they are exempt from having to write to the zinester about their zine. If no one ever offered feedback and made connections this scene would die.'

For Bailie, communication is a vital part of the zine writing experience. 'If you're not receiving feedback, what's the point? You wouldn't be involved in the scene at all, you'd just keep your publications to yourself. But the point is that you want to share, you want to experience that sense of community, because it's comforting (mostly) and exciting to find like-minded people who share your passion.'

Other projects have been run to increase the access people have to zines, working to strengthen the community. *The Zine Yearbook*, a yearly anthology of small press writing, was started by Jen Angel and Jason Kucsma in 1996, and is now in its eighth year. Each edition is a collection of excerpts from publications printed within a certain year and with circulation of less than 5,000 copies. This snapshot of independent publishing is produced in book format and distributed to shops making it much more accessible than many of the zines it features. This allows the general public a way into the zine world, thus alleviating a common concern among many zine writers who work to make the network as open to everyone as possible, without compromising its independent nature.

Zine writers have realized that the strength of the zine community lies in communicating directly with one another, helping to provide resources and shared knowledge so that other people can start to write their own zines. One such conference organized by Jason Kucsma in 1999 developed into the Allied Media Conference. An annual event giving all those working in all forms of independent media – zine writing, film making, art activism – a physical space to communicate. Such events put independent media in a stronger position to work against the corporate control of the mainstream. Only by working together can people form a strong alternative.

During the 1990s in the US the riot grrrl movement championed the zine as the ideal format to spread their collective manifestos and more personal viewpoints. In the spirit of bringing young women together to discuss their experiences and the impact of riot grrrl, the format of a conference seemed ideal. Conferences specifically devoted to the zine highlighted the importance placed on these little paper magazines that could be easily produced but could contain so much powerful information. Such events also tried to encourage wannabe zine writers to put pen to paper, so workshops were organized to give people the confidence and the push they might need in order to begin their own zine. Established zine writers gave talks on different aspects of zine-making and by supplying pens and paper and printing facilities encouraged others to get writing during the course of the workshop. Dozens of new zines began in this way, fuelling the increasing numbers of those already in circulation.

One organization working currently as a resource for potential zine writers to put their words into print is Grrrl Zines A-Go-Go. This organization was formed in 2002 and travels to community venues and non-profit organizations in San Diego and Southern California and holds zine and book-making workshops. Elke Zobl[10] is one of the main organizers of this group effort and she explains their aims:

'The group especially focuses on the empowerment of teenage girls through the production of zines and artist books. The DIY ethic is the cornerstone of the political aspect of Grrrl Zines A-Go-Go. We believe zine-making embodies the phrase "The personal is political" by encouraging active participation in the creation of one's own culture and independence from mainstream media. We think that this is especially important for teen girls who discover a new avenue for expression that is uncensored; something that they can produce alone, without the need for experts or expensive tools – their tools are their minds and a pen – anyone can do it. It is a truly democratic form of media; everyone who reads a zine can create one. Every reader should be a writer and zines make this possible, removing the fear of writing and emphasizing the process for each person.' Such an outlook illustrates how self-publishing is viewed by many as an activity to share, and not in any way elitist. The sense of community and co-operation which runs through the zine network is best illustrated by the presence of such organizations.

Zine Archives and Libraries
As zine writing developed over the decades the numbers of zines produced was immense. Those involved in zine networks realized the relevance of what they were doing – creating a valued alternative to the mainstream media. As well as the organization of zine conferences, zine festivals and workshops, zine resource centres have been set up where people can go and learn how to produce zines, and there are independent zine libraries where you can go and read vast zine collections. One novel idea aimed at exposing people to independent publications who might not otherwise see them, is the Bookmobile bus: a Vintage 1959

air-stream trailer which travels around America and Canada sharing zines. This volunteer-run tour takes a collection of artists' books, zines and other independent publications to promote non-corporate media to groups as diverse as schoolchildren, prisoners and the elderly, groups who may otherwise never see the potential of do-it-yourself publishing.

Over recent years other organizations have began to be interested in zine writing as a cultural phenomenon, and academic and public libraries, as well as online archives, have begun to work on archiving zines. Stephen Duncombe explains the need to research and archive zines, 'They are something that is a bit of an anomaly today: a culture that people produce and distribute themselves, instead of merely consuming something made by experts and sold by corporations. While zines themselves may be relatively unimportant, the implications of this DIY ideal are huge. What would happen if we all decided to produce politics in this way?' Viewing independent publications as historic documents that need to be preserved and researched is an idea that is growing in momentum. Zine writers have begun to donate their zine collections to libraries for preservation, following the lead of *Factsheet Five's* Mike Gunderloy, who in 1993 donated five hundred boxes of zines to the New York Library. In a sense, this work of archiving zines is grounding the zine network, providing a physical space for readers to experience a sense of the scope of the scene.

Elke Zobl, who documents zine history on her site grrrlzines.net, explains why she feels that the voices of marginalized groups producing zines need to be preserved. 'I am drawn to zines because they reflect the unfiltered personal and political voices of people from different backgrounds, countries and interests. We don't get to hear those voices, especially those of girls and young women,

women of colour, working class women, queer and transgender youth – in mainstream, adult-run media. Historically, these voices have been erased and forgotten and that's why they are so important to document and preserve.' She continues, 'Zines document not only people's daily lives and their participation in social and political life but also the cultural zeitgeist and certain historical moments. They are vivid and important examples of alternative self-publishing. Because print zines often have a short publishing lifetime and are difficult to catalogue, many libraries have not archived them. The same is true for online zines – they are not preserved at all. Right now I am working on a database to document and preserve e-zines for the future. In the years to come, grrrlzines.net will be important archival documents illustrating a long tradition of feminist alternative and grass roots publishing.'

Some zine writers feel that academic interest will dampen the creativity of the zine, confining it to academic circles perhaps, and archiving will lessen the sense of immediacy. Others view this interest as a valuable opportunity to preserve generations of zine writing.

The Queer Zine

In the 1970s, following the emergence of punk, those punks that were gay felt dissatisfied with the options of either participating in the hardcore punk scene or the mainstream gay scene. Neither scene was willing to accept them fully: they could either be queer in the punk scene or punk in the queer scene. As many individuals identified with both scenes, they realized they would need to create their own new and radical scene to challenge the accepted boundaries of each – and so Queercore was born.

The first zine with queer content began in New York in the early 1970s. Ralph Hall, an activist in the post-Stonewall radical gay movement called Gay Activists Alliance, produced his zine *Faggots and Faggotry* under the name *FIRM – Faggots International Revolutionary Movement*. The zine was filled with homoerotic line drawings, poetry and political commentary. The content was largely personal, including reflections on love, sexuality and politics. It was radically different from anything else being produced at the time and, in the early days of the punk zine, proved to be both different and shocking. As with the later riot grrrls, whose identification of a need for a very particular kind of zine meant their publications gained a wide readership extremely quickly, the queer zine rapidly evolved and, accompanying the growing numbers of queer individuals in punk music, became a force to be reckoned with in DIY culture.

The term 'homocore', which would later become interchangeable with the more inclusive word 'queercore', first appeared in the title of the influential zine by Tom Jennings and Deke Motif Nihilson in 1988. Dissatisfied with the current zines they were reading, which typically focused on the often macho, sexist and homophobic hardcore punk scene, they found inspiration in the writing of Bruce La Bruce and GB Jones.

JDs Zine

Lesbian filmmaker and musician GB Jones and her gay male friend Bruce LaBruce had begun their zine, *JDs,* a few years earlier in Toronto, Canada, in 1985 and filled its pages with news of the queer music scene that was beginning to take shape. They were disillusioned with the tendencies of punk culture to be tailored towards the straight male and were angered by its often overtly sexist and homophobic attitudes.

Neither did they fit into the traditional gay club scene, which dominated 80s gay culture and favoured music by pop bands such as Erasure and Boy George. Political action and social pressures had already begun to establish social spaces for gay people to meet and socialize but these had quickly developed into a homogenous culture with strict codes of dress and behaviour. Queer punks, such as Jones and LaBruce, experienced a sense of exclusion from these seemingly accessible spaces. Jones explains that, by the time they started *JDs* in 1986, '…all the *JDs* gang had been thrown out of every gay bar in Toronto… It was obvious we weren't consumers of the 'right' clothes, shoes, hairstyles, music and politics that the rigid gay and lesbian 'community' insisted on: we didn't subscribe to the racism and misogyny and their ridiculous segregation of the sexes, either. Plus we were poor.' [11] Such factors alienated the pair and their friends from the standardized gay experience. Without access to support from the gay community they needed to create their own alternative. LaBruce explains their position, 'We weren't so much trying to build a community as create the illusion that there was already a fully-fledged, swinging movement of queer homosexuals happening in Toronto, even though there was only two dykes and one lonely faggot.'[12]

He continues, 'One of the main impetuses behind *JDs* was to rant against the direction the punk movement was going in at that time. The early punk scene was much more adventurous and sexually experimental, particularly as it emerged in London and New York in the late 70s and Southern California in the early 80s. Like the early gay scene, it was a refuge for all sorts of people who engaged in nonconformist behaviour, from criminals to oppressed minorities to sexual outlaws of all stripes. By the mid-80s however, with the advent of hardcore, a certain sexual conservatism crept into the scene. The macho posturing of the speed metal heads and the skinheads and the other mosh pit habitués resulted in a regression to a kind of high school mentality, with the jocks on centre stage and the girls and fairies on the periphery like wallflowers. So with *JDs*, we tried to poke fun at the macho boys by putting them in compromising, homosexually charged contexts and pointing out the homoerotic nature of their antics. We would get visiting band members drunk and make them take their clothes off and take pictures of them with large phallic objects beside them and publish them in our movies and fanzines. We were brats in that regard.'

In response to their sense of alienation and exasperation at the narrow lifestyle choices offered to them by the hardcore punk scene and the mainstream gay scene, Jones and LaBruce turned to the traditionally punk medium of the zine to express their views. By creating *JDs*, they aimed to reach others with similar attitudes in order to network, share ideas and develop an alternative culture, which would blend queer and hardcore identities.

JDs is seen by many to be the catalyst that pushed the queercore scene into existence. La Bruce explains the reaction. 'Sitting behind our little desks at 3am in the morning with our glue sticks and scissors and pencils and take-out coffees, we never thought that our little fanzine would become an international phenomenon with fans all over the globe. We obviously connected with a disenfranchised minority within the minority who felt they weren't being represented.' The zine had a fairly long lifespan, it ran till 1992, and its influence exceeded these years in print.

Interview with **GB Jones**, co-founder of *JDs* zine and member of the queercore band fifth column.

Was *JDs* a conscious reaction against the punk and hardcore scene?

'*JDs* was a conscious response, as opposed to an unconscious reaction, to the punk and hardcore scene but bear in mind that those scenes weren't taken particularly seriously. Our goal, vis-à-vis the punk scene, was to antagonize.'

Were you consciously trying to build a queer community?

'Yes and no. We were vigorously uncompromising but aware that like-minded people were out there, ready for a change and astute enough to appreciate our aesthetic.'

Why do you think there was a need for a queer community away from the mainstream gay culture?

'Unlike the punk scene, which did manage to initiate its own culture, the gay world was largely in a position of being passive consumers of products not created by itself. Our projects were directed towards rectifying that situation for a select audience, to posit alternatives on various levels for those aware enough to appreciate the value of a self-determined culture and those alienated by the restrictive gay community. We were just as eager to provoke the gays and lesbians as we were the punks.

Mainstream gay culture is essentially a mirror of repressed straight society, of which I include large segments of the so-called 'alternative' scene. Foucault's notions of sexuality and gender interested me far more than the adherence to 'labels' that inhibit both straight and gay culture. Ideas about undifferentiated sexualities — the creation of an unfettered liberal underworld where all pleasures are possible – was my inspiration.

The gay community was, and still is (although to a much lesser extent, post-queercore), very segregated. Men and women didn't interact socially and magazines and other cultural productions were similarly separatist as policy dictated. Also, gay culture was entirely insular and most attempts at communication never strayed beyond the borders of that closed world. "Preaching to the converted" is the expression used to describe such limitations. Exceptions would be pleas for tolerance such as "We're human too!" and others of that pathetic ilk. *JDs* centred itself aggressively in the midst of various supposedly "straight" milieus like the punk, anarchist and fringe art worlds, welcoming any and all reactions. I'm opposed to that kind of restrictive self-ghettoization, as it's symptomatic of the repression of the individual that I think is intolerable.'

Did you expect the response you received?
'Having our mail constantly opened at the border and frequently seized made us aware that *JDs* was definitely causing a reaction. Being banned from the Montreal Anarchist Bookstore and having Toronto's gay bookstore, Glad Day, refuse to sell *JDs* also made us cognizant that we were regarded as incendiary. However, these attempts at censorship did little except fan the flames. Likewise, outraged letters about *JDs* that appeared in various publications only increased interest. If one applies one's will towards change, success is a definite possibility.'

Do you think the queercore scene has developed or changed since the 1980s?
'It has developed, largely on its own terms, as a visible and

43

viable alternative. And, whether it will continue to have an impact on mainstream gay society or more subterranean cultures will be dependant on the current crop of kids if that's a concern for them. The most important aspect of its evolution is that there now exists a complex, extant written, musical and visual culture that's been instigated and perpetuated by its participants, outside of the mainstream mono culture, that's unique and still as vital for those involved today as it was then.'

How important is the DIY ethic in queercore?
'An important aspect of creating your own culture is the ability to do it yourself. The means of self-representation are in your control, free from censorship and misrepresentation. It's an important step in developing one's aesthetic which is something few people seem willing or able to do these days.'

How important are zines as a means of communication within the queercore scene?
'Zines were, obviously, a significant instigating factor in the formation of many movements and subcultures, from the dadaists of the 1930s, to the punks and on up to the queercore scene. It's been an important first step, resulting in performances happening and bands forming, along with films and videos and other means of communication necessary for a movement's materialization. New zines continue to surface, preventing the stagnation that would occur without the influx of new ideas.'

Homocore Zine
JDs reached Tom Jennings and Deke Motif Nihilson in San Francisco who took the potential merging of the hardcore punk and queer identities as the title of their zine –

Homocore. Although they were based in the apparently queer-friendly city of San Francisco, they felt that their involvement in the punk and hardcore scenes made them outsiders. They explained their attitude in the introduction to the first issue, which appeared in 1988: 'We're outlaws if we don't follow the usual rules and don't want to be part of mass culture. We're mutants if we try new things, things that are honest and human, like making our own cultures, preferably lots of them, all with room for each other.'

Their punk attitude of being social mutants, opposed to mainstream culture, appears as their dominant attitude. They viewed their sexuality as only one part of their identity but one which limited them from finding their place in punk. The counterculture which celebrated the outsider figure and often used elements and images of queer culture was often wary of including the gay punk fully in the scene.

Followed by others who were similarly disillusioned by the choices offered to them, the queercore scene began to grow and take shape. Zines such as *JDs* and *Homocore*, as well as *Bimbox, Holy Titclamps, Scutter* and Vaginal Crème Davis' *Fertile LaToyah Jackson* became required reading material. These expressed the sense of dissatisfaction felt by many as well as championing the new queercore music scene that was beginning to develop. Zines acknowledged that their origins stemmed directly from the existence of *JDs* and *Homocore*. Larry Bob began writing his zine, *Holy Titclamps* in 1989 and explains: 'I was living in Minneapolis and in 1988 I'd found out about zines like *Homocore* and *JDs*. I'd been into punk rock, and I was out as gay, but didn't know many other people who shared both those interests. Those zines showed it could be done, but nobody else in my town was doing it.'[13] Those writers who began *JDs* and

Homocore made it possible for others in a similar position to realize that they could share what they felt with an audience by starting their own zine.

SPEW

A loosely connected network of creators who supported each other's work steadily began to develop. However, these individuals were not linked by one particular geographical location and so much of this support and sharing of work was conducted through the mail. People had managed to find the connections and support they were looking for but had few opportunities to meet one another face to face. This began to change in May 1991 when the first national queer zine gathering was held. Named SPEW by organizer Steve LaFreniere, this event held at the Randolph Street Gallery in Chicago was regarded as a watershed event in the history of queercore, bringing together a wide array of artists, musicians and zine-makers.

They adopted an approach different to that of a typical convention, feeling that it would place limitations on what they saw to be an important opportunity for networking. They explicitly listed that there would be: 'NO panels. NO workshops. NO keynote address. VANLOADS of noisy dykes and fags.' Instead, Randolph Street Gallery was divided into a display area for zines and merchandise, a video area and a performance area. Most of the major queer punk zines were in attendance, including *JDs*, *Bimbox* and *Fertile La Toyah Jackson*.

A second SPEW, organized by Dennis Cooper and others in Los Angeles, took place in the spring of 1992 and attracted even more participants than the first. The third incarnation of SPEW was held in May 1993 at the Buddies in Bad Times Theatre. The organizers tried to create a space that avoided the mere buying and selling of zines by holding a series of informal discussions which allowed people to talk and share experiences and new ideas. Performance was seen as an important feature of the convention and around three hundred people arrived for an all-ages show with local bands.

After the initial rush of queer zines during the late 80s and early 90s, this unique form of zine writing did not end. It has continued ever since, zines growing in numbers and influence, and being read by people across the globe. Like other zine forms, the queer zine has made use of the internet and now many more appear online. The subject matter has widened and the early queercore zines, having opened the discourse on sexuality, gender and identity, have been joined by transgender, transsexual and genderqueer voices.

Zine Feminism

Zine culture has primarily been male produced. As a product of its time period, it has historically consisted of male writers involved in sci-fi fandom, 60s independent newspapers and those at the forefront of punk. Eventually, women who were interested in the potential power of independent media but did not see their own experiences reflected in the existing publications decided to produce their own. Many decided to focus on feminist issues, which they felt had not been given attention in either the mainstream or underground press.

This boom in feminist publications began in 1970 with *It Ain't Me Babe*. Published in Berkeley, America, *It Ain't Me Babe* lasted just a year, but its anger and energy was contagious. It inspired writers in Washington DC to produce *Off Our Backs* a few weeks later and this quickly became one of the most respected feminist papers of the era. The next to generate interest was *Ms.*, which made its debut in 1972. This glossy magazine has been criticized as being more conservative than others of the generation but still held an important position amongst the pioneers of independent feminist publications.

The Riot

Third wave feminism attempts to take notions of feminism away from any stale academic assumptions and tries to make it relevant to the lives of all women. These early feminist magazines are part of an earlier tradition, vital in establishing the presence of women both in society as well as in the independent publishing world. The riot grrrl movement of the early 90s was a part of this third wave ambition and organized a subculture of young girls who wanted to express themselves and their experiences as well as their feminist beliefs. They used the zine as an important tool with which to explain their ideas, print their manifestos and call for others to join their growing culture. The term 'riot grrrl' was first used in zines by musicians and activists in America – Kathleen Hanna from Bikini Kill (and later Le Tigre) and Allison Wolfe from Bratmobile. They presented this as a clear cultural vision and printed their aims for realizing its potential in riot grrrl manifestos, which then appeared in their zines.

Kathleen Hanna's own manifesto, printed in her zine, explained her realization of the need for the riot grrrl movement: 'BECAUSE us girls crave records and books and fanzines that speak to US that WE feel included in and can understand in our own ways. BECAUSE we wanna make it easier for girls to see/hear each other's work so that we can share strategies and criticize-applaud each other. BECAUSE we must take over the means of production in order to create our own moanings. BECAUSE viewing our work as being connected to our girlfriends-politics-real lives is essential if we are gonna figure out how what we are doing impacts, reflects, perpetuates, or DISRUPTS the status quo.'

These ideas found their way to the audience of both Hanna and Wolfe's bands and the scene began to gain momentum. Here women redefined feminism for the 90s and recognized each other as manufacturers of culture as opposed to participants in a culture that they were forced to accept. They were encouraged to reclaim the media and produce their own cultural forms.

As well as by forming bands, one of the primary means for them to produce their own cultural experience was by producing zines. This process allowed them to assert their independence while at the same time calling for others to join them. The zines that they produced were unique in that they focused on the experiences of young girls who spoke frankly about their experiences. Influences for these zines were taken from the whole history of zine culture. They most closely resembled the punk zines of the late 70s, versions of which were still being produced as grunge grew in popularity and was driven by many of the same ideals. Riot grrrl zines were also similar to the early dada publications, as part of their stand against mass media involved them taking and subverting images from mainstream magazines, such as fashion features or advice columns; a similar practice to the dadaists' reworking of recognized mass cultural images for their artistic goals. Many writers would have felt that the zine medium was theirs alone and had never been used before. This is part of the beauty of the zine. It can be used as a blank model for people to capture their own experiences and ideas in print.

The riot grrrl scene was always wary of any media interest, sensing that their actions would be distorted by the mainstream press and that they would be represented as hysterical women. The issues that they tackled were weighty, such as feminism and sexual abuse, and it was felt that these would be trivialized in media accounts. They were concerned also that certain bands would be celebrated in the music press as new and exciting only be ignored once the novelty of girls creating music wore off. To control their own media representations, the instigators of the scene, as well as others who caught their infectious enthusiasm, decided that through zines they could create their own form of supportive community. In 1992, a media blackout was called by the key figures in the scene where no one involved was encouraged to speak to the mainstream media. Zines were now vital in spreading the ethos to new audiences. The bands provided the soundtrack to the scene and zines was the means of sustaining the unique social networks that developed.

British zines such as *Ablaze*, written by Karen Ablaze, and Erica Smith's *Girlfrenzy* were linked to this new wave of riot grrrl zines as they drew strength from what was happening in America. *Girlfrenzy* began in around 1993 as a means to get women to participate in the arts. Smith explores her motives for starting the magazine, 'I wanted to encourage women to write and draw and perform because (particularly ten years ago, but even now), women tend to be more reluctant than men to push their work out to an audience. *GirlFrenzy* pre-dated riot grrrl, and things have changed a lot since then.'[14] Her aims were clear, and mirrored the ambition of riot grrrl zines – to encourage women to begin to publish their own work. These type of zines returned to the collective approach to zine-making which disappeared slightly during punk in the 70s. Once more, the need to try and support each others work called for a collective effort.

Other zines associated with riot grrrl realized how important it was to empower girls through zines. One in particular was *FAT!SO?* – Marilyn Wann's manifesto for fat empowerment, calling for women to be happy with their bodies and challenging anyone who disagreed. Started in July 1994, this zine developed a few years after riot grrrl began, but encapsulated the motives for many of the zines started by the riot grrrls. The popularity of this zine proved that young women were waiting for this form of media.

That these young women turned to riot grrrl zines as a form of mutual support is described by Elke Zobl: 'I can say that overall grrrls turn to zines for a variety of reasons: for personal expression, an outlet for creativity, to break out of isolation, in search of friends, a community and network, and as a form of cultural and political resistance. For many, especially those living in small towns in the middle of nowhere, zines are a great way of connecting with like-minded folks around the world, without ever meeting them in person. Zines are a way of saying: "You are not alone! Come share your experience and we'll learn from each other!"'

Zobl continues, to explain that this sense of reaching out for a sense of community is universal and that while riot grrrl zines may seem to have died out by the end of the 90s, they are still being produced today. 'Although zines (as well as riot grrrl and grrrl zines) have been declared by some as dead, I am still finding lots of amazing grrrl zines and won't buy into the "zines are dead" cry. If you look at zines with

an international perspective, you will see that there are
many more zines created which fall under our radar
because they might not have a website, may not be called
"zines" (*samizdat* for example), are written in a language
you don't speak and are circulated in local networks. Just
recently I found young women currently creating zines in
the United Arab Emirates, Peru and Israel. And I think this
is so exciting to see that young women in so many places
create their own zines. So I think zines are very much alive
and thriving! You just have to make the effort to find them!'

New Feminists

Towards the end of the 90s, the third wave of feminists
began to truly find their voices through the riot grrrl
movement. As the movement grew in strength and the
potential for a large audience was realized, zines began to
broaden their scale. In particular, *Bust, Bitch, Venus Zine,
Chickfactor* and *Rockgrrrl* emerged – zines which developed
into slick independent magazines but retained their
underground ethos. This new wave of female-published
magazines came directly from the riot grrrl movement but
lost many of the characteristics such as the cut and paste
style and the angry ranting articles. This was a more grown
up version of the riot grrrl publications. Although
continuing to be self-produced, these later publications
typically refer to themselves as 'magazines', drawing
attention to the fact that to be taken seriously, many felt
you had to move away from your zine origins.

Each of these magazines focuses on issues affecting
women, as well as looking at female musicians and artists,
from a feminist perspective. Such magazines allowed young
feminists a channel through which to network and the
writers enjoyed the liberating zine-experience of being

able to print whatever they wanted. Fed up with being misrepresented in the mainstream press, the importance of the community that they created cannot be underestimated. This new network of zines coincided with the indie zines of the 90s, as the communities now forming were similar and with many overlapping principles.

Interview with **Lisa Jervis** of *Bitch: A Feminist Response to Pop Culture* – a zine which has grown to a magazine (with a print run of 45,000 copies in 2003).

Why did you decide to start Bitch? How did you go about setting it up?
'My coeditor, Andi Zeisler, and I were basically sick of our day jobs and sick of our love/hate relationship with pop culture. We wanted a public forum in which to air our thoughts on what was all wrong (and the few things that are right) with the way women, gender, and feminist issues are treated in the media.

We really just dove into it without knowing what we were doing or knowing what we were getting into.'

Which zine or magazine has most influenced you?
'I was a huge fan of *Sassy* back in the day. It was thrilling to see a glossy magazine for girls that dared to contradict the others of its kind by running more serious articles, making fun of fashion and beauty coverage (even though they had it too), and being a lot less prescriptive about behaviour.

Certainly seeing the vast array of zines out there was something that, when we started, clued us in to the world of possibilities in self-publishing. It was fantastic to feel a part of this community of alternative women's magazines that started just before and right around the time we did: *Bust, Hues, Maxine*. Sadly, two of those are gone now, and others have come and gone (*Fabula, Moxie*), but more are popping up all the time (*Fierce, Venus zine*).'

What style and content decisions did you make while developing *Bitch*?

'We really wanted it to look nice, and as slick as possible with the resources we had (which at first were really not a lot, in terms of both money and equipment but also experience and savvy). We drafted our founding art director, Ben Shaykin, who was just starting out in his design career at the time. The three of us all have a real affection for and excitement about magazine conventions, so we wanted to use those as much as possible. We obviously had (and have) huge issues with the content that many magazines (particularly women's magazines) feature, but we've always embraced the modes of presentation that glossy magazines use.

At first we were really far from that, with a half-legal size and no colour at all--and what look like in retrospect some really amateurish choices. As we grew we got more experienced and were able to improve the production.

The content, on the other hand, is conspicuously opposed to many glossy magazine conventions: we don't cover new products at all. We don't run big pictures of stuff. Our articles are all about stuff to think about rather than stuff to buy or stuff to do (i.e., service journalism).'

Why did you decide to distribute the magazine on a large scale rather than writing a smaller scale zine?

'That was something that came organically out of the growth of the magazine. Our first print run was three hundred, and we distributed it by me putting them all in the back of my station wagon and going around to local bookstores and asking if they would put it on the shelves. It did well and they started telling their distributors about it, and we had also contacted feminist bookstores nationwide, and they started to pick us up and also tell their distributors. So we picked up some other distribution channels and kept growing – from 300 to 1000 to 1500 to 2500, and so on. We increased the size to something more standard, added colour of the cover, got a barcode, got more and more distributors...it was a natural process, and it was always spurred by demand from the stores. It wasn't really so much of a conscious decision as an evolution.'

What do you consider be the state of mainstream women's magazines in the US? Were you consciously creating an alternative to these magazines?
'Sometimes it feels like those magazines have changed – actresses instead of models on all the covers, racier coverlines, a little more diversity of body type in the fashion coverage – but really, those are fairly superficial things. The raison d'etre of these magazines – to sell makeup and clothing and whatever else to their readers on behalf of advertizers – hasn't changed.

We definitely see ourselves as creating both an alternative to and a response to these glossy women's magazines.'

Do you think zines can successfully build communities?
'They definitely can. I certainly feel like *Bitch* is a part of a community of independent publishers, as well as a smaller sub-community of independent feminist publishers. There's a lot of support and ad trading and advice-giving and resource sharing etc that goes on and I know those things are going on everywhere.'

Do you feel that *Bitch* is part of the zine community?
'I don't think there's anything coherent that could be called "the zine community" – people have too many strong and conflicting opinions on what's a zine and what's a magazine and all the issues that go along with that.'

Is *Bitch* a zine or a magazine?
'I think of *Bitch* as a magazine, because our goals have always been growth. I know that some people would never consider us a zine because of our size, the fact that we have colour or because we have a barcode. People have their own definitions of what makes a publication a zine or not. My favourite definition of all time comes from Tom Lupoff, who was the magazine buyer at Cody's in Berkeley and then worked for several small distributors before starting his own distribution company. He always said that a zine was something done for love and not money. Even though *Bitch* is my full-time job now, that has always been the case for me. By that definition we're still and will always be a zine.'

What do you see to be the limitations of zines – either in paper form or on the internet? Do they exclude anyone?
'The internet obviously has higher barriers to entry (for both readers and makers), but once you have internet access and a computer, then it's cheaper and easier to make or read something online than in print. But both take resources, no doubt about that. For me, part of the beauty of print is that anyone with five dollars can just walk into the bookstore and get one.

A whole other element is readership – and yes, zines are exclusive by nature, in that they tend to be about niche topics.'

What impact do you think the internet has had or will have on zines and magazines?

'It's made it much easier to find out about them, and to connect with other people making them. It is easier to make a zine now because you can do it online if that's easier for you, or you can get access to advice and info about making a print zine. People thought that the internet was going to herald the death of print, which was a crock even in the boom days. The feeling of a printed document is never going to lose its appeal or be replaced by an electronic alternative.'

Both *Bitch* and *Bust* magazines have made the move onto the internet, whilst also remaining available in paper form. Other third wave feminist writers have made the decision to only publish on the internet, making use of the new technologies available to them. 'The F Word' is one such website. Published in Britain, it focuses on the experiences of third wave feminists. As a form of independent media, it can publish whatever it wants without any constraints.

Mama Zines

The rise in popularity of the zine has meant that more people have been inspired to start their own. One such group which has found, through zine-making, a means to write about their experiences, is parents. The popularity of zines over the past thirty years has meant that many of those who have grown up reading them have now started families. Faced with this new experience, several turned back to the zine format to record their new lives. If people wrote zines with boundless enthusiasm about the latest punk bands then once they had children, and being a parent became a fundamental part of their identity, there was no reason why they shouldn't also want to record this new experience. This followed a growing trend of discussing alternative parenting, which began in the 1960s and 70s. The counterculture of this era affected parenting values and many people were looking for a way to bring up their children that worked alongside their social and political beliefs.

In 1990, a young single mother of a two year old daughter started her zine *The Future Generation*. After living within an anarchist community, China Martens had become used to a particular way of working with people, of supporting one another and sharing resources. On becoming a young mother, she felt isolated. She explains, 'I was in new territory and felt a total minority group. Most punks weren't parents and most parents weren't punks.

I felt I was in the middle of a revolution – so many things were changing from the way I had seen when I was growing up. Ways of acting, thinking, and living. Ways of approaching injustice. Almost everyone I knew didn't want to be like their parents, so then when you turn into a parent – having basically rejected the society one grew up in – how do you parent? There's something about motherhood that changes your world completely, and the way you found you could live as an independent "liberated" individual doesn't quite work the same way anymore. You get left out and left behind. Especially because as a subculture parent I was in the total minority. I was never in the beginning of punk but so many people talk about how in the beginning you could identify others by simply looking at them: it was an "us against the world" mode (for better or worse) at some point; when I became a mom I felt like that, if I saw anyone different, let's say sitting on the curb breastfeeding their child, I was like, "Hey, let's be friends!" or at least "How is it going with you?" '[15]

She was looking for a sense of community. 'I was writing to try to build community – to find a few other people even – that was the whole point, to communicate with others.' It is this sense of isolation and the urge to join a wider community that often attracts people to publish their own words, to reach out and find similar people and express what they are feeling. For China, this was coupled with her frustration at the lack of resources available for people like herself, who wanted to raise a child from a punk perspective. She saw the zine as 'a punk and anarchist medium', and one which was perfect for her needs to explore her new vision.

It was this need that motivated her to start her zine, which she filled with her own personal experiences as well as lists of childcare resources and articles on her vision of how to raise a child without compromising your own values. Although previously involved with a community where zines were common, she explains, 'I wanted to start a zine about motherhood because it was the biggest issue affecting my life and how I saw the world – this was before the internet – I wanted to communicate with others about our experiences in the world, the ideas we were part of, and share resources. I pretty quickly identified that we needed a support system and we needed to create awareness. I was growing as a person, at this time the culture around me seemed as much about building our own positive alternatives as about rejecting and protesting the negative dominant social system around us.' To China, writing her zine was a political act. 'My highest aim was to push this society to be a better place for my child, to resist the dominant war like exploitative capitalistic systems as a rebel mama, to create a support network and alternatives like Squat Daycare or something. I don't think my highest aims were achieved but then I was still coming from a more youthful and idealistic state – ask anyone what were their aims at age twenty-two... You know what I mean? Especially coming from a background of growing up in the Reagan Era and taking part in protests. Things were kind of wild sometimes. Then again, some of the fires of resistance have been kept burning and some communication has come out of my zine – but it's been a small thing. At the same time, it was my birth of a zinester and of sharing my writing – and that is something that goes on with me. I see awareness growing all the time around me of motherhood, parenting, and youth issues – so things are moving along. Was my zine a part of this? I don't know really. It never was that big. But then again, diverse small autonomous personal communication... these little effects matter.'

This sense of a change in parenting values was felt by many other parents, from those who hungrily poured over the details in her zine, to those who started their own. China realizes that those who have joined her and produced their own zines are part of a growing movement of parent zine writers. 'There is a diversity in parenting zines, of course, this subject is broad you know? Smash alienation. It's so hard, you know, it's still so very hard.'

Hipmama is probably now the most well-known of parenting zines. Started by Ariel Gore in 1994, when she was a single mother on welfare and a full-time college student, it began life as a print zine and has now grown to include a website. In 1996, Bee Lavender asked if she could produce hipmama.com, and included discussion boards, as well as girlmom.com, mamaphonic.com and Yo Mama Says. Sticking to its original aim, it explores the experience of being a parent, and not just a rosy, idealized version of parenthood. It tries to represent all forms of family and explore the issues which may not be addressed elsewhere. For those who have grown up reading and writing zines and living in praise of independent culture, it is a valuable opportunity to see that there are others living similar lives and facing similar challenges. Other young mothers began producing zines about their experiences, including Katherine Arnoldi who created her graphic novel *Amazing Story of a Teenage Single Mum* in 1998, based on her experiences of having a baby at seventeen years old.

The zine *The East Village Inky* by Ayun Halliday has a different perspective, as it explores the life of one particular family in New York City. As with all zines, the first in the generation focuses on the direct need for information and support and then, once this is covered, the next zines are freer to explore their subject.

Interview with **Ayun Halliday** on *The East Village Inky* and parenting zines.

How long have you been involved in writing zines? Was The East Village Inky your first zine?
'I'd always wanted to write one, but could never find a subject that was compelling enough to sustain the enormous amount of labour that producing one requires.

I doodled around with a couple of one shots that I handed out to five friends or so – a poetry zine that I xeroxed at work, a little booklet called *Nature* that I made when I was on a writing retreat on a mountain in New Hampshire. There was only one other woman there, and I was there for free because I had agreed to feed the benefactor's cat while she was on vacation. Every morning I would discover the previous night's feline trophies: the dismembered carcasses of baby bats, baby bunnies, field mice... I was already scared to be out there all alone in the woods and these little corpses just about sent me over the edge... so rather than writing the "NOVEL!!!" I was supposed to be working on, I made this little zine about finding dead animals and my nervous walks through the woods.

All this to say, yes, I suppose *The East Village Inky* is what counts as my first zine.'

What were your original aims for this zine and do you think you achieved these?
'I'd spent nearly every weekend for the decade leading up to my daughter's birth performing my own material in this rag tag late night show called "Too Much Light Makes The Baby Go Blind". The show had attracted a cult audience and in my own small potatoes way, I had the pleasure of knowing that my work had regular, repeat consumers who were not personal friends of mine. Finances and the desire to spend as much ape-like quality time with my baby meant that this outlet was no longer available to me post-partum. So, I sought to have a creative outlet that would be read (and hopefully admired by others). I wanted to get mail where once I got applause. I wanted to at least break even on the money issue. I wanted to be reviewed in publications that review zines. And I wanted it to feel like fun... the writer (and former zine publisher) Pagan Kennedy referred to this as that tongue-between-teeth feeling of concentration a child enjoys when wholly consumed by some project.'

How important was it to you to build a community or were you, at first, writing for yourself?

'I place a high value on community and romanticize it and don't always achieve it. I've got lots of little communities – my kids' wild and woolly public school, my friends from college, people who write zines and the sort of books I do... and then the people who read them too.

There's a stage where I write for myself (foreplay), but the money shot is when someone else reads the book, sees the show, buys a friend a gift subscription to the zine.'

What do you think of the wave of parenting zines being produced today? Do you feel part of this?
'I think they're all helping to keep their publishers wigs on straight during the most trying years of raising small children. Some of them stand out due to their writing – there are a lot of universals to the behaviour of small children and the adults who serve them, so when someone brings a fresh, specific perspective to the piping public profanities, the refusals to eat, the endless adventures in excrement, that's true artistic achievement! Some of my favourites are *Housefrau, The Future Generation* and *Stretchmarks.* There's a really spiffy looking one called *Mamalicious* that I like too – it seems like it has the potential to become *Bust* for mothers.

I do feel part of it, partly because many of the fledgling publishers are kind enough to send me a copy with a letter saying that *The East Village Inky* was an inspiration. *Hipmama* and *The Future Generation* were around for years before I came along (I discovered them when I was trying to promote my early issues). I think maybe those two with *The East Village Inky* inspired some people to take up creative arms against a sea of troubles...

Another thing I'll say for parenting zines is that they ensure that early childhood is documented in some way.

My diary entries that were numerous before I had children are now non-existent. Most of the pictures are smiling and/or celebratory. Zines can document the nitty gritty as it unfolds. Then years later you delve back into an early issue and are shocked at all the details you'd forgotten, recorded for the ages in the zine. A copy of *The East Village Inky* mulched into view the other day when I was putting up new shelves in my bedroom – I hadn't seen one of those in at least four years. What a blast from the past – there was this whole detailed section about the choreography of getting visitors into the crowded entryway of our three hundred and forty square foot East Village apartment – our friend Sarah stepping into the bedroom immediately because she knew she couldn't fit past the kitchen counter with her baby-backpack carrier, her husband's shoulder scraping the clock off the wall, Inky tumbling around underfoot...the minutiae just slips down the old mental drain when it isn't compulsively set down...'

Craft

As riot grrrl zines are decreasing in numbers, many of those people once involved in the zine community are moving into a new form of DIY endeavour. The act of crafting – sewing, knitting, doing crochet and in fact any form of craft as long as you can do it yourself – has recently taken over. The trend has made use of the trail established by previous DIY cultures and zines and blogs have been produced about the crafter's activities.

Betsy Greer of the craft blog Craftivism.com, explains her own DIY heritage: 'As a teen, I was really involved in riot grrrl and see definite parallels in the craft community now that I saw with punk and DIY culture ten years ago.'[16]

This is a new phrase of independent culture, one which is closely connected to zine culture. Whereas a decade ago, young women in the punk underground were predominately writing paper zines, in the early years of the 21st century, many are sharing craft tips, patterns, designs and recipes with one another using a self-publishing network. As with zine culture, the channels are rarely commercial, they are people sharing resources and ideas with another independently from the cultural mainstream. Paper zines exploring craft, both theoretically and practically, are being written and distributed along the existing zine network. The majority of these craftsters are, however, distributing their work and ideas via the internet. As zines are finding their place online, many of those active in the craft community are looking first to the internet as the ideal place to share their ideas.

Betsy Greer's Craftivism.com, Leah Kramer's craftster.org and Jean Railla's Getcrafty.com are just a few of the multitude of sites, forums and blogs dedicated to the new wave of craft. Their creators adopt many characteristics of the zine format, expressing their own personal views independently of the mainstream media while at the same time reaching out for interaction with those who view the site. The discourse created between creator and reader is blurred as interaction is encouraged. One dominant feature of such sites is the use of online forums, where those who view the site are asked to share their own crafting ideas. This interaction, as it was as part of the zine community, is of vital importance here. The sharing of ideas and skills is fundamental to this craft community, which promotes accessibility and community – key aspects of the DIY movement as a whole.

For many, this new wave of craft as a lo-fi activity, is a

form of feminism. Jean Railla of Getcrafty.com explains in the introduction to her recent book, her attitude that this resurgence of craft activities is a form of 'new domesticity' – a way for women to link feminist principles with the idea that crafting is an enjoyable and valued activity and one which should not be rejected as part of a oppressive culture. She writes, 'Get Crafty is a manifesto for what I call the "New Domesticity", a movement committed to recognizing, exalting and most of all enjoying the culture that women have built for millennia.' [17]

Those involved attempt, in part, to reclaim the idea of domesticity and the skills that were passed down previously by women within families.

Greer feels that far from being a passive activity, it is a revolutionary and political act. As she sees it, 'Craft has taken on a revolutionary role. Instead of knitting, weaving or sewing because we have to, with all of the technology that is available, people are *choosing* to. It is in this choice to spend one's leisure time making something that could be easily purchased where there is resistance.' This sense of resistance and activism has always resonated through the DIY community and encompasses many of the celebrated features of lo-fi culture – that the pleasure of producing something yourself on your own terms can also be a conscious rejection of oppressive cultural and political values. Greer continues, to explain that this new wave of craft and craft writing in the underground community is not entirely new. 'It has to be recognized that thinking about craft as a political act is relatively new, which is why I want to study the past two hundred years or so of craft, in order to better understand the timeline. It's especially interesting when paired with the feminist movement, as well as craft resurgence in times of war.' In linking the current craft revival with current social situations, Greer makes an interesting point. Just as previous communities have been driven to self-publish by social conditions, many in recent years have similarly adopted the tradition of crafting as a form of resistance.

She explains further: 'One of the best things I read when I started to think about all of this was Faith Gillespie's piece in the book *Women and Craft* (1987). Especially this quote, 'Our turning to craftwork is a refusal. We may not all see ourselves this way, but we are working from a position of dissent. And that is a political position." And then I began to realize that maybe I was actually on to something instead of just thinking too much.'

There appear to be parallels between the changes in zine networks and this new craft movement. Not only have many made the decision to publish, promote and interact online, but other changes in zine writing seem to resemble the new craft approach to publishing. As riot grrrl ethics have developed into magazines such as *Bitch*, *Bust* and *Venus Zine*, seemingly those who previously may have been involved in riot grrrl are now taking part in this new movement. For those women who grew up with the early riot grrrl movement ten years ago, instead of leaving the DIY network they have instead begun to develop a new direction for their energies. This new craft network can be seen as a new phase in DIY culture, one where those involved in earlier DIY movements can express themselves and build new communities are they grow up.

Interview with **Leah Kramer** of craftster.com

Do you think craft is a revolutionary act?
'I think that the young, hip, crafters today who are

reclaiming crafting for themselves and making it fit their own personalities and styles are doing something revolutionary. There are many examples of this on Craftster and then there are people like the woman behind SubversiveCrossStitch (www.subversivecrossstitch.com). She took the cutesy act of cross-stitch and made up patterns that are irreverent and funny and acerbic.

Also, if you think about the rise in popularity of knitting, it can be seen as a revolutionary act. In cities like London, NY, San Francisco and Boston, it's becoming extremely popular amongst twenty to thirty year-olds to hang out in coffee shops and bars and knit. Or to knit on your bus or subway commute. It's so common to see this in Boston (where I live) that I don't think people think twice about it anymore. But for those first few brave souls who said "I'm not an 80-year-old grandma but I love to knit and I'm gonna do it in public!" I applaud them for paving the way.'

Is it a part of third wave feminism? Has the current rise in craft followed any existing networks (such as those established by zine, DIY or riot grrrl communities)?
'I do see the popularity of crafting as an important part of ever-changing definition of who women are. My own theory is that there was a point in time where women really had to distance themselves from domestic activities in order to break down the roles that were defined for them. But now that women have come so far and have proven the many roles that they can take on, those that have the desire to do crafty things can feel more free to embrace them.

As far as whether the rise in popularity of crafting has followed any existing networks you mention, I'm not entirely sure because I haven't actively been involved in those. But I can definitely see that happening in theory. When you get a bunch of creative, strong-minded women together, these things happen! I think that zine communities and mail art communities (like nervousness.org) do a lot of swapping of creative works with one another. This idea is also very popular on Craftster where people trade crafted goods based on a certain theme. This idea probably came from zine and mail art communities.'

Also, why do you think there has been a recent rise in people taking part in craft activities?
'SOCIAL: Crafting has become a very social activity. Stitch n' bitches and other crafting meetups are a great way to relax and chat and actually do something productive at the same time. INDIVIDUALITY: I think that it's fashionable right now to want to create wearable things that no one else has. MONEY SAVING: The state of the economy drives people to save money by making gifts and things for yourself rather than buying. SOCIALLY CONSCIENTIOUS: There is a sort of anti-brand/anti-corporate feeling growing stronger as people become aware of what goes into mass-produced goods. And making things yourself helps you appreciate how much work can go into things like clothing and can make you wonder how they can be sold so cheaply. ENVIRONMENTAL: On Craftster you can easily see the popularity of crafts that involve cleverly reusing throwaways. This manifests itself in ways ranging from crafts to make out of AOL CDs you get in the mail, to tips on reusing thrift store clothing, fabrics, sheets, pillowcases to make clothing, quilts and handbags. Finding a way to remake existing things can also be a big money saver and it also gets you lots of extra points for ingenuity.'

DIY Literature Online

The Web Journal

A recent development in the history of self-publishing and one which is a direct result of the growth of the internet, has been the use of the internet for people to produce sites which, operating similarly to the personal zine, examine the writer's own life. This type of publishing began almost as soon as the internet became widely accessible. Personal web pages were created by people who wanted to talk about themselves, their families and interests. This trend developed and these many sites began to take on the format of online diaries. These online journals or 'e-diaries' present an intimate look at their writer's life. The idea of presenting your personal thoughts and details of your life in such a public forum may seem daunting to many, but it quickly became a popular use of the internet.

The key to the popularity of these narrative presentations of the writer's life is how simple they are to produce. People who would never have attempted to write a paper zine, now have online journals and communicate with a potentially huge 'invisible' audience. Not so many years ago, people would have needed specialist programming knowledge to attempt such a project. This is now not the case as websites such as Diarist.net and Diaryland.com sprung up which allowed users to easily publish their own online journals. Typically they cost nothing to produce and take little more effort that filling in a template.

As many people are living increasingly busy lives, some find it useful to use an online journal to update friends about what they have been doing. Although in a public domain, this can be quite a private means of communication between friends. As people talk about their everyday lives through this medium, a high percentage can be mundane, but some are wonderfully idiosyncratic, much like the best print zines. Readers often have to read through the less interesting sites to find the gems. The benefits of the internet mean that updates can be posted instantly and previous entries are archived. A reader can feel as though they have a little window into the mind of a diary site's creator and can follow the action as their life plays out. There is greater opportunity for a reader/writer relationship and the fact that comments can be made instantly via email provokes communication, be it from friends, enemies or total strangers.

As with any previous form of self-publishing, a community soon grew from this new genre of confessional writing. Journals are linked together between groups of friends or by similar interests, creating a strong community, eager to read what each other is writing. In this way, the writers are also the audience. During the late 1990s, the rapid increase in the popularity of these online journals meant that conferences began to be organized. The first of these was JournalCon in Pittsburgh, Pennsylvania in October 2000, which enabled people to come together and discuss this new trend in self-publishing.

Online journals are not an entirely new development in self-publishing the idea of publishing your thoughts, ideas and details about your life has existed in the zine world for decades. Personal zines, for example, share many similarities with the online journal. However, this is a much more accessible medium, involving far less effort from either writer or reader. Where there were only hundreds of personal zines, there are now tens of thousands of online journals.

Online journals often seem like semi-fictional works, with the writer using themselves to create a character to present to others via their site, and often count amongst the most popular of websites. As the identity of the writer is obscured by the semi-anonymity of the online experience they can shape and mould their personality to fulfil any role.

Short story writer, Amy Prior, has noticed this trend of creating an online persona through a web journal; moulding yourself into a character that contrasts with your everyday personality and life. As she explains, 'You take out huge truths and put in huge truths.' This clearly draws close parallels with personal zines, such as those of Aaron Cometbus and Dishwasher Pete – their lives becoming almost fictionalized through their accounts.[18]

Many writers who previously wrote personal zines have begun to produce versions of their zine on the internet using the online journal. This has proved controversial to those who prefer paper copies, and think zine writers are giving up too much by being based solely online. In fact, some zine writers choose to use the online journal almost as a scrapbook of ideas to be later developed into articles for their paper zine. In this way, they lead a self-publishing double life – making use of the immediacy of the online journal whilst preserving the aesthetics and traditions of a paper zine.

The Blog
The blog, or weblog, is a recent phenomenon and its growth has been rapid. In 1998, there were only a few weblogs in existence. The term had only been adopted the previous year by Jon Berger, who used it to describe the small but frequently updated websites that were being produced to chronicle their creators' online life – as opposed to their everyday existence. Often like a little scrapbook, these sites contained posts from the writer,

arranged in reverse chronological order, and links to different sites which the writer felt worth recommending to others.

Jesse James Garrett, editor of *Infosift*, was working on his weblog and began to compile a list of sites similar to his own. The rapid growth of the weblog is well illustrated by his list, which at the beginning of 1999 counted only twenty-three in existence. He started sending his list to a friend, Cameron Barrett, who began publishing the list online as Camworld in November 1998. Others who had similar sites began to send them to him and Camworld swiftly became a comprehensive record of the weblog community.

Peter Merholz announced in early 1999 that he was going to pronounce it 'web-blog' and inevitably this was shortened to 'blog' with the weblog editor referred to as a 'blogger.' The trend rapidly grew and before long it became impossible to keep track of all the new sites that were appearing. Whilst Cameron Barret made the decision to list only the sites that he had found himself, other webloggers began to try and produce a comprehensive document of what was happening. In early 1999 Brigitte Eaton compiled a list of every weblog she knew about on her Eatonweb Portal.

Since its emergence, the word 'blog' has become almost interchangeable with the online journal. People are not only including information about their activities online but also their own lives. The weblog format can be easily used as an online diary and people can use it to write about their day-to-day experiences or as a creative outlet.

There are many different types of blog. There is the 'topical blog', focusing on a specific niche, often a technical one; the 'friend blog', a distributed networked journal on the web, composed of short, frequently updated posts written by friends connected through their similar interests; a 'collaborative' (collective or group), which is obviously written by more than one person and focuses on a specific topic; also the 'political blog', where an individual will link to articles from news websites and post their own comments.

Of all the above, the political blog is perhaps the most interesting, particularly as it resembles the original radical publications. One of the earliest and most popular examples of this genre of blog is found at the site www.AndrewSullivan.com, which hosts the personal blog of Anglo-American journalist and writer Andrew Sullivan. He is a freelance writer, reporting on the war in Iraq from Iraq Kurdistan. Having previously worked for the *New York Daily News,* Sullivan realized a need for independent reporting of the conflict and to fund this venture he raised almost $15,000, donated by the readers of his weblog. His weblog was regarded as a legitimate information source and for many it became the favoured port of call for news on the Iraq War. The quality of his work has since been recognized and he has been shortlisted for an Utne Independent Press Award for online political coverage.

This blog is a clear example of quality independent journalism, but is the blog a new advancement in journalism, similar to that achieved by the radical newspapers of the 60s? To begin with, blogs were viewed as a new wave in journalism – the opportunity for anyone to report the news for themselves. Obviously this is an idealistic premise, but one which did have relevance. The problem with many blogs is that although they intend to report the news impartially, as they are primarily concerned with their creators' lives and personal biases the reporting is often flawed. Although they work as a form of participatory media, they cannot essentially be regarded as a form of journalism.

The online journal and blog appear as recent phenomena, a new way of working with the media for personal or political expression. They are the most recent of all self-publishing methods and appear to be among the most easily accessible. The blog has recently been paid much media attention, achieving popularity similar to that enjoyed by the many zines produced in the mid-90s, and despite being based to an extent on pre-existing formats of self-publishing.

Amy Prior connects this new trend of online journals and blogs directly to the personal zine heritage of the early 90s. Individuals in both the queercore and riot grrrl movements used autobiography extensively in their paper zines as a means to connect with their reader and develop a persona through which to discuss their ideas. Now people appear to write accounts of their lives online with a similar aim. She explains that, 'There has always been a culture of shared experience but it wasn't in the mainstream. Riot grrrls particularly wrote about really private issues and self-published them. Self-publishing was important in order for them to share these experiences. It happened to some extent in earlier punk zines. When punk was feminized by the riot grrrl movement it became more personal.'

Many riot grrrl writers were among the first to start web journals as a form of progression from their zines. They seemed to move from producing zines in paper form to communicating through message boards on the internet in the mid-90s, then on to writing their own live journals. They retained various quirks and qualities of their paper-based zines, such as the sense of honest confession and a documentation of the everyday, traits which have since been embraced by many of those whose first self-publishing efforts are posted online.

This confessional style of writing has moved from the cultural underground and become almost a mainstream activity. Prior explains that, 'It was an underground thing and now it's part of the mainstream. Every teenager probably has a web zine now. And it came from zine writing. It is definitely a similar type of writing.' She feels this new trend to be part of our current 'culture of confession'. At a time when people are experiencing a sense of social alienation and many are clamouring to become celebrities, the online journal and blog serves both needs. This new medium offers a chance for individuals to express themselves and place details of their lives in front of a potentially huge audience.

The E-Zine

It isn't only personal zines that have begun to make an appearance on the internet. Since the paper zine apparently reached the peak of its popularity in 1995-6 with readership figures tailing off in 1997-8, zines of all types have been affected by improvements in technology. Previous developments, such as offset printing and the photocopier, helped the zine gain momentum as the means of production became more accessible, but the rise of the PC and internet have resulted in radical changes in zine format across the board. With the rapid growth of digital culture, and so many zines making the transition to the web, the internet has breathed new life into an old idea. SchNEWS is one such publication that has made the transition successfully.

Interview with **John Hodge** on SchNEWS online.

When and why did SchNEWS go online?

'SchNEWS went online in stages. Firstly someone put a

subdirectory type site on their website which gave the text in bare-bones form; from April '95, Issue 20. There was a launch, in late '97 which involved putting PDF files of the issues and in late '98 it got its first .org.uk address. SchNEWS went online officially cos it was there already, even though very much as a side issue to the paper copies and annuals etc initially.'

What have been the main benefits and costs of going online?
'SchNEWS is run with donations, one of which involves a friendly web server who has given us free webspace for years. The main benefit of the internet is that 10,000 people get the email version of SchNEWS a week, and 10,000 people visit the site each week – as opposed to the 3-5000 we usually print. So even though the paper is still considered its main form, statistically it exists as a PDF file the most.'

What are your top five online news sources and why?
'www.indymedia.org.uk: a good round-up of protest stuff in Britain. If you treat the world-wide set of Indymedia sites as one resource, it's an amazing global news service. www.corporatewatch.org.uk: good critical articles about corporations including issues like privatization, GM or climate change. www.zmag.org/ZNET.htm: good for essays about world politics. www.guardian.co.uk: to get the football results.

A lot of issues, like climate change or GM or road protests, are dealt with best by groups who are specializing in that topic, for example Rising Tide or Road Alert; but these might not be the places you'd go for general browsing.'

What irritates you most about news websites (design and content-wise?)
'Some of the newspaper websites don't give you access to the full article unless you're a subscriber. The Indymedia sites can get cumbersome if there's loads of posting to trawl through, and some of the postings are questionable.'

SchNEWS deals with big issues. What do you make of the argument that independent media must go beyond separatism and push issues into the mainstream to achieve lasting change?
'Unless you're happy writing for an audience within a narrow confine, in which case you'll make less impact, then you might as well try to reach as many as possible. It's always a fine line for SchNEWS to occasionally do things to promote the site or the book or whatever, without sounding like you're haranguing the readers with crappy marketing gimmicks. As for toning the material down to reach a so-called broader readership, we've built up a loyal readership by staying true to a certain ethic about not being seen to sell out – so we have to stick to our guns.

Recently I've got an insight into the world of zines, which are great but in many ways are happy to stay as a sub-culture thing. I wouldn't want that.

The web is a different playground, things like coming up in google searches when people put in key-words on subjects you have articles about are big factors, and you can get random readers.'

Trends in design are towards increasing interactivity on news sites eg: readers forums and 'email the author' functions. Critics argue this emphasis on engaging presentation can sideline content. Do you agree?

'I think it's great if the author can be responded to – if the author is able to create a useful debate/dialogue with the readers. On the other hand feedback questionnaires often just look like market research. I think wikipedia is an interesting exercise in reader participation, it's an online encyclopedia which is built up with entries supplied and edited by readers.'

Unusually, SchNEWS doesn't run photographs on its website. Why not?
'SchNEWS in the newsletter doesn't have pics cos it's text only, apart from the weekly cartoon. So the website inherits this format, but the cartoons are on it each week. Also using photos often runs into image copyright issues which is another thing. Not that we rule it out in the future.'

What innovations/changes would you like to see on online news sites over the next few years?
'Much more streaming video. We've started having short films we've produced on our website SchMovies and gradually as everybody gets faster internet it's more of an option. And hopefully the commercial media would get into offering clips for free online.'

Internet filtering is becoming commonplace in workplaces, libraries, schools, in the UK and overseas. Has SchNEWS ever been monitored by any authorities to your knowledge? And has it ever been blocked from the internet? (I imagine you might not be able to access it from Saudi Arabia or China for example?)
Somebody contacted us once from Leeds to say that their internet connection at work, in govt/council, blocked SchNEWS (and it's not as if we swear very often so it

wasn't that). We don't know of that much blocking of SchNEWS. One block is the way other sites will appear higher in google searches cos they paid money or get promoted by big corps etc.

It's assumed that police will monitor us from time to time to see what's going on with a protest campaign or whatever, but – "touch wood"– we haven't had cops in the office yet.'

With the development of the online zine, which is far quicker and easier to produce than any hard copy, to many people the print zine appears to be less valid. However, there are debates as to whether e-zines restrict the zine to being simply a hobby of those who can afford a computer, thereby creating an elite form of zine experience that is not accessible to everyone. Perhaps this argument is less valid now that the use of the internet has increased dramatically and most people can access the web in some way. Chip Rowe, founder of *This is the Spinal Tap Zine* and *Chip's Closet Cleaner*, is one zine writer particularly interested in new technology – he has a version of his *The Book of Zines* online. He explains that if zines are only accessible via the web, 'They exclude people without online access. But if they are sold, they exclude anyone without money. And if they are in print, they exclude people who don't ever see a copy. So I think you always have limitations.' He is in favour of the zine moving onto the internet, 'I think it's had a tremendous impact – print has its qualities but the internet can give you a much larger audience – and although zines are personal and done to entertain the author more than anything, who doesn't like feedback?' A few years ago he produced an issue of his zine, *Chip's Closet Cleaner* in disc form. The idea was that people could simply load this disc and read the zine on the screen and print their own copy. Then he realized that by using a PDF file, which could be accessed online, readers could either read the material on screen or print it out for themselves. If you preferred the quality of a paper zine you could download the zines you wanted and keep a hard copy. This appeared to be a great solution but not one which anyone else has followed.

John Marr, who produces the zine *Murder Can Be Fun* wrote an article called 'Zines are Dead' in 1999, in which he considered the future of the zine. He realized that, 'The quirky spirit of zines hasn't died. It's just migrated to the web. If I were starting out today, no way would I mess with hard copy – I'd go straight to the net. It's cheaper, easier and faster.'[19] Although many people feel that the spirit of the zine is not compatible with modern technology, the internet has made zine production much easier and potentially far more accessible.

One problem facing paper zines was that once all the copy had been written, printed and then distributed to readers it was already out of date. With the online zine, new articles can be added as soon as they are written. This means that information can be spread much quicker – adding to the sense of urgency felt by the many zinesters.

The economics of the online zine make sense. Avoiding the costs of printing and distributing a zine, it is much easier to produce a zine for very little money.

Moreover, communities can be created with much more ease through the internet than could ever have been achieved through the postal network, largely because email addresses can be added to the webzine and so readers can contact the editor almost instantly. Though this creates a more detached means of communicating than in person, it does mean that people all over the world can communicate with ease, with the advent of message boards and guestbooks which can be attached to sites enabling readers to network with one another as well as with the editor.

Although e-zines offer their readers an instantaneous zine experience, the ease of virtual communication can limit personal interaction. Ericka Bailie of Pander Zine Distro explains. 'While the internet has made it easier to get information on zines out in the world it has also hindered personal contact. When I started Pander, I didn't have a computer and none of my fellow zinesters had email addresses, we wrote each other actual letters.' This personal sense of communication has been lost with the rise of the e-zine but there is opportunity for communication on a wider scale than ever before. The numbers of hand written letters exchanged between zine writers may have reduced, but email does offer an instant form of communication.

Other zine writers have argued that the essence of the zine cannot be transferred online. Bruce La Bruce, of the queercore zine *JDs*, explains, 'When we started *JDs*, there was no email, no internet, etc. So making DIY fanzines and using the mail was our only way of communicating internationally to other like-minded individuals. But the zines were much more tactile and personal than websites, their modern counterpart are: they were objects that you could carry around with you, manifestos you could share, gifts you could give. They were more romantic than electronic media is.'

Other zine writers have expressed a similar attitude – that the paper zine and the postal network are part of the pleasure of the zine writing experience. John Marr laments in his article 'Zines are Dead', 'Back when I started putting out my zine *Murder Can Be Fun* sometime in the mid-80s, my daily trip to the PO box was the highlight of my life…

A good batch of mail could make up for the crappiest day at work. I subscribed to credos like "A day without mail is like a day without sunshine" and "There is no sight sadder than that of an empty mailbox." But that was then. These days, my mail lacks both quantity and quality. No longer do I schedule my afternoons around my branch's 5.30 closing. I only make the trip two or three times per week. And if I miss a day, it's no longer a personal tragedy.'

For writers such as Marr, this experience of receiving letters from their readers was a highly rewarding feature of zine writing. Many such writers feel that the internet cannot offer the same experience. The internet can build a virtual community but not the aesthetic romance of a personal letter.

Zine writers have often been thought of as not embracing modern technology and the prevalent characteristics of the zine reinforce this idea, as many writers followed the dada-influenced punk aesthetic of the cut and paste style, revelling in the amateur production methods. Many did not use computers to layout their work, often producing text on typewriters, feeling that the aesthetics of the zine tradition were a vital feature and that that computers could not replicate this style unique to the zine-style. In fact, this use of past production methods in a nostalgic way is also a more general feature of the DIY community at large.

The design of the zine has been adapted by those who made the move onto the computer screen. Editors still used the traditional cut and paste style but it was now more difficult to create, with images needing to be scanned into the computer and arranged to look as though they were just glued together on paper. Other editors embraced the new technology available to them and produced more complex, impressive sites.

The use of the internet in zine-making has revolutionized the process. Ideas are now transmitted further than ever before. The DIY ethos of the scene fits in perfectly with the original idea of the internet – that it would be a non-commercial means of communication, with no geographical limitations, so many more people can communicate. The motivation for the zine remains the same; it is just the medium that has changed. There are now millions of online zines, web journals and blogs, resembling the DIY culture of previous decades and creating similar distribution channels.

The first zine writers to make use of the internet did so in 1991, during the very early stages of the web functioning as a means of mass communication. They did not produce websites, but rather text only files that were distributed via email. Though the audience for this form of zine was originally small, the response proved that the zine did have the potential to work on the internet. This was proved as the zine community online began to grow. In 1992, a Usenet discussion group called 'Alt.zines' was set up for people to discuss zines.

There has been confusion over the move of the zine onto the internet and the blurring of the distinction between the zine and the e-zine. The term 'e-zine' has come to mean 'electronic magazine' without the past associations with zine culture. The e-zine is instead taken to be any form of magazine available on the internet, even if the publication is commercial and the motivation is monetary gain. This form of online magazine appeared after 1991, when the ban on the commercial use of the internet was lifted and internet growth sped up.

This reference to this form of magazine as an 'e-zine'

stands in contrast to the original premise of the zine, as a media culture set apart from mainstream cultural interests. There are subsequently a number of people, often those with previous knowledge and experience of zines, who are keen to differentiate between the two.

Just as there have been debates about the death of print culture as a result of the rise in use of the internet, some people have felt that the zine would also quickly become obsolete. It is true that many zines have made the move onto the internet, realizing the benefits of the medium, but many have also kept hold of their print roots and kept producing paper versions of their zine.

Following in the footsteps of Chip Rowe and his *Chip's Closet Cleaner* another print zine publisher who was amongst the first to make the transition onto the web was Jeff Koyen, publisher of the music zine *Crank*. He started by advertizing it via email and then set up Crank.com to catalogue past issues and issue updates. Others soon joined him.

One writer who realized that the internet offered more opportunity to reach a wide audience than the print zine was Jean Ecoule, founder of the British online music zine trakMARX.com. He explains as follows: 'The reason we chose to do a zine online was that the costs of setting out, printing and distributing a hard copy zine meant we'd never have got the thing off the ground. We considered our subject matter and our poor attitude – and after absolutely no fraught editorial meetings – we decided we'd 'carry on' the DIY legacy of *Sniffin' Glue* by making use of the internet.' Their position online meant that they could reach a wider audience than they would have been able to if they limited themselves to distributing paper copies. 'We had no idea how successful this would be when we started up in 2001 – it was a case of pissing in the cyber wind, to a certain extent. All we really knew was that the mainstream hardcopy music press had disappeared so far up its own arse that in many ways the record-buying public were being regularly insulted – on a weekly and monthly basis. We felt we could do better. So we did.'[20]

Although they felt that they were directly challenging the mainstream music press, as punk zines had done in the 70s, they wanted to retain some qualities of the independent fanzine.

'TrakMARX was designed as a fanzine and will always remain so. We have no advertizing and never will – so the options for making money out of it are absolutely zero. The zine is meant to be printed from the internet, stapled together and passed around friends and associates with similar tastes and anti-corporate beliefs.' Their independent attitude has won them readers. 'Initially, trakMARX got hundreds of hits a day, we now have a readership in excess of 20,000 world-wide and get taken seriously by enough of our subjects and peers to make it all worthwhile. We publish five issues a year – roughly when we feel like it – and we all enjoy it very much indeed. We are well aware that not everyone in the world has a computer or a printer but we don't have access to a printing press and our dads don't own IPC – so we see it as a compromize essential to our publication. If we're that good trickledown will come into play and the "DIY print & distribute" ethic will prevail.'

The first major independent publication to establish a presence on the internet was *Mother Jones*. As early as 1993, the magazine began to make its online presence felt when its editors first developed a website. Richard Reynolds recognizes the opportunities that the internet raises for the magazine. 'The opportunities offered by the internet were apparent to us from the start, and we were fortunate enough to have a staff member who was a techno-genius who came to us after becoming frustrated with the corporate world. We began posting the content of the print magazine online in November of 1993 and by 1995 we were using the internet to offer huge searchable databases of political campaign contributions.' This development was a giant leap from the original production of the magazine, which started in the 1970s when it was set in hot type, a 19th century technology using molten lead. The use of computer technology was very different from the process of setting hot type, but just as appropriate for the magazine in this new stage in its history. The popularity of the magazine has greatly increased and the website now receives 1.25 million page views each month. The new technology offered by the internet has also meant that a more diverse group of people are able to access the magazine; many of those finding it online may never have come across the print version of the magazine.

Punk Planet's editors also realized that producing an online version of their magazine would be a good way to reach new readers. However, in order to survive they still need to sell copies of their print magazine, and so only included a limited amount of its content on their website. The site therefore serves as a form of advertizing for their magazine, as well as explaining what they are all about to the uninitiated.

The internet has meant that independent publications can have a space alongside the mainstream publications and their potential to affect more change than ever is obvious. The world has changed considerably since the first zines and independent magazines appeared, and with the internet (and the vast amount of information it makes available) now being a part of daily life for many people, the zine is a valuable addition.

As mentioned, some zine writers see the internet as a threat that will ultimately divide the zine community. However, it seems more likely that it benefits the zine community, in much the same way as the beginning of *Factsheet Five*. Mike Gunderloy's efforts enabled zine writers to communicate with each other, pushing the community to grow during the 80s. The influence of the internet is similar, with zine writers easily able to see what other writers are doing and further develop – strengthening the community.

After all these changes that underground self-publishing has gone through, it is probably the internet which has brought about the most change. As Stephen Duncombe realizes, 'The real thing that changed zines was the rise of the web, and then later blogs. The web democratized self-publication, spreading it to many more people.' However, he warns that by this development, the do-it-yourself publication may lose some of its 'intimate underground edge'[21] – the very independent essence that has made it unique.

Zines Past and of the Future

Interview with **Teal Triggs**, co-editor with Roger Sabin of *Below Critical Radar: Fanzines and Alternative Comics From 1976 to Now* (Hove: Slab-O-Concrete, 2000) on contemporary zine culture.

Do you think there is a characteristic visual style of the zine that still hold true of contemporary zines?
'Prior to the development of desktop publishing, I would suggest fanzines did have a characteristic visual style that

emerged out of the way in which the fanzines were made and produced. Often, this consisted of typewritten and hand scrawled texts, use of Letraset or rub down lettering, photobooth snap shots, collage imagery from mainstream publications and/or hand-drawn illustrations. This style also emerged as a result of using 'cut and paste' techniques taken from whatever magazines, bits of paper, crayons, etc the producer had around them. Also, when punk arrived in the UK, a politics of resistance translated into a subcultural graphic language manifest in the use of 'threatening' ransom note lettering, anarchist symbols, underpinned by an intentionally 'shocking' and aggressive use of swear words and slogans, intentional misspellings and incorrect use of punctuation.

Punk, however, is not the only genre of fanzine. The broad range of titles currently published cover zines on the subject of football (*Red Attitude*), beer drinking (*Beer Frame*) and thrift shopping (*Thrift Score*) to the more recent punkzine *Open up and Bleed* and riot grrrl publications (e.g. *Heavy Flow, Sista Yes!, Aggamengmong Moggie*). Despite the subjects which are celebrated and the variety of production techniques – from the DIY to DTP fanzines continue to adopt many of these earlier visual conventions.'

Are there any specific techniques that zine editors make use of? If so, where do you think this came from?
'Today you have e-zines appearing as online websites using the latest versions of Flash to more conventional handmade zine DIY methods that still use the photocopier to great effect. DTP revolutionized the production of zines (much like the advent of the Apple Mac impacted mainstream publishing practices) and provided a stripped down version of an earlier DIY aesthetic. Riot grrrl fanzines are a good

example of ways in which fanzine producers maintained the graphic language originally fostered by punk zines such as Mark Perry's *Sniffin' Glue* or in the States, V. Vale's *Search and Destroy*. These zines established in the late 1970s a very distinct graphic style. At the same time another strand of zines emerged out of the tradition of dada collage and related visual techniques of art movements. Often these fanzines were produced by people knowingly experimenting with visual techniques and concepts. Jamie Reid's early Suburban Press is the result of a producer's interest in visualizing the antics of situationism first used by King Mob Echo and other British anarchist groups in the late 1960s.'

What, in your opinion, is the current state of the zine?
'Over the last few years fanzines have made a transition from the underground into the overground and have become 'hip' accessories. Take zines such as the *Shoreditch Twat* – an east London production which picked up on the hip vibe of Hoxton Square. There has also been a trend of fanzines turning into full-blown mainstream magazines especially in the States (e.g. *Bust, Oriental Whatever, Giant Robot*) or producers have authored books (e.g. *Cheap Date, Punk Planet*) which are collected anthologies of writings from their original print fanzines. Retailers such as Diesel clothing and Urban Outfitters picked up on this as well creating 'faux fanzines' using a DIY ethos and often commissioning 'authentic' fanzine writers to promote their products. All of this has combined to raise an awareness of fanzines and profile (see Utne Reader's small press column written by fanzine enthusiast Chris Dodge), articles in national newspapers and mainstream news publications such as *Time* magazine.

At the same time the graphic design community has

continued to 'plunder' from fanzine aesthetic. Early examples include *Details* and *i-D* style magazines whose origins began in fanzines and eventually became a mainstay of a youth publishing industry. Chicks on Speed's *Will Save Us All* album still carries the hand-drawn lettering and performative nature of art-based punk. The list goes on.'

Are more zines being produced? Are they more political?
'I would say that there is a resurgence of fanzines especially print based in circulation today. Somewhere I read that thousands of football titles are in existence where each club has a handful of members producing unofficial publications.

This of course doesn't take into account the plethora of titles created by fans of music, political groups or other interest areas.

I would also say that fanzines are more political – although it's hard to generalize and it depends on your definition of "politics". I believe with the emergence of riot grrrl, there has been a more overt sense of political views taken through fanzines – views which incorporate feminism and the whole "independent" scene. At the same time you still get fans of Pez dispensers and second-hand clothing shops which carry their own "political" position.'

Are paper zines in decline with more zines being produced online?
'In the early 1990s the positioning of online publishing initiated a number of heated debates within the community. While the websites maintained the DIY ethos through such "amateur" productions, many sites have become promotional or supplemental vehicles for the actual print publication. I think print based zines are here for the duration. People need tactility of materials,

accessibility and interaction on a face-to-face social level such as handing out zines at local music gigs.'

How do British zines compare with American zines?
'American zines tend to cover some really zany subjects and have a higher profile on the newsstands. Alternative publishing in general tends to be more visible and perhaps as a consequence you also see fanzines more professionally produced – less of a DIY attitude. It is hard to generalize as there are pockets of activity in both countries where fanzines visually still reflect the personality of individual producers and maintain the spirit of independent publishing.'

Self-publishing of the Future
The production of independent literature has certainly changed since the early days of the sci-fi zinesters. It has evolved in form and style but at the core of each new development or trend individuals retain the same ambition – to publish their own writing away from commercial constraints and reach an audience much like themselves. Whether this writing was in the form of a story, a political rant, a celebration of a cultural scene, a manifesto or personal confession, the primary need was to be heard, to communicate. The resultant networks have been remarkable. Strong communities have been built, supportive of one another's work. Some can be seen as idealistic, flawed, or egotistical, but each provide an alternative cultural experience. Publications are in print that would never have been commissioned by a commercial publisher or printed in a professional magazine. This has never been a one-sided dialogue, but a means for communication between writer and reader, a means to find allies and transmit ideas.

Technology has certainly played an integral part in the rise of do-it-yourself literature. With each new development, there has been a change in independent printed output. The printing press, the photocopier and the internet have all played their part. Each has made the means of production more accessible and so the writer is able to reach further and more people are encouraged to take part. Some styles have changed, others have remained the same, but these printed efforts will remain as a form of cultural artifact, a record of the activities of underground culture.

PART II: THE HISTORY OF SELF-PUBLISHING

Zine beginnings

Science Fiction Fandom

The zine did not begin with the internet e-zine, the riot grrrl zine calling for a feminist revolution in the 1990s, the punk zine of the 1970s, or even the chapbook of the 1950s, but with science fiction fanzines produced in the 1930s. Modern zines cover every imaginable subject ranging from music, politics and fiction to sports and travel but to start with there was just one genre – sci-fi.

It was during the 1920s that science fiction magazines began to appear on news-stands across America. For the first time, fans of sci-fi could now read original stories in magazines that had been printed professionally (referred to early on as 'prozines') – magazines like Luxembourg businessman and inventor Hugo Gernsback's *Amazing Stories*.[22] Initially published in 1926, this was one of the very first sci-fi magazines and Gernsback's aim was to give his readers a basic understanding of factual science through the stories he printed. He called this 'scientifiction', a combination of science and fiction, which later became 'science fiction'. Although the scientific information was often rudimentary, the magazine was made popular by the inclusion of writing by authors such as Jules Verne and HG Wells as well as Edgar Rice Burroughs'[23] stories.

The editors of *Amazing Stories* made an important and, at that time, radical decision, which would become the starting point for the zine. They decided to feature letters pages within their publication, inviting readers to contribute and offer feedback, and printed not only the names but also the addresses of those who sent in their letters. This enabled fans to start communicating with each other, at first writing letters to be featured on these pages and starting debates, then writing to one another directly and sharing ideas independently. Correspondence clubs were formed, with the purpose of introducing fans to one another, giving enthusiasts a chance to exchange their views and stories via the mail. The once isolated hobby of the sci-fi enthusiast began to grow into a community of fans.

Just like the independent music communities which would develop in the 70s and 80s, through the letters pages of alternative rock magazines such as *Maximumrocknroll*, the sci-fi fans of the 1920s soon began to organize themselves into groups across America. When clubs such as The Science Correspondence Club, founded by Walter L Dennis in Chicago and sponsored by *Amazing Stories*, proved to be popular, it was an obvious progression for sci-fi fans to start writing their own versions of the magazines they were reading. These amateur magazines did not just try to replicate the professional magazines but instead created their own medium and produced small print-runs of mimeographed pamphlets (using an early duplication machine producing copies from a stencil) that were cheap and easy to produce and distribute. The network of fans developed their own terminology or 'fanspeak' to describe what they were doing within their growing community. They called these new magazines 'fan-magazines' or 'fan-mags'[24], which in the 1940s were dubbed 'fanzines' by one of their most popular writers – Louis Russell Chauvenet.[25]

The earliest of these fan-mags was *The Comet*, produced by Roy Palmer for The Science Correspondence Club in May 1930. This publication has been credited by many as being the first ever fanzine and it ran for many years, later being renamed *Cosmology*. Spurred on by the network that was forming, others quickly followed. Again through the pages of the professional magazines, the fan group The Scienceers was set up in the Bronx, New York by Mort Weisinger[26]. They used a mimeograph to begin another fanzine in the early 1930s, which proved to be a success and became well known – *The Time Traveller*. Among the first subscribers to *The Time Traveller* was Ohio teenager Jerome Siegel[27], who was inspired to begin his own fanzine, *Science Fiction*, in 1932. Siegel later joined forces with illustrator Joe Shuster[28] to create one of Marvel Comic's biggest heroes – Superman. The writers of *The Time Traveller* achieved success through their fanzine. Within two issues they had moved on to printing it as a typeset magazine and its editors, Mort Weisinger and Julius Schwartz, began to be respected in the professional sci-fi world. Through their magazine they became increasingly well known in the sci-fi community, and were soon able to access news about the sci-fi scene directly from the offices of the professional sci-fi magazines. They were becoming professionals themselves. By 1934 they had began representing sci-fi writers, acting as their agents, and Julius Schwartz later worked on updating the images of Superman and Batman when they were developed for major films. Although their roots were in independent publishing, printing on a small scale to a limited audience, both Schwartz and Weisinger developed their interest in sci-fi into well-documented careers.

This trend of independently published sci-fi zines grew and the 1930s, 40s and 50s saw many more sci-fi fanzines join these three pioneering titles. But why, when it took time and money to produce each issue and distribution would not have been high as it was a relatively underground network, did anyone choose to make these little paper documents? What was it about these publications that inspired such passion? Why would anyone spend their entire week's wages producing a zine? The motivational force behind zine production in the early part of the 20th century is pretty much the same as it is today, and stemmed from a variety of reasons that continue to be relevant.

Many of the fanzine writers aspired to write in the prozines someday and believed the production of a fanzine provided them with a springboard to further these aspirations – which in many cases it did. For example, Ray Bradbury and Arthur C Clarke emerged from amongst the New York fan group The Futurians (1938-45) to later become prominent writers.

Other fans simply enjoyed the experience of writing about subjects they were passionate about and relished having a platform from which to air their views.

There were also those for whom the sense of community was the most important factor. This often stemmed from an academic interest rather than from a simple need to belong, these people were interested in the very nature of their being a fan and their relationship with the genre about which they were writing. Andy Sawyer, Science Fiction Librarian at the University of Liverpool Library, notices this feature. 'The particular aspect of sci-fi fandom which as far as I'm aware doesn't appear in any other fandom is that sci-fi fans very quickly began to write, not just about sci-fi, but the experience of being a fan. Science fiction was like the water in which fans swam, but the interesting thing was fandom itself, its collective and individual idiosyncrasies.'[29] He terms these fans 'obsessive communicators' who felt compelled to write their views down on paper, to write to one another, to join groups –

any means to talk about their passion. The act of publishing these fanzines developed into a hobby. It developed from a documentation of one genre, detailing all its interests and quirks, to a wider means of communication. Sci-fi fans had realised that fanzine writing was the perfect way to talk to one another.

Although the subject matter seems at first to have nothing in common with what was to follow, the sci-fi fanzine was the first critical stage in zine history. It is here that fan journalism began, where fans began to realize that they could write about their interests and participate in the media. In many ways, the sci-fi fanzines are similar to the zines of today. They are produced by cheap and accessible technology and attempt to bring together a wide group of people with a specific interest. Ilona Jasiewicz of long running London-based zine *Radium Dial* agrees with these parallels: 'Modern zines are probably derived from sci-fi zines, yes, as zine culture definitely attracts outsiders and fanatics, and in the 30s and 40s was probably still pretty underground, marginalized and ignored by the mainstream. You could draw parallels between this pattern of emergence and the development...of the underground music scene too: the mainstream overlooked both, so the people involved created their own network of newsletters, magazines, clubs, conventions etc.'[30]

The concept of the fanzine spread to other groups of people and fans of other mediums, such as music, comics and film also began to write about their interests. In time, the 'fanzine' moved away from being a publication written by fans and developed into what is known today as the 'zine'. It developed into an important form of independent publishing, which provided the ideal means for communities to communicate.

The Beat Generation

In the late 1940s, a group of young writers began to think about self-publishing as a way to distribute their own writing. These writers became known as the 'beats' – men and women who, in an increasingly conservative post-war America, decided that their only option was to reject society and write. Their successes are widely known, Jack Kerouac's *On The Road* and Allen Ginsberg's *Howl* are cult classics; however, it is less well known that these authors did not simply write but also published and promoted their own work.

Beat writers are often romanticized and considered cultural icons for being rebellious individuals. However, it wasn't just the lifestyles they pioneered or the literary talents they displayed that made them different, it was the way they adopted the idea of self-promotion through independent methods of publication. This interest in self-publishing developed more through necessity than choice. As their writing often did not mirror the literary or political views of established magazines or publishers, finding anyone to print their work proved to be difficult. Poet Gary Snyder, for example, found that his poems were continually rejected from *Poetry Magazine*. (Founded in Chicago by Harriet Monroe in 1912, this has become the oldest monthly devoted to verse in the English speaking world.) Snyder, who was interested in Chinese and Japanese culture and poetry, as well as writing mystical poetry himself, was an important source of inspiration for many beat writers. He introduced them to the teachings of Zen Buddhism, as well as to the natural beauty of the American landscape and was soon captured in fiction by Jack Kerouac. Numerous camping and hiking trips have been documented in beat memoirs and fictions with Snyder, or a Snyder-inspired character leading the way.

Robert Duncan was another writer who had difficulty in getting his work published. His work was considered to be controversial and after his essay 'The Homosexual in Society' appeared in the August 1944 issue of Dwight Macdonald's left-wing journal *Politics* his poetry was refused by *The Kenyon Review*. This essay angrily likened the difficulties faced by a gay man to the positions of Jewish and African-American men in contemporary society. This subject matter was seen as far too controversial to appear in print.

Following rejection after rejection from the mainstream press, many writers made the decision to create their own outlets, their own channels through which to try and get their work and that of their contemporaries to a receptive audience. Steve Clay, who wrote extensively on the self-publishing activities of writers of this period in his book, *A Secret Location on the Lower East Side*, realized the importance of such actions. 'One might even say that without the small presses and self-published magazines many of these writers would not have been published, would not have received early support to help their work develop and blossom.'[31]

This route of independent publishing later proved to be the right one to take for both Snyder and Duncan. Their work appeared in numerous independent publications and Snyder later achieved success when his first book *Riprap* was published in 1959 and he went on to win a Pulitzer Prize in the mid-70s. Duncan's reputation as a major poet was established in the 1960s in three collections, *The Opening of the Field* (1960), *Roots and Branches* (1964) and *Bending the Bow* (1968). Without the operations of the underground press, both poets may never have achieved such success.

One option for seeing their work in print for many of

these writers was to produce their own chapbooks. These were aimed at small audiences and so were mimeographed publications printed in small quantities. Being lightly-bound, cheaply produced paperbacks (somewhere between a magazine and a book) that were generally funded by and published by individual writers, with the simple aim of getting their writing read, these small scale publications are often considered the forerunner of the literary zine published by writers today.

Despite the diverse writing that they produced, ranging from political social commentary to experimental poetry, these writers of the 40s and 50s were generally supportive of one another and began to help publish each other's work. It was important to them that their own writing and that of their contemporaries was printed, their ideas heard and that they reached other Americans feeling similarly dissatisfied with the cultural experience offered by the mainstream.

In the mid-1940s, beat edited magazines began to appear. Although seemingly radical at the time, the idea of these magazines was not entirely original. They closely followed the earlier model of the 'little magazine' – those literary reviews such as *Little Review and Poetry* published in England and America in the early 20th century. Ezra Pound was one writer particularly known for working on these reviews. He worked in a foreign correspondent role for *Little Review and Poetry,* helped found both *Blast* and *The Exile,* and worked on turning *The Egoist* from a feminist magazine into an avant-garde literary review. The poet William Carlos Williams was also a dedicated supporter of small literary reviews, he edited *Contact* from 1920 to 1923 and published a further three issues in 1932, and was later leading writer at *Pagany*. That many beat writers celebrated the work of modernist writers such as Pound and Williams[32] is well illustrated by their revival of these 'little magazines' in the 50s, thus linking the two literary groups.

This collective promotion, found in both the modernists of the early 20th century and the beat writers mid-century, can be traced back further in American literary history to the work of writers in the mid 19th century such as Ralph Waldo Emerson, Walt Whitman (who self-published the first edition of his collection of poems *Leaves of Grass* in 1885) and Emily Dickinson who collected her poems together in single copy self-published booklets. These writers have been documented as having a direct influence on the beat writers both in terms of subject and style as well as in this trend of self-publishing.

For many beat writers, their work was first printed in small magazines produced by their friends, such as *Yugen, The Floating Bear Newsletter, Measure* and *The Black Mountain Review*. For a change, it was the writers who were in control. Well-known writers of the 50s, such as Jack Kerouac, as well as Diane Di Prima (one of the most prominent female authors of the beat scene) and others including Philip Whalen, John Weiners, Gregory Corso and LeRoi Jones, not only contributed to, but also edited these new magazines. A strong sense of artistic community was established by these small scale, self-published magazines. Steve Clay argues that 'These communities developed in some sense out of necessity. It takes many people working together to put together a magazine.'[33] For once, and because of their own self-publishing activities, young writers were consciously celebrated as new literary talents rather than instantly rejected as too rebellious and confrontational.

Yugen, The Floating Bear and *The Black Mountain Review*

The American poet, playwright and novelist LeRoi Jones[34] (who later changed his name to Imamu Amiri Baraka when he converted to the Muslim faith) became an important figure in the New York literary scene and together with his wife Hettie Cohen[35], started the literary magazine *Yugen* in New York in the late 1950s, with the aim of promoting new writing. This was a low production publication – Cohen worked on the magazine layout at the kitchen table.

Jones later joined poet Diane Di Prima[36], who was by this point also an established figure of the New York beat scene, to produce *The Floating Bear Newsletter*. Di Prima was a particularly interesting member of the bohemian New York crowd of the 50s and 60s as she was one of the few female writers to gain prominence. From a young age, she devoted herself to writing and has spent her adult life pursuing a career in literary and performance arts. In 1965, she moved from New York City, where she had been writing while supporting herself by working in bookshops and as an artist's model, to upstate New York to participate in Timothy Leary's[37] psychedelic community at Millbrook.

The Floating Bear Newsletter ran from 1961 to 1969. This monthly newsletter contained a selection of writing submitted to *Yugen*. Jones and Di Prima co-edited the publication for the first two years, until 1963 when Di Prima took over as the sole editor. At its start, this was a consciously non-profit-making venture and the newsletter was free. The act of giving the writing away without commercial gain was at that time considered a radical act. However, due to financial constraints, subsequent issues asked readers for a contribution towards printing costs and people sent money, stamps or donations, which allowed the magazine to continue running until its demise in 1969.

The newsletter proved to be an important method of communication, enabling contemporary writers to form networks, and providing a means through which writers could keep each other informed about their writing. Such collaboration and communication has always been paramount in forging any kind of artistic community and it was through this newsletter that writers began to develop their own community. Being small and cheap to produce, issues of the newsletter could be turned around with relative ease. It was the swift production that helped to form the community, as writers were quickly able to see what others were doing.

Although *The Floating Bear Newsletter* ran for eight years, successfully promoting new writers and channelling their energies, it was seen by some to have more controversial aims. In late 1961, Di Prima and Jones were arrested by the FBI on the charge of including obscene material in the ninth issue of the newsletter. Jones defended the case himself, which proved successful as it was eventually dismissed, but the accusation illustrates the challenges that these writers faced when trying to distribute their writing. In a conservative era, any challenge to authority – here provided by the content of the magazine as well as the fact that individuals were self-publishing at all (the widespread opinion being that this should be left to 'professional' publishing houses) – was viewed with great suspicion and such charges weren't uncommon for writers and their publishers.

Avoiding censorship was not the only challenge faced by emerging independent magazines lacking the reputation of the more established literary publications, there was also the problem of reaching a sufficient audience. Readership was initially low, but with a supportive literary community developing in the late 50s, concentrated around cities –

New York in particular — these underground magazines typically had just enough support to survive. Gilbert Sorrentino's *Neon* magazine for example, which he started in 1956 with friends (including the writers Hubert Selby Jr and Fielding Dawson) at Brooklyn College, New York, and which was intended to feature fiction from their peers, survived on an average audience of just two hundred readers per issue.[38] Editors had to work hard to keep their magazines up and running and their motivation rarely involved monetary gain.

Founders of these publications could afford the expense of publishing their work only because, at the time, printing costs were low. With the dollar strong after World War II, books could either be printed abroad or using new technology which had just become available and revolutionized the printing process — making it cheaper and easier than ever before to begin publishing. Writers now had direct access to the means of production and it was no surprise that they used these to publish their own work. Steve Clay explains how these improvements in available technology lead to an increase in self-published work at this time. 'I subscribe to Marshall McLuhan's[39] assessment that new technology allows [maybe even forces] old technology to be put to different, often artistic, purposes. The widespread development and acceptance of offset printing left a lot of letterpress equipment on the market for little or no money — poets and others could take control of the production of their works within such a context.'[40]

Their principal ambition was to develop a new literary scene where the writing that they wanted to produce and read could be published. This scene was widened by the links between the beat writers of New York and San Francisco and those working at Black Mountain College in

North Carolina. Black Mountain College, an experimental school founded in 1933 and located in a rural mountain community, became home to many avant-garde poets, such as Robert Creeley, Robert Duncan, Denise Levertov and Charles Olson. Their writing at first appeared in the literary magazine they called *Origin*, which ran from 1951 to 1956, but when Robert Creeley (born 1926) began to teach at the school at the request of Charles Olson he instead founded *The Black Mountain Review*. Creeley admired Olson as an older contemporary and was a poet himself. He published several books of his own poetry during the 50s but did not receive widespread recognition until his book *For Love: Poems 1950-1960* was published in 1962. Robert Duncan was another poet associated with the college. On leaving California in 1938 he moved to New York to become involved in the bohemian literary scene, which by this point included the writer Anaïs Nin. When he returned to California in 1946, he met Charles Oslon (in 1947), developing a friendship that resulted in Duncan being invited to teach at the college in 1956.

Those poets associated with Black Mountain College and published in its *Review* were pioneering a new form of poetry. They believed that poetry should take on a spontaneous form and transmit the poet's emotional and intellectual energy to the reader.

Creeley and Duncan became the link between these experimental poets of the Black Mountain College and the beat writers of the San Francisco Renaissance, and the *Review* became a place where the writing of Allen Ginsberg and Gary Snyder could be read alongside that of regulars such as Charles Olson.

As with the poetry coming out of Black Mountain College, where writers tried to break from the rigid verse form common in post-war America, the magazine was highly innovative. Running from 1954-1956, it quickly became a place where new experimental writers could hope to be published. William S Burroughs' first published work, for example, appeared within its pages after rejections from many other publications for being too obscene and vulgar. The founding of this magazine allowed writers to find a supportive forum to publish their work in an independent publication that could avoid the constraints imposed by mainstream publishers of the 50s.

With the rise in popularity of beat writers, between the 1940s and 1960s, both the numbers of independent literary magazines produced and the popularity of these magazines increased. The readership of *The Floating Bear Newsletter* soared from 117 copies for the first issue in 1961 to 1250 copies by the final issue in 1969.[41] The calibre of writing which these magazines generated was slowly realized   as many writers began to find relative success in the mainstream publishing world. You only have to look at the contributors to the final issue of *The Black Mountain Review* published in the autumn of 1956 to realize the standard of work that these 'first time' authors were submitting. It featured work by Allen Ginsberg and Jack Kerouac, as well as an extract from William S Burroughs' *Naked Lunch*. All of these writers struggled to find suitable publishers initially, but later, through exposure by their own form of independent publishing, achieved mainstream success.

The Small Press

In their independent magazines, editors had celebrated the discovery of new talent in America, but many young writers were often still no closer to being offered a publishing contract. The next logical step was to begin publishing their own books, and many writers and editors subsequently began to establish their own small presses. These small presses initially concentrated on publishing works too long for magazine publication, as well as collections of shorter pieces that had previously appeared in the magazines. They were developing their own form of publishing and sought their own audience, but although contemporary and progressive, they were also following the burgeoning American literary tradition of self-publication.

New Directions

New Directions was one such American small press that appeared to serve as a model for others which followed it. This was founded in 1936 by James Laughlin while he was still an undergraduate at Harvard University, majoring in Latin and Italian. Laughlin was disappointed by the conservatism of his teachers and took a leave of absence in the middle of his sophomore year. At Harvard he had gained more of an education in literature than he could ever have hoped for, as he travelled to France and spent time with Gertrude Stein and Alice B Toklas and then on to Italy to visit Ezra Pound. However, in 1935 Pound, critical of Laughlin's own poetry, suggested that he become a publisher instead – and Laughlin took this advice. Keen to avoid working for the family steel business, he made his first steps into the world of publishing, when returning to Harvard in 1936. Using money from his father, he began to run New Directions from a small cottage in the grounds of his aunt's house in Norfolk.

From the outset, Duncan committed New Directions to publishing the best of avant-garde literature. Along with printing the experimental writing of many of the beat writers, he also published the work of established writers, and authors as well-known as Ezra Pound, Hermann Hesse, William Carlos Williams, Henry Miller and Dylan Thomas appeared on its list. The first book Laughlin published was *New Directions in Prose & Poetry* (1936): an anthology of experimental writing which included contributions from e e cummings, Henry Miller, Marianne Moore, Gertrude Stein, Ezra Pound, Wallace Stevens and William Carlos Williams. Laughlin worked hard to promote the work of his authors, becoming somewhat of a travelling salesman for the title, selling copies straight from his car.

It was fortunate for the beat writers, who admired many of these writers that New Directions began publishing and were eager to be published alongside them, that the magazine was willing to not only feature the work of such celebrated authors, but also encouraged new talent. Many of the beat writers were thus able to find someone willing to take a risk by publishing their work, and through the exposure that the better-known authors afforded the magazine, reached a far wider audience than they could have hoped for.

City Lights

Many small presses which began in the 50s with the ambition of publishing the work of new writers followed the example of New Directions. One such publisher which grew with the model of New Directions in mind was City Lights Books. In the summer of 1953, Lawrence Ferlinghetti and a partner started the City Lights Pocket Book Shop in San Francisco as an outlet which would only sell books in paperback edition. Independent bookshops such as this allowed low budget, often home-made publications a chance to be sold from its shelves.

But Ferlinghetti didn't just want to sell books, he wanted to make them. When his partner left a year later and he became the sole owner, Ferlinghetti began work on an idea which he had been developing for sometime and expanded the business into a publishing house. As a poet himself, he realized the need for a publisher who would be prepared to publish the writing of his peers in such a way that it that could be sold at a low cost. He began to publish the Pocket Poet Series, which was a series of cheap pocket-sized volumes of poetry. A collection of his own poems, *Pictures of the Gone World,* was the first book to be published by City Lights in 1955. As the San Francisco Renaissance, a new movement of American poets who adopted a freer verse style linked with both the New York literary scene and the writers at Black Mountain College, raged through the 50s and 60s, City Lights became a popular publishers as well as bookshop. Ferlinghetti gave new writers a chance to be published, among them Allen Ginsberg whose poem *Howl* was published in 1956 as Number 4 in the Pocket Poets Series. Ferlinghetti also contributed to the literary magazine culture of the time by producing *The City Lights Journal* to print the work that he was not able to publish in book form.

Other small presses which formed in the wake of the model provided by New Directions included LeRoi Jones' Totem Press, founded in 1958 after beginning his own writing career in 1956, as an offshoot of his *Yugen* magazine. Totem Press worked alongside another small publisher, Corinth Books, and together they were successful in publishing the work of Jack Kerouac, Allen Ginsberg, Gary Snyder, Diane Di Prima and Gregory Corso.

In the mid-60s, Diane Di Prima also took up the challenge of publishing the work of new writers and established The Poets Press with her husband Alan

Marlowe. During the five years that it was in operation (1964-1969), this highly successful independent press focused on the writing of innovative avant-garde poets and published twenty-nine books of prose and poetry by writers such as Audre Lorde42, Clive Matson and Herbert Hunke.

White Rabbit Press
Of the many small scale independent publishers that were started during the late 50s and 60s, not all of them produced professionally constructed books. Instead, using the technology available to them, they printed their own magazines using a mimeograph press. One such publisher was Jack Spicer's San Francisco White Rabbit Press. He produced *J,* his own mimeographed magazine and was keen to feature unpublished writers within its pages. He accepted contributions from a box kept in a bar in the North Beach, San Francisco. Although based within the heart of the beat poetry scene, Spicer kept himself aside from this movement. The rise in popularity of particular writers led him to feel that they had forgotten their underground roots. In particular, he disliked Ferlinghetti at City Lights, feeling that he was too commercially successful.

These small press pioneers, and others like them, helped others realize that it was only through controlling their own means of production that writers and editors like themselves were able to get their work and that of their contemporaries into the world. They realized that they could not wait for literary America to somehow 'discover' them: they would have to do something for themselves if they wished to be heard. Perched at the edge of 'respectable' society, these writers were typically young and impatient, wanting to be free and experimental in a post- war era where they felt they were expected to jump into life as fully formed adults. The emphasis in their work was often adventurousness, innovation and indeed youthfulness itself. As they were not able to reach an audience through the established channels of the conservative literary world, they had to find their own way, forming the necessary networks and working together to establish their own forms of media. If it were not for their inventiveness and determination, many of the subcultures which have grown directly from these early beat writers would not have enjoyed the benefit of their influence.

The literary world that they created relied on self-publishing and self-promotion. Through these networks, a community grew. Words were not just confined to paper, there were also live events, where writers had the chance to speak directly to their audience. The most famed of these was the now legendary reading in 1955 by Allen Ginsberg at Six Gallery on Fillmore Street, of his poem *Howl*. The sense of excitement and anticipation of this event fired the beat writers into wider recognition. This primal interaction between writer and audience, typically seen as only possible through the live event was a vital element of the scene. The act of self-publishing their work mirrored this interaction, writing was put directly into the hands of the reader. This is what made the beat writers' activities such an important stage in self-publishing history – they could reach their reader directly, create a sense of community and mutual participation. It is this essence that other self-publishers seem to be attempting to recapture.

The Fiction Zine

The Story Tellers
When they could not find publishers to take on their work

beat writers turned to self-publishing and produced independent magazines and established their own presses to gain exposure for their work and find an audience. Improvements in technology in recent years have further facilitated the process by which writers may publish their own work much more easily. Steve Clay, whose book *A Secret Location on the Lower East Side* focuses on the self-publishing efforts of the 20th century, compares this directly to the activities of the beat writers. He explains that: 'Desktop publishing brings the possibility of publishing into the economic and skill level range of more people than any previous form of print production. This has resulted in an explosion of new publications.' This explosion of self-publishing has not only been in the form of self-published books, but also zines.

Due to their specialized nature, the impact of small press journals often reached no further than the avant-garde literary world. However, the zine would prove to be the ideal format for writers to use to begin to publish their own work. For the first time, writers were not pressurized into producing a whole volume of their own work, they could print just one story or poem alongside the work of others.

With new technology making it cheaper and easier than ever before to produce a zine, this tradition of self-publishing continues to broaden the literary landscape. The surge of fiction zines, as well as poetry zines, in the latter part of the 20th century (due in part to the developments in technology that Clay mentions) has proved to be a vital part of the literary community's development.

A number of independently produced poetry zines joined the existing poetry scene which placed emphasis on performing your work aloud. The zine became another way to present poems to an audience. However, in recent years the poetry zine network appears to have shrunk, in terms of the numbers of people taking part, alongside the decrease in other genres of paper zines. This is in part due to the ease in which people can now self-publish their own work in such a way that mirrors the professional presses. Nazmia Jamal, active in the British poetry zine community in the late 90s, explains, 'People are moving away from the cut n'paste postal community more towards vanity pressing.'[43] There have been an increase in numbers of people choosing this option – publishing volumes of their own work independently rather than working with others to produce collaborative zines.

A similar change can be seen in the fiction community, with people often self-publishing their own work and others starting their own presses. Cities across America, such as New York and San Francisco, have developed strong networks of independently owned presses, operating away from the mainstream. These follow in the tradition of those started in the 50s and hold similar fiercely independent ideals, being determined not to compromize what they want to publish for commercial success. Writers now have the option to work with these presses, often well established in the literary underground.

There is also the relatively recent practice of writers publishing their poetry on the internet. For some, this seems an unlikely format, Jamal says, 'The internet is a strange medium for poetry. I think that people prefer performance or paper.' Others have embraced the new technology and countless e-journals of poetry and fiction can be found online, linking together a virtual literary community. Even if they don't chose to publish their work online, writers can produce their own websites and publicize themselves – reaching a potential audience for their work.

An interview with London-based short story writer and editor **Amy Prior.**

How do fiction zines work?
'I think that a fanzine is really about music. Whereas fiction zines are an inspiration in terms of ways of making networks for distribution of new writing. You can also use them to distribute writing in networks that already exist – in music, film and other arts. It's sort of borrowing from networks that are already there.'

Are they any particularly important fiction zines?
'There was *Between C and D: Writings for the Lower East Side.* That was definitely a fiction zine – around in the late 80s. It was responsible for publishing many risk-taking US writers' early works – people like Dennis Cooper, Lynne Tillman. Kevin Williamson also did one called *Rebel Inc* – a really influential literary zine in Scotland. *Rebel Inc* is now an imprint of Canongate and publishes new edgy writers. It started off as a zine in the early 90s – publishing writers like Irvine Welsh, Alan Warner and Laura Hird. It only lasted for five issues. Kevin Williamson was very much influenced by football and music fanzines then moved on to fiction. He was one of the first to organize crossover literary events, which involved music and DJs and was quite influential in starting that approach – in the UK at least. He brought those *Rebel Inc* writers to a wider audience.'

Do you think that those people writing fiction zines are trying to move into writing professionally? Do you see it as a starting place for writers?
'I can't think of any fiction zines that have lasted more than two or three years. Mostly what happens is that these

communities are created and get a certain brand – like the 'New Scottish Writing' – and then suddenly big publishers will pick up on it and start publishing their writers.

But then you get more personal zines, like *Pagan's Head* by Pagan Kennedy. She brought the idea of the zine to the public. She's a classic example of how a person can produce a zine. Kevin Williamson was trying to form communities of new writers. She was trying to further her own writing. What I find interesting about this is that she did a book about her zine, which she uses to analyse what she is doing and what it brought her. One thing she talks about is the fact that she was becoming quite a professional writer, getting her work published in some quite big journals, but she started this zine out of anger because she felt that she had to conform to an aesthetic if she was to succeed as a writer.'

Do you think that zine writing can be a form of rebellion for a writer?
'Yeah, you can write what you want and don't have anyone peering over your shoulder saying that you have to be writing about suburban America for example (there was a big thing in the 80s when Pagan Kennedy was writing her zine where everyone was writing about golf and suburban America). She was thinking that she was doing it out of reaction, but it was also helping her create material that seeped into her fiction (sort of like Virginia Woolf did in her diary). She could write whatever she wanted and it helped her find her voice. She wrote in her zine about things that other people weren't writing about – she had historical stuff and stuff about her family. She was drawing on all these issues that continue to have an influence on what she is doing now. So her zine was a way of exploring

her own ideas that she wasn't able to do in a writing programme at college.'

It's like a public version of a diary?
'It's like a diary and it's not fiction, it's autobiographical, but then the autobiography feeds into the fiction. So it's similar to the blog or the web journal on the internet.' (See 'DIY literature online' for material on self-publishing on the net).

So that is also a form of self-publishing, a way to get people to read your writing? Getting ideas together to use later.
'The problem with web journals is that you need someone to creatively shape the work to make it into fiction. One of the problems is that we have a culture of autobiography – people writing about their 'real lives' – but we don't have much of a culture of people who read fiction. We do get a lot of good writing in zines but it's good autobiographical writing. In music fanzines people write about their own experiences.'

What are the motivations for people writing or continuing to write fiction zines? Are they looking to be published by mainstream publishers?
'I think some sort of sharing with a wider audience is important. It depends what route you take. Some people taking a route through college might have their work published through that. One problem is that we don't have enough zines.'

Are there any current fiction zines?
'All those that I know about are historical. The latest I can think of is *Rebel Inc* and that was the 90s.'

Why aren't there any anymore? Is it because it's now easier to get your work published on the internet rather than physically publishing something?
'Yes, and it's also partly because we have a culture of autobiography, so people publishing on the internet are doing live journals. Where people might have tried to write fiction ten years ago now they write journals.'

Is self-publishing more common amongst poets?
'There are huge networks for poetry. There's the Poetry Society, loads of poetry zines and the Poetry Library. Generally if you aren't writing poetry then you are writing a novel. Short fiction isn't that highly valued so there need to be more networks to share short fiction. There are a few readings but they are more low-key readings. There are more readings than publications, which takes time. Also you have to think about festivals – in San Francisco there's a lot going on. Also these things grow out of small presses. There needs to be things feeding the independent presses. There needs to be more younger writers, taking risks in terms of form or content – in more DIY kinds of ways.'

What form of community do fiction zines create?
'If I do a reading, I often look different to other writers doing the same. My friends all work in other art forms. To me, one way of forming communities is to look at communities that are already there, linking up with other art communities. The crossover between different art forms is so blurry now. Someone like Miranda July is doing short fiction, film and live art for example. All the boundaries are blurred now.'

Are you interested in working in other art forms?
'I am interested in showing my work in different ways, ways

that don't involve standing up in a bookshop and reading. I am interested in broadening my horizons and operating beyond the literary community.'

Do you need fiction zines because the line between different art forms is blurred, or is it blurred because there aren't specific fiction zines and related supportive networks? Is it better that you have to try and find your own route with less support?

'I do have my own communities. I sometimes develop work in workshops with other writers. I have international networks through my collections. But there are differences between local and international networks and local networks are important.'

Are fiction zines generally a reaction against mainstream publishing trends?

'It's a way of developing work. Someone like Dennis Cooper wouldn't have been published without this. It's finding your networks to make new work. *Between C and D* worked to show emerging writers who weren't shown in the usual literary magazines. It's also a way of showing work in different places. They showed people's work in galleries. Lynne Tillman had her work shown in art catalogues.'

So they have more freedom to do what they want, to find their own places to show their work?

'Yes. And build on networks that are already there. There is an amazing US magazine called *BOMB*, which includes people from different art forms interviewing each other – like a recorded dialogue. It came out of the crossover of different types of artists supporting each other.'

So you are interested in the idea of building new networks or finding existing networks through which to show your work?

'My preoccupation is showing work in places that aren't bookshops. Why do you have to show in a shop? Why does someone who wrote a story have to stand up and read it? A writer isn't necessarily a performer, and the audience also gets preoccupied by the person who wrote the text rather than the text. If you want to show to more than one person at a time – not through them just reading the story in a book – you need to construct different environments for them to do that. You can have a gallery environment, a film environment, a sound/audio environment. Your audience will also then be more of a crossover. You'll be bringing literature out of a bookshop into more of a general cultural arena.'

Does mainstream publishing get influenced by what the underground writers are doing?

'I suppose the only way they are influenced is by poaching writers, not by creating networks. They just pluck people out.'

How do writers view that?

'I guess it's like music. It depends on the person and how they are affected by it. If they just cut themselves off from their community then that will affect their work.'

Do you think self-publishing is viewed as an amateur form of press? When does something stop becoming a zine and become vanity publishing?

'I suppose when money is involved, when you are paying. It's a different production; you can't just use a photocopier.

Investing money in it changes things.'

Fiction zines tend to be collaborations, featuring the work of different people. What if someone produces a zine of all their own work? Is that viewed differently? Are they trying to get published?
'I guess it depends on how sustainable it is.'

Why do you think people don't tend to just publish their own work in a zine? Is it because networking is part of the experience?
'Maybe nowadays someone who wanted to do that would have their own blog or web journal. Also it is a lot of effort to do something that is just your own work. It's more intensive. Doing something on your own is always more difficult. It's much better if you have distribution networks. With a music zine you automatically have a means of distribution. You can go to gigs and sell them and make friends. With fiction zines you feel like you are trying to tap into something else to get your audience. You can't go up to someone and say, "Do you want to buy my short story? I published it myself." So that's why you need networks and if you haven't got something really big to sustain them then it can't work.'

So the way you work and distribute is different from other types of zines?
'I had short stories published in a zine in about 1996. We used to hand them out at gigs. They were all stories. People seem to do that with autobiographical zines, shared experiences, but not with fiction. Fiction is shared experience but also art.'

Artists and the Zine

Art Rebels

Many visual artists working in the 20th century recognized the zine as a means of cultural resistance, embodying the political significance of creating your own work and distributing it yourself. This is what the sci-fi zinesters and the beat writers realized – the potential of developing your own sustainable cultural underground, using the zine as a primary tool of communication. Many visual artists believed that individuality lies in the creative process rather than in passive consumption, and many art movements of the 20th century, in turning away from the seemingly elite world of traditional art practices such as painting, began to follow the route that the independent writers had previously taken.

The dadaist, gutai, fluxus and situationist movements, for example, took many ideas from the independent press. Members of each group realized that if they could cheaply and easily reproduce their work, it would enable them to interact with a wider audience and allow them a chance for mass collaboration. During the first half of the 20th century, technological developments in the printing industry meant that artists had this new opportunity to distribute their work for themselves. Artists would play with mass-producing images and in doing so could constantly reinvent the medium within which they were working. Many held an almost utopian ideal that the interaction between the artist and audience was a vital one and that the spectator held as important a position in the artistic process as the artist. They experimented with this idea by using the mass distribution of images, the concept of fly posting – where an image would be distributed as street art – and the production of rubber stamps that could be used to produce multiple images. Such methods were designed to change the widely held perception of art as elitist and instead establish the idea that it could be universal and accessible. Artists began to realize that they did not need to operate within the mainstream art world but could co-exist just outside, developing global networks through which to distribute their cryptic art.

Dada

During the first decade of the 20th century, dada artists began creating what can be seen as a design template for the modern day zine. Dadaism (whose name derives from the baby-talk syllables 'da-da') was a radical international movement in literature and art that called for a complete break with tradition and the systematic destruction of culture and of civilization. Its origins can be traced to Cabaret Voltaire, a small bar and variety hall opened by Hugo Ball and Emmy Hennings in 1916, in Zurich, Switzerland. Here artists would gather; both to escape the draft and to create work in response to the widespread conflict. These people had little choice but to use the method of underground publishing to make controversial statements, to get their ideas heard and to shake the bourgeois sensibilities of the art world. Active between 1915 and 1922, the artists within this dada movement experimented with techniques such as collage, detournement[44] (the practice of subverting established images, demonstrated most simply by the adaptation of comic strip captions) and appropriation (illustrated by their taking of design elements from mainstream culture and adapting them for their own purposes).

The movement spread from Switzerland to Paris, Berlin,

Eastern Europe and New York, where younger artists, such as Marcel Duchamp, Tristan Tzara[45] and Francis Picabia[46] became enchanted by the new ideas. Experimenting with different images and materials dada artists would produce little books: art zines containing collages and rubber stamp art which would be reproduced and distributed. Self-publishing was popular and magazines such as *Cabaret Voltaire, Dada, 291, 391* and *New York Dada* were circulated, designed and printed by artists themselves. Many of these techniques would later be adopted by the surrealist movement in their publications, and later still the situationists would pick up on the same techniques in their publications.

The visual techniques that these artists used in their art books and magazines later appeared, more than sixty years after the early dada movement, in the 'cut and paste' style of the punk zine of the 1970s.[47]

The editorial style that the dadaists commonly adopted would also later influence coming generations of zine writers, with long ranting columns expressing radical points of views. Techniques such as detournement and appropriation have reappeared in zines ever since. In the 60s, *Oz* magazine controversially altered a comic strip featuring Rupert the Bear and riot grrrl zines of the 1990s often used elements of mainstream culture, such as adapting adverts from women's magazines or subversively using the image of the Barbie doll. Such subversion of established culture is a way for a subculture to force a space for itself within the mainstream. The dadaists developed an accessible design and writing style, which suited their agenda and would in turn suit zine writers from punk onwards. In modern zines, text runs in unconventional ways, over collages and around pictures; humour is used, whether through sharp satire or silly jokes and puns; self-reference is common and so debates and ideas are often impenetrable without prior knowledge and the sensibilities of the mainstream media are attacked and criticized. Rather than being a recent invention, the origins of all these verbal and visual techniques and forms of content can be traced back to the dadaists of the early 20th century and hundreds of paper zines and magazines since produced have shared similar characteristics – from original British punk zine *Sniffin' Glue* in the 70s to the underground American music magazine *Maximumrocknroll* beginning in the 80s and still in print today.

Situationist International

As well as the dadaists, the group known as 'The Situationist International' were also pioneers of many of the features and styles found in later zines. This Paris based artistic and political movement was concerned with radically redefining the boundaries of art in the 20th century. They did not want people to see art as a specialized activity but rather as a part of everyday life.

The movement originated in the Italian village of Cosio d'Arroscia on the 28th July 1957 with the fusion of small European art groups calling themselves 'Lettrist International' (itself a splinter group of The Radical Lettrists) and 'The International Movement for an Imaginist Bauhaus'. Later, The London Psychogeographical Society joined them. Earlier anti-art movements such as dada, surrealism and fluxus can also be included as amongst those movements which exerted an influence upon the situationists.

The work of the situationist movement is typically abstract and difficult to understand, but they certainly supported a policy of attempting to spread their ideas through self-publishing. Producing their own pamphlets explaining their complex agenda was a perfect way to ensure that their words were not misrepresented.

Guy Debord, a central figure in the situationist movement, had been influenced in his adoption of the technique of self-promotion by the lettrists who understood the need for a group or individual to distribute their own ideas in their own way. In 1948, the lettrists distributed posters around the Latin Quarter of Paris reading: '12,000 Youths Will Take The Streets to Make the Lettrist Revolution.' They wanted to spark a youth rebellion, but a radical youth culture wasn't yet in place.

As well as publishing twelve issues of its journal *Internationale Situationiste,* The Situationist International issued a stream of publications, among them *Potlatch* – a name referring to the gift-giving practices of Northwest Native Americans. They developed a new means of distributing their publications. Aside from passing them out themselves, they mailed them to people chosen at random from the phone book. It was accompanied by an anti-copyright notice that, 'All texts published in *Potlatch* can be reproduced, adapted or quoted without any mention of the source.'[48] They wanted readers to feel that the work was their own and did not belong to a distant writer. This became a key ideal that later writers would take hold of, from the radical newspapers of the 1960s to the punk zines of the 1970s. In underground culture, writers have always tried to forge a close bond with their reader.

Although the movement never had more than around twenty to forty members at any one time and ended in 1972, the impact of the Situationist International on independent art has been widely recognized and its influence remains today. Many people have noticed the similarities between The Situationist International publications and many zines which were produced later, both in the visual style, rebellious attitude and means of distribution.

The Bay Area Dadaists

Like the dada artists, who produced publications which reflected their radical attitudes towards art, the emerging Bay Area dada group of the 1960s was also engaged in self-publishing, taking advantage of new affordable print technologies. The number of artists self-publishing at the time was as impressive as their work was varied. Infamous artist, Monte Cazazza edited *Nitrous Oxide*, Patricia Tavenner published *Mail Order Art*, Mancusi produced *The New York Weekly Breeder*, Gaglione introduced *Dadazine,* and later with Anna Banana, he wrote *VILE*.[49] Chickadel compiled *Quoz?* and *The West Bay Dadaist*. Rick Soloway distributed the *Nu Art Review*. Opel Nations was printing *Strange Faces* and Irene Dogmatic published *Insult*. Such publications pre-empted the later popularity of DIY publishing. The headline of the second issue of *The West Bay Dadaist* read 'Do-It-Yourself' and many generations to come did just that.

Fluxus

Artists of the fluxus movement, which started around 1962, consciously attempted to play with the preconceived idea of art. They wanted to rid art of its oppressive sense of the commercial and instead infuse it with a sense of theatrical humour. They followed the attitude that art should be accessible to all and indeed, that anyone could produce it.

The movement was started by George Maciunas, a Lithuanian architect and designer who co-owned the AG Gallery in New York. In 1960, he met the composer La Monte Young[50]. Young became active in the avant-garde art scene and, between 1960 and 1961, with the artist Yoko Ono[51] organized a concert series at Ono's New York loft. Maciunas and Young both became involved in showing work at Maciunas' gallery and began organizing 'happenings' – small scale abstract art events, which ranged from readings to strangely themed parties.

Young and Maciunas were not just connected by their involvement in art but also by their interest in publishing. In 1960, Young guest-edited the literary journal *Beatitude East* and was given the task of including conceptual art in the publication. With the help of Maciunas and others, in October 1961 the collection became a self-published journal entitled *An Anthology,* which included experimental music and event scores; poetry, essays and the work of artists like Nam June Paik,[52] Dieter Roth[53] and Emmett Williams.[54] That this journal included details of experimental music is indicative of the part music played in the art movement. Many of its artists were influenced by the avant-garde musician John Cage. A large number of those originally involved in the movement had attended Cage's course in Musical Composition at The New School of Social Research, New York, in the summer of 1958.

At the start of 1963, Maciunas published the *Purge Manifesto,* outlining the aims of the fluxus movement and openly declaring war on what he saw to be, 'The world of bourgeois sickness, "intellectual", professional and commercialized culture.' This became the battle cry for the fluxus art community, a direct attack on commercial art. The New York art scene began to buzz with this new artistic community who tried to set themselves apart from the established art world.

To break from a system where art critics were all-powerful and money inspired art, the fluxus artists tried an approach which would, rather idealistically, make all artists of the movement equal. It was envisioned that all artists should sign their artwork simply 'fluxus' without adding their own names. This was an attempt to build a sense of inclusiveness within the community – there were to be no egos. Other artists preferred to use pseudonyms, which they often referred to as 'combat names'. The idea was not to produce a piece of work in isolation, which would later be sold, but instead to create an artistic movement where the overall ideals were more valued than the individual artist.

While the early years of the 1970s saw a steady rise in the number of publications, the figures rose dramatically from 1975 onwards. From 1970-74 the average number of mail art shows world-wide was four per year, from 1975-80 the average was up to thirty-four.[55]

Mail Art

These ideas about the universality of art that the fluxus movement was championing also existed in the mail art movement. Credited as having been started by Marcel Duchamp in 1916 when he first circulated his ideas by postcard, this movement has developed into a world-wide network. A small scale artwork 'in progress' is sent out via post to other artists with directions for the next artist to add to the work and pass it on. By this process, art is created with many different collaborators, many of whom may have never met in person. Other projects were created by artists sending out mass-produced images to other artists, or sending found objects to a chainletter. Mail artists played with the idea of a mass media culture and developed a new form of cultural exchange, which was relevant to their experimental ideas. Existing today, mail art continues to be a fun approach to art. Participants often make the very act of mailing an object part of the art, devising projects where they challenge each other to post the most unusual object they can think of (using the idea that you aren't required to package an object to send it through the post) – including anything from a potato to a vinyl record with the address painted on. Such games echo back to the activities of the fluxus artists and their love of happenings and the obscure.

This way of spreading ideas through the mail network was often viewed by the postal system as suspicious. This was also a problem experienced by the zine network. Having to rely so heavily on the postal system caused difficulties, as they would be reluctant to deliver controversial or seemingly subversive material. Dedicated mail artist and member of art-punk band Throbbing Gristle, Genesis P Orridge encountered difficulty when he sent handmade postcards featuring naked figures through the post in the late 1970s. The post office objected to the undisguised material that he was sending and pressed charges of indecency in 1976. In his statement to his solicitor he explains his role as a mail artist and the important need for this type of communication in the art world: 'I want to be a part of popular culture, involved with everyday life and responses, not an intellectual artist, in an ivory tower, thinking I am special, revered and monumental. I don't really want to make myself precious, and my work and myself are inseparable.' To him, his mail art project was a valid means of distributing his art to his audience. This mirrors the zine process and the fundamental aim of all zine writers – to share what they are thinking with others.

Decos

In a recent manifestation of mail art that exists today, a

little booklet called the 'deco' (decorated friendship book), passes from person to person through the mail in an envelope with each recipient decorating a page including their name and address before passing it on. These mini art projects often have themes, which can be anything. When the booklet is full it is then returned to the person who originally started it; a simple idea relying on the principle that people will take part and that the booklet will be returned. Participants have to trust each other and, when this works, this practice helps create a network of similarly creative people – or at least the illusion of such a network. The quality will of course vary, depending on whether participants take the project seriously or are only half-heartedly involved. This contemporary method of mail art provides an unusual opportunity for individual creativity, with the added advantage that by following the zine trail through everyday postal systems, it offers people who may not be artists the chance to take part.

New York Correspondance School

Ray Johnson, the man who pre-dated Andy Warhol in his use of images borrowed from popular culture, was one of the most influential figures in the mail art movement. Born in Detroit, Michigan in 1927, from 1946-48 he studied at the Black Mountain College in North Carolina alongside Robert Rauschenberg and Cy Twombly, with faculty members Joseph Albers, Robert Motherwell, John Cage, Merce Cunningham, Buckminister Fuller and Willem and Elaine DeKooning. Johnson started the New York Correspondance School in the early 1960s, which became an international network of artists who would use the postal system to exchange artwork and ideas. The purposeful misspelling of 'Correspondance', changing a noun into a verb, consciously played with the process of interaction. As with the sci-fi scene of the 1930s, where fans began to communicate via the pages of the magazines they were reading, the mail artist could communicate through newsletters and listings of the addresses of participants. Communication was the key and through the network that was forged, art and art-making practices were explored, linking artists' lives to their art.

In the mid-50s, Johnson – nicknamed the 'the most famous unknown artist' – became an important figure in the New York art scene. 'Ray didn't talk about it, he just did it,' says long-time friend Toby Spiselman, 'That's why you don't find art magazines lying around quoting the art philosophy of Ray Johnson'.[56]

One of the first artists to use celebrity as content, by 1955 Johnson was working with images of Elvis Presley, Marilyn Monroe and James Dean. Making collages, which he called 'moticos', he often displayed his work in cardboard boxes to be shown in Grand Central Station or on the street. He was not particularly interested in displaying his art in galleries (though in the early 70s the Whitney Museum of American Art in New York would hold the first major mail art exhibition) but would rather give it away or display it in locations where anyone could see it. Mark Block, author of the web article, 'A Brief History of Postal Art,' explains that, 'Ray told me in 1991, "They just wanted them as objects. 'Aren't these nice! Put them in a museum with nice lighting.' Not the ideas... I wanted to paste things on railroad cars. Nothing to be seen by anyone except coyotes."'[57] This was a sort of anti-elitist game that many artists were playing, one where art was fun, a means to explore the idea that anything, however trivial, could be art.

A number of artists' own self-produced publications emerged from the mail art network. One of the most prominent was the New York Correspondance School's *Weekly Breeder*. This single-sheeted weekly newsletter was started by the artist Ken Friedman from Fluxus West. Following the spirit of collaboration at the heart of the mail art network, *Weekly Breeder* twice changed hands during its lifetime: from Friedman, to Stu Horn in Philadelphia, then on to Bill Gaglione and Tom Mancusi of the Bay Area dadaists in San Francisco, who published it until 1974. In the final issue, the Bay Area dadaists claimed this publication to be a 'dadazine', thus linking the new zines which were being produced at the time to this earlier form. The mail art network has many characteristics similar to the zine network. Both are democratic forms of communication where people can contact others who may have similar ideas. With the advent of these art magazines and mail art projects, those interested in such cultural forms increasingly began to realize that they were a part of a wider network.

As the forerunner of mail art and the New York Correspondance School, and along with these offshoots, the fluxus movement's adaptation of an underground means of production and distribution of artists' work, provides a useful illustration of how groups existing in isolation from one another have been prompted to reinvent the DIY concept for themselves, tailoring it to suit their own needs. The spread of the DIY ethic also suggested that the need for people to share their work with others, and the recurring need for collaboration between creators, was universal. Significantly, a principle and recurring goal behind the DIY approach is one of community building – the idea is not that individuals simply encourage each other to 'do-it-yourself' but rather that groups are formed under the collective urge to 'do-it-ourselves'.

Interview with **John Held, Jr**: Art curator, writer and editor of irregular American periodical *Bibliozine*, published in connection with research the editor was conducting for his book *International Networker Culture: An Annotated Bibliography*.

What do you think the role of do-it-yourself ethics is in art culture?

'Mail art is to art, as zine culture is to self-publishing. They are both based on DIY ethics. Concurrent with the rise of modernist art in the beginning of the 20th century, an alternative strain of artistic thought emerged. While the majority of the artists of the time continued the tradition of developing their technique in classical mediums, entering prestigious exhibitions, pursuing commercial success in nascent gallery structures and establishing reputations as a prelude to a professional career path, an international undercurrent appeared. Russian transrationalism (*zaum*),[58] Italian futurism[59] and the outburst of dadaism in Switzerland, Germany, France and Eastern Europe, envisioned artistic practice as salvation from the poverty of the competitive spirit in modern life.

This tendency, born from the turbulence of World War I, exhausted itself with the coming of a second global conflict and the American Depression, only to resurface at the end of hostilities after World War II and with a more prosperous America.

Central to this was John Cage, first as a mentor to a younger generation of artists at Black Mountain College, and later as a teacher at the New School for Social Research, influencing many artists associated with the fluxus movement. Another of his students, Allen Kaprow, unaligned with fluxus, popularized the 'happening', which harked back to the practices of the zaum, futurist and dada artists, taking art out of the studio and attempting to blend it with life. Likewise, Ray Johnson, who attended Black Mountain College with Cage, began developing the postal system as an alternative art medium, taking art out of the galleries and fostering a more intimate approach to the artistic process.

The democratic nature of this approach to art-making resists judgements of quality in pursuit of an open system, in which anyone can participate. Histories of this alternative path, like judgements of quality, are often avoided to insure that no hierarchical structure is established at the expense of this fluid structure.

Ignorance of the history of alternative art denies its importance in a society that associates artistic accomplishment with commercial success. In many ways, the practices of alternative art encouraged and anticipated the open nature of the internet. This historical vacuum encourages the prevalence of commercial enterprise at the expense of more creative uses of emerging mediums. An investigation of alternative art, therefore, can fortify our knowledge of parallel uses of new communication technologies.'

Which art movement do you think was the first to produce printed material resembling the zine?

'I've been doing a lot of research on the pre-revolutionary Russian avant-garde, especially their use of the rubber stamp in producing artists' books. These books are very much like zines: produced inexpensively with stapled bindings. The covers were sometimes made from wallpaper.

In reaction to the academic conservatism of the symbolists who preceded them, the artists of the pre-revolutionary Russian avant-garde challenged the basic assumptions of both the art and life of their time. Their face-painting reflected a desire to merge art with life, while their use of the humble rubber stamp in their books brought the artefacts of daily living into their art. Alexei Kruchenykh's rubber stamp poem from *Worldbackwards* (1912), stands as a benchmark between the old and new arts, the title shedding insight into the Russian avant-garde's fervent desire to reconstruct the world during the new century.

Cubism, futurism, zaum and supremacist styling rushed by in frenzied attempts to capture and convey the spirit of Russia in revolt. Post-revolutionary political regimes incorporated and then rejected avant-garde visions of harmonizing art and life. Screened from the Western art world for much of the 20th century, their bold initiatives are now being unearthed, exemplified by an exhaustive re-examination of their published works in the Museum of Modern Art, New York, 2002 exhibition, "The Russian Avant-garde Book, 1910-1934."

Mail artists have known about the Russian avant-garde since the late 1980s, when Soviet artists Serge Segay and Rea Nikonova (Eysk), spread knowledge of zaum poetry throughout this international artistic network. The activities of the Russian avant-garde found a receptive audience among mail artists, as both groups were producing alternative expressions of the dominant art of the day.'

Do you think artists and mail artists use the self-publishing network in the same way as zine writers?
'Very much so. And there is quite a bit of overlap, for

example, the literary works of Al Ackerman and John Bennett, who both participate in mail art and contribute to zines (Bennett publishes the zine *Lost and Found Times*). Mail art is an alternative art system, having its own exhibitions (no fee to enter, all work exhibited, documentation to participants). Artists can build resumes by their appearance in mail art shows, just as zine writers gain experience by having their works published in zines.'

Is DIY as important in the art world as it is in music scenes?
'I don't think so. I think the music industry pays more attention to its "underground" than the mainstream art world, which barely acknowledges the existence of mail art. Mail art is generally a gift, and not shown in commercial galleries. Therefore, it's not taken seriously by a commodity driven culture.'

Is it a conscious decision, turning away from the mainstream art world?
'Very much so. Duchamp said that the artist of tomorrow, "would go underground" in an attempt to retain the spiritual qualities in art production. This is all but impossible in the commercial mainstream, which pits artist against artist. Mail art is based on co-operation and collaboration, rather then competition.'

Do you think mail artists and zine scenes use the same methods?
'Yes. Both are created in similar fashions. The venture is financed by the individual. It often combines both the work of the artist/publisher, with those of his collaborators. It is distributed in a pre-existing network.'

Do you think the 'cut and paste' style which has developed has any particular importance? Why has it become a dominant style in DIY?
'Its importance lies in an alliance with photocopier reproduction methods. Photocopying melds disparate graphic sources (and texts) into a unified whole. When computers replaced photocopiers as favoured production tools, these methods were carried over, proving that one medium rarely 'replaces' another, but instead, improves upon the former.'

How important are the ideas of network and collaboration in mail art movements?
'The mail art network is based on collaboration and networking. An alternative name for mail art is the 'Eternal Network', which was the name given by fluxus artist Robert Fililiou to describe a circle of collaborators, in which some were leaving, some entering, with a core group always present to impart a knowledge of the past. A mail art project, like the "Brain Cell" project by Japanese mail artist Ryosuke Cohen, which gathers images from throughout the mail art network and situates them on a single sheet of paper, accompanied by a list of names and addresses of contributors, is impossible to conceive of without the aid of a network of artists in collaboration.'

What are your favourite mail art concepts/project ideas?
'"Brain Cell", by Ryosuke Cohen. Here images from various mail artists are gathered on a single sheet of paper printed by a gocco printer.[60]

"Mohammed Center of Restricted Communication", by Plinio Mesculiam. Mesculiam would send out his letterhead to artists. They would do something on the page and attach a list of twelve names and addresses. Mesculiam would then colour photocopy the page, assign it a "unit number" and distribute it to the artist and the twelve named people.

"AAA Edizione", by Vittore Baroni and Piermario Ciani. They've been publishing a series of paperback books on mail art, rubber stamp art, and artist postage stamps.'

Do you see any similarities between communication via the mail art movement and the internet?
'Before the dotcom generation, mail artists were paving the information highway, reaching across vanishing borders to establish contact with like-minded individuals through mediated communication. Instantaneous communication via computer has certain undeniable advantages over the postal system. But art via the mail still possesses certain preferential characteristics. The shared touch of the paper, the varied textures of presentation and the duration one waits for a reply all adds to the mystery of postal correspondence.

Many strategies developed in mail art have made the transition to the internet. Mail art shows, where all entries are accepted, have made the leap to the internet. A call for entry goes out (via email). Jpegs are sent by contributors. They are gathered on a website by the organizer. Same as mail art.'

Political Zines

The Radicals
The 20th century saw the development of offset printing – a relatively cheap and accessible way to reproduce the written word. Since the 19th century, newspaper copy had been set in hot lead type on a linotype machine and then

printed on a huge press, with operators who required technical training and which called for major financial investment. The development of cold-type printing made newspapers quick, easy and cheap to produce. Now anyone with ideas and a typewriter could produce their own newspaper. In the mid-1950s and early 1960s, people began to realize the potential of this development and started to make and distribute magazines and newspapers. Some opted for the small scale, just a few dozen copies passed out to friends, whereas others produced large copy runs of newspapers which they then distributed on a national or international scale.

There was a new audience for these publications, a new generation of young people who were not content with the established press of their parents. The sense of social and political dissent of the post-war era gave way to the 60s, which brought with them social changes almost unthought of a generation before: more people were able to go to college, recreational drug use increased, the contraceptive pill contributed to the sexual revolution. This has long been documented as a time of social liberation, a time where pre-existing values were dismantled.

However, throughout this time of change, the mainstream media of the United Kingdom and America almost refused to shift from the model it had assumed decades earlier, and was slow to realize that times were changing or that the counterculture was growing. In fact, the media was often condescending towards the behaviour of those involved in sub-cultural activities, treating them as something of a joke and refusing to print unbiased coverage of the events taking place involving the counterculture or its underlying political activism. As the printing of small scale magazines and pamphlets had long been seen as a valid political and social tool enabling the communication of opinion, many people turned to self-publishing, feeling that the established press was not reflecting their own experiences and viewpoints. This rebellion was infectious and the underground press movement grew rapidly. By the late 1960s there were one hundred and fifty underground newspapers in the US with a total circulation of about two million readers. This was during a period when many mainstream newspapers were shutting down due to a decline in readership.

The writers and editors were typically college students and post college drop-outs, stretching coast to coast across America. The situation was similar in Britain where there were countless young people dissatisfied with their jobs or universities. This was a group waiting for action who needed to be organized – and as a long-established means of communication, the newspaper was the ideal tool. In its basic form, it is a way to communicate to a large group of people; the events of different cities can be relatively quickly and easily transmitted to readers across the UK. The underground press used this network model as a way to build their community and by forging links with other individuals grew in strength. People were encouraged to get involved and help to bring about change. This was not a one-sided news transmission but a dialogue between writer and reader.

These newspapers echoed the predominant themes of the day, such as student rights, minority rights, anti-war activities, women's rights, gay rights, anti-capitalism and the class struggle. Students realized that reading newspapers was a passive experience where new information was rarely given and instead old ideas or 'known' truths were simply reworked and recycled. In the US they tried to tackle the

141

government head on and printed political exposés of the Pentagon and the CIA, the police and the government. This was at a time when the establishment press was not yet printing serious investigative reports on government activities or presenting any extreme or antagonistic social views.[61] This new generation of publishers wanted to inform their readers, make previously undisclosed facts public. As the underground culture bloomed in the 60s, it was thought that the establishment needed to be attacked directly in order to bring about change. These rebel papers made their contribution as a form of protest alongside the well-documented marches and sit-ins. They embodied a sense of the moment as they tried to bind together the bohemian ideals and the new art and culture with the political ideas of the rising New Left, the civil rights campaign and the peace movement.

The catalyst for the founding of many of these American papers was the political unrest of the country during the late 50s. This was an explosive time, where the sense of uncertainty experienced by the core of the population created social change. Fear and anxiety took hold during the 1940s as Cold War mentality spread. Eastern Europe came under the grip of communism and the Soviet Union flexed its muscles by detonating an atomic bomb. The Korean War further shook Americans' confidence. As their military battled for three years to prevent Korea from joining the Communist Bloc, 54,000 American soldiers were killed.[62] The Vietnam War increased this sense of social uncertainty. With the exception of critical coverage that Tet Offensive received, reporting its attacks on many bases and cities in a well-planned campaign in late January 1968, the mainstream media generally supported the government's actions. However, underground newspapers had the confidence to attack the war from the beginning. They had no allegiance with the government and were therefore in a much better position to criticize its actions. Opposition to the US military involvement in Vietnam began in the mid-1950s and grew during the 1960s. This anti-war sentiment soon added to a momentous rising demand for the creation of a counterculture that would help a generation of rebels develop agendas and strategies for securing civil rights for everyone.[63]

One of the most frequently recurring subjects of most of the American underground newspapers of the 1960s was the writers' fierce objections to the Vietnam War. The mainstream papers were typically conservative in nature and backed the government, so the underground press was the natural home for this counterculture concerned with the peace movement.

During this time, a surprizing trend of zine-writing developed amongst men serving in the US army. Many of those drafted into the army did not hold views typical of those who would have joined voluntarily. They were against the war and wrote these zines for other servicemen who had the same objections. These unauthorized papers angered officials who attempted to control their writers through threats and disciplinary action, but the network grew and popular zines included *Bond: The Voice of the American Servicemen's Union 1967* and *Fun, Travel and Adventure at Fort Knox Kentucky.*

Blending art with politics, the emergent newspapers would also feature articles about the new art forms that were developing. Rock music was fast growing into the soundtrack of the 60s and was written about extensively in many of these new newspapers. As new cultural icons appeared, the people celebrated in the underground press were very different to

143

those written about in the mainstream media. The contributors wrote extensively about new art scenes and consciously tried to take art away from its allegedly pretentious roots and make it more accessible to everyone.

The rise of drug culture, associated with artistic movements, followed the development of counterculture. The use of psychedelic drugs at this time encouraged individuals to perceive themselves as existing outside of, and perhaps in opposition to, conventional societal norms. With an altered mindset, their concept of self was increased and filled them with a sense of self-importance that made writing about their own lives and experiences vital.

Whether this was all a revolutionary fantasy, a generation styling themselves as social outlaws, or a valid social movement beginning at a grass roots level with radical literature and turning into an important social force, they spread their ideas through the self-published printed word like never before. This took self-publishing to a new level, involving more people than ever before, and enabling print runs to be in the thousands rather than the hundreds. The underground press was making a real effort to effect as much change as possible.

Radical Style

With no existing model to follow, the editors and writers of these publications could make their own rules and develop their own ways of working. This was truly a DIY experience, writers sometimes forfeiting payment for the love of working on an independent paper, the editors often having little or no prior experience, and if they had, it would have come from working on established mainstream publications or on school newspapers.

The sense of being amateurs, ordinary people trying to

work for themselves, was seen as something to be admired and it was rarely felt that individuals were working on these newspapers as a route to moving on to a larger paper. This was just what they wanted to be doing – creating a new network of news reporting that would bypass the official governing bodies and print news stories that more closely resembled the truth.

This sense of freedom allowed writers to experiment with unconventional visual styles and forms of writing. Editors rejected the traditional format of the newspaper, with its rigid columns, and instead experimented with bold colours and unusual layouts. New forms of graphic design were developed, psychedelic imagery and stylized fonts would dominate the page, headlines and graphics were often drawn by hand, articles were not set conventionally and often ran upside-down or sideways, colours would be allowed to bleed into one another during printing to produce new and unusual effects. Papers were often amateurish in appearance, with words consciously being misspelt or misused. These new design techniques appealed to the new youth market. Confrontational, provocative language and colloquial slang was used to express passionate, often angry, views. Writers tried to shock their audience, to make the experience of reading these papers as different as possible from the mainstream press. This was rebellion in print, an anti-establishment stance on journalism.

New subjects were approached, which would have never before been seen in print, and new styles developed. Editors included personal essays as well as the news, giving an insight into the minds of the young of both the US and Britain. First hand accounts of news events developed into what is now known as 'New Journalism'. As they were often writing about the issues that they were involved with, the writer became part of the news story. They were conscious that the reality of a situation was often not presented in the establishment papers and wanted to expose the truth behind the stories, working hard to uncover the facts. This was a different way to working than the established papers. The amateur beginnings of these writers and editors meant that they were typically idealists and so felt confident to tackle issues that others had not.

This idealism did have its drawbacks. Alongside the best of the newspapers were far less impressive ones. Many small scale newspapers were full of radical political rants. Reaching a small audience, they sometimes printed the views of just one individual and so were often not representative of any larger social movement. The contributors' enthusiasm for change could also come across as ignorant or arrogant. Idealized concepts of progress were viewed with cynicism by the mainstream press and many of the population. So when a writer appeared ignorant of the wider implications of the issues they were raising and naïve about the consequences of their actions, they were often patronized by society at large.

The radical press can only really accurately represent those groups that make up the writers. The underground press of the 1960s was run predominately by white, middle class men and so the interests of this group were primarily addressed. Although newspapers did tackle the issues of broader civil rights movements, this was limited as it came from a more privileged and distanced perspective. Many papers concentrated on the issues affecting college students and difficulties faced by young men drafted into the army during the Vietnam War. It is true that they did effect great change in the distribution of radical new ideas but it must be remembered that the writers and editors were still often addressing those issues that most affected their own lives.

As contributors largely used a form of journalism where editorials contained the writers' own personal views, and as these writers were typically male and this was over fifty years ago, there was underlying and often overt sexism. In 1968, a male writer from the *San Francisco Express Times* interviewed a female anti-war activist on her return from accompanying released American POWs from Hanoi. Writing the interview up in the confessional style that was so common in the underground press, he included the fact that he was attracted to this women and made many comments about her physical appearance. This caused outrage amongst many readers, but is a common example of the type of attitude which was prevalent.[65]

The Village Voice

In the autumn of 1955, at the time when writers were sending out their radical writing and experimental poetry to their readers in the form of self-published books and magazines, Dan Wolf, Ed Francher and novelist Norman Mailer made the decision to launch a weekly newspaper in New York City. They held aspirations of creating a vital new form of newspaper which would speak to those rebellious souls who did not already have a regular news publication to call their own. This newspaper, which they called *The Village Voice,* would change the shape of the underground press and exercise great influence over similar publications hereafter.

The writers were in control. Francher and Wolf were editor and publisher respectively. They were joined in the planning stages by Jerry Tallmer and John Wilcock. Modest financial investment came from Francher and Mailer's own pocket. Mailer's influence on the newspaper has long been debated but, according to Wolf and Francher's own 1963 account in *The Village Voice Reader,* his involvement has been exaggerated. He was not involved with setting the editorial policy of the magazine and after writing a series of columns, he withdrew, critical of the direction which the newspaper was taking.

They all had different backgrounds. Tallmer and Wilcock had both been freelance writers and so had some background in newspapers and magazines. Wolf's only writing experience was gained producing entries on philosophy for the *Columbia Encyclopedia* and handling publicity for the Turkish Information Office. Like many young men at the time, three of them had been overseas during the war and had gone back to college when it was over. As with many young men of this generation, they were affected by this early experience of conflict and were not ready to slip straight back into a society which they felt to be conformist.

This was one of the first of the new underground newspapers, pre-empting the cultural revolution which would spread into the 60s. Focusing on the Greenwich Village community of New York City, it featured news of local arts events, which were growing in popularity with the rise of new 'Off-Off-Broadway' theatre, avant-garde film, downtown galleries and the jazz scene, as well as articles on wider social and political issues. It worked hard to expose corrupt landlords and dishonest government officials. The paper was rooted in the issues of the community, but soon took on the characteristics of a national newspaper with writers contributing from all parts of the country. The paper attracted talented young writers who could not be printed in the mainstream press. They welcomed passionate journalism, tired of the bland reporting that they saw in other newspapers. It grew to attract writers such as such as the aforementioned Ezra Pound (one of the major figures of the modernist movement in early 20th century poetry), American novelist Henry Miller, African-American novelist James Baldwin, poet e e cummings and playwright Tom Stoppard – high profile writers who would appear alongside those seeing their words in print for the first time.

So, why did the first of the new wave of underground newspapers begin in Greenwich Village? A bohemian community was already established in the Village, a location which had long attracted artists, musicians and those individuals looking for an alternative lifestyle. At the start of the 20th century, it was a staunchly working class neighbourhood, made up of mainly Italian immigrants who worked in Lower East Side garment shops, factories or in construction. Cheap rents drew those looking for the ideals of the bohemian lifestyle, a way of life that tended to include working in low income jobs so that low rents were a necessity. From the turn of the century to the 1920s, the district became a location for artistic communities. As tends to happen when an artistic community colonizes an area, it became fashionable to live there and so those with money flocked in and renovated the old houses and built large apartment buildings. Rents become too high for most bohemian types, and much of the original artistic community began to disperse, though the place remained surrounded in the bohemian myth. It became a model for similar neighbourhoods in other large cities. This ideal was fuelled by *The Village Voice* newspaper which was firmly linked with the bohemian lifestyle, celebrating the widely held artistic concepts of the Village, which may have no longer been entirely accurate. However, during the late 50s and early 60s, the place buzzed with creative energy –

young artists, musicians and writers gathered here. Living in bohemian-glorified poverty, they congregated in coffee shops, bars and bookshops, believing that the place symbolized freedom and independence. Locations have always been vital in building a sense of community, the shared space necessary to allow people to feel that they are living similar lives. Though it may not have been as authentically bohemian as in the 1920s, attracting those more affluent hipsters, it was still something of a Mecca for those with aspirations of this kind. *The Village Voice* thus became the paper for these later bohemians of the mid-50s

The inspiration for creating the paper was the contemporary artistic and social scene but the aspirations of the editors and writers remain less clear. It was certain that from the start they wanted to produce something different. They could relate to their audience as they were living similar lives and could comfortably address the young audience, the bubbling of like-minded individuals who existed before hippies became a cultural phenomenon. It was the sense of starting from the beginning, of building a new type of newspaper with no previous experience, that was both the challenge and triumph of the paper. As Wolf and Francher explained in their *Village Voice Reader*, '*The Village Voice* was originally conceived as a living, breathing attempt to demolish the notion that one needs to be a professional to accomplish something in a field as purportedly technical as journalism. It was a philosophical position. We wanted to jam the gears of creeping automatism.'[66] They claim that they were trying to make a distinct change in contemporary media, to create something new. If they had known more about the publishing process then they would have created something very different, but it was this amateur status that sparked enthusiasm in others and provoked a passionate response to the paper as it grew in popularity. It was also this sense that they were creating something new and exciting that spurred talented young writers to aspire to write for the *Village Voice* or start their own publications. They were able to amplify the emerging voices of the counterculture movement at a time when few others were willing to listen.

The mainstream press at the time was more concerned with writing about larger institutions and presenting the business affairs of the nation in a positive light. *The Village Voice* rejected this stance and instead worked to expose corruption on a national scale. They printed works of groundbreaking investigative journalism years before other mainstream papers moved in this direction.

Although the paper is seen by many to be the first of its kind – a new radical publication published regularly for the restless youth of America – it can also be read as having missed many of the opportunities that it could have created. Norman Mailer was one of the most outspoken critics of the paper. As mentioned, he was one of its founders and wrote a regular column before withdrawing in opposition to the way the paper was developing, reportedly wanting a far more outrageous and rebellious paper. In *The Village Voice Reader* he explained that Francher and Wolf, '…wanted it to be successful; I wanted it to be outrageous. They wanted a newspaper that could satisfy the conservative community – church news, meeting of political organisations, so forth. I believed we could grow only if we tried to reach an audience in which no newspaper had yet been interested. I had the feeling of an underground revolution on its way, and I do not know that I was wrong.'

To some extent, they were both right. Mailer pre-

emoted the cultural revolution that would follow but
Francher and Wolf realized the need to slowly build a
community in order to create any long lasting cultural
change. But they did not create the 'hip' paper that Mailer
imagined. He found it too liberal in its views, almost an
establishment figure of the underground rather than a new
vital newspaper. Mailer soon left, but the paper continued
and developed almost into an institution, which remains
prominent today.

The Realist

One of the first papers to exist along side *The Village Voice,*
though seeming a world away from its serious ideals was
The Realist. Founded in 1958 by a twenty-six year old
comedian named Paul Krassner, this was a strange new
publication covering anything from spouse swapping and
abortion to gossip and rumours about public figures. The
paper was highly unpredictable and never restricted, by
Krassner or anyone else. Its eccentricities made it popular –
circulation rose steadily from 600 to 150,000 over the
period it was published. However, *The Realist* was not a
serious paper through which to explore the issues facing
the underground or a manifesto for its future. Perhaps the
time was still not quite right for the radical new press that
Mailer had envisioned a few years earlier.

The Bohemian Others

If *The Village Voice* is seen as the parent of the new wave of
radical newspapers that emerged in the 60s, then the
subsequent new papers that followed can be seen as
rebellious children. There were other radical papers located
on the Lower East Side. During the mid-60s, an emerging
New York paper *The East Village Other* managed to make

The Voice seem conservative in contrast. There were others, similar in nature. On 4th Street, there was *The Guardian* – a newspaper with national distribution of Old Left origins that briefly became the primary paper of the New Left. *The Rat* was a local paper that tried to combine a counter-cultural spirit with revolutionary politics. It failed to survive because of divisions among the staff on social issues, particularly concerning feminism. *The Guardian* survived similar internal battles, but eventually folded after it lost Old Left financial support. It is these internal battles which unfortunately commonly restrict such revolutionary ideas. Impassioned people working together will probably have different ideas and if there is no effort to compromize then projects will suffer. That *The Village Voice* remains today may be because of its editors' caution about running headlong into revolution, instead creating steady foundations for what was to follow.

The East Village Other

The East Village Other was probably most similar to the type of newspaper that Mailer felt Francher, Wolf and himself ought to have started, but it wasn't until 1965 that it arrived. *The Village Voice* had begun a new wave of newspaper publication, which would develop throughout the 60s. However, as it focused on community actions and attempted to report unbiased news, its intentions seemed limited to many younger writers who wanted to find a platform for their confrontational political views. Poet Allan Katzman was disillusioned with the mainstream press, which he saw to be more interested in making news – 'pseudo events' which were created by reporters. He was fed up with what he felt to be boring and repetitive news with no moral stance and no real opinions.[67] He envisioned a newspaper which would cover serious political issues such as the Vietnam War, but on realizing that no one else was going to take the project on board, he decided to do so himself. Along with painter Walter Bowart, Katzman co-founded a biweekly newspaper in Lower Manhattan, within the nonconformist community of the East Village, and called it *The East Village Other*.

This newspaper did not separate fact from opinion, a direct contrast to the mainstream press and following the approach begun by *The Village Voice*. Katzman and Bowart were soon joined by John Wilcock, who had written a weekly *Village Voice* column for nearly eleven years. He was disillusioned with this older, more established paper viewing it as set slightly behind the times, unwilling to write about new issues until they became mainstream. He considered *The Village Voice* to be written for an older audience. *The East Village Other* targeted a younger audience, fuelled by a passion for change. It was now the mid-1960s, and America was changing. The counterculture was widespread and growing in strength.

They had a wider vision; they looked beyond their local community and wanted to cover politics, civil rights and arts on a wider scale. The content was provided directly by events occurring in the country at the time.

The articles they ran were often concerned with the rise in drug use and the loosened morals that the youth culture celebrated. The paper ran a reader correspondence section called 'tripstripstrips', comic strips, 'Where It's At' (the hipster's calendar of events); a photo feature dubbed 'Slum Goddess' (a 'poverty playmate' from the tenement next door); and some editorial ramblings, aptly entitled 'Poor Paranoid's Almanac'.

Every few years, a new audience wants a new media experience to call their own. In the 60s, an audience which had grown out of beat culture into hippiedom was ready: new young readers who wanted something different, something that was their own. *The East Village Other* reflects the vision of less naïve second-generation hipsters, still believing in the feasibility of an alternative to mainstream culture, but no longer surprized at the corrupt nature of this mainstream or the possible failings of the underground.

This second-generation audience increased the numbers of similar newspapers that were were founded. Over the next three years their collective circulation grew to 270,000.

It wasn't long before what *The East Village Other's* writers and audience would call 'the establishment' became interested in the paper, eager to understand it from a cultural viewpoint. In the late 1960s, Allen Katzman was regularly asked by uptown reporters to write for other newspapers and to give talks on what he was doing. He refused, in the knowledge that mainstream audiences would not understand, however much they wanted to find out about this new culture.

Los Angeles Free Press

On May Day 1964 at the Renaissance Pleasure Faire, Art Kunkin handed out the first issue of the *Los Angeles Free Press*. The idea had begun to develop only two weeks earlier when the thirty-nine year old recently unemployed master machinist and tool and dye maker from Brooklyn had asked if he might be able to promote his plans for the new weekly newspaper at the event. Deciding to produce the first issue in time for the faire, and with an initial outlay of only fifteen dollars, he quickly worked to produce five thousand copies of an eight page tabloid. This was a collective effort, and along with college students, dressed as Robin Hood and 15th century peasant girls, Kunkin and his team handed out free copies of the magazine to crowds at the faire. With the added publicity that this stunt provided the paper attracted interest and achieved a circulation of paying customers reaching 50,000 within three years. The *Los Angeles Free Press,* known affectionately as the 'freep' was generally acknowledged to be one of the first of the important underground papers of the 60s. Kunkin himself claims it to be the 'first alternative paper of the period, the largest…very political and intended to be the record of the cultural and political 60s.'[68] The movement was growing and by the end of the decade there would be an estimated four hundred regularly and irregularly published underground papers in existence in America.

The *Los Angeles Free Press* began to establish the idea that readers could be involved in the news gathering process. Kunkin explains his early idea that the *Los Angeles Free Press* was, 'Information To Change The World, A Newspaper Where Every Reader Is A Reporter,' whereas the commercial paper, the *LA Times* was 'News about the Status Quo'. In one editorial, he explains that at many times in his paper's history, the readers became the news gatherers. On June 23rd 1967, at the Century City anti-war demonstration against Lyndon Johnson, a violent outbreak by the Los Angeles police was reported by two *Los Angeles Times* reporters with a pro-police slant. The *Free Press* gave the demonstrators an opportunity to tell their side and printed their articles and photographs. This concept would later be taken up by independent newspapers in the 1990s as the internet enabled writers and readers to communicate with ease.

The Berkeley Barb
Emphasis from Greenwich Village as the centre of the underground gradually shifted to San Francisco, with the

movement that spread across America emerging from the dissatisfied individuals of the 1950s and developing into a widespread force by the 1960s. As a burgeoning hive of artistic activity, San Francisco provided the perfect environment for a counterculture community and its members gathered here en masse, often attending the University of California at Berkeley, looking for an alternative lifestyle. This community needed a newspaper of its own and Max Scherr stepped forward.

First published in August 1965, *The Berkeley Barb* was one of the first and most influential of all underground newspapers that chronicled the counterculture movement as it swept through the San Francisco area. Scherr, a fifty-one year old New Leftist who ran a local bar called Steppenwolfe decided that Berkeley needed a newspaper to reflect these changes. Throughout the 1960s he joined the patrons at his bar to complain about the conservative politics of America and about the way in which newspapers were reporting the news. He was particularly frustrated by the growing gap between the era's newspapers and their readers. What was really going on in the country was not being reported in the news, and people like himself did not seem to have a voice. Scherr decided that he would be the one to create a newspaper to report local and national news and champion social action. He sold his bar for ten thousand dollars and put all his money into founding the paper.[69]

The source of funding for a newspaper dictated the extent to which it could be political. Editors had to be realistic and, although printing these newspapers was not as expensive at it once was, they still needed to fund the large print runs. The financial backer ultimately dictated how outspoken and honest the editors could be, which of their opinions they could air and which they had to censor.

There were some newspapers, such as *The Berkeley Barb*, that were financially independent. These publications were usually funded by an initial outlay from the editor and were then reliant on advertizing revenue. Although not supported by an outside body, as such papers still had to rely on advertizers to provide money they had to exercize some level of self-control over what they printed, in order to retain these advertizers.

By mid-1966, Scheer was a common sight on Telegraph Avenue, San Francisco, wandering through the coffee shops trying to sell his paper to anyone who was interested. He was extremely passionate about his cause, risking his own money to fund the paper. Of course, there were times when he barely broke even, but there were also times when his paper looked like it was going to be a success. For example, in May 1967 he produced the first colour edition and promptly sold 75,000 papers. From this point onwards, the paper really took off as the counterculture was reaching its peak. By late 1969, the paper was distributed nationwide with a circulation of 93,000 and with forty members of staff working alongside Scherr.

This was a more political form of bohemian life. The peace movement was gathering momentum and the infamous 60s 'sit-ins' and campus protests became widespread. From the start, *The Berkeley Barb* covered civil rights and anti-war movements and became the social conscience of every social, political, musical, and mind-expanding event held in the San Francisco area over the following decade.

Not only did they write about what was happening, they also took part, managing to implement real change in the community. One example of this was the fight for 'The People's Park' in San Francisco. This plot of land, which lay up Haste Street from Telegraph Avenue and contained community housing of members of the counterculture, was bought by the University of California in the late 1960s. The community was outraged that many would lose their homes, angry protests followed and the work was delayed. On April 18th 1969 *The Berkeley Barb* called for people to congregate on the site to work together to build 'The People's Park' – a community park for local people. The University decided to take back their private land to continue with their building plans and so bulldozed the park, provoking further anger from the local community. Angry protests followed, escalating into violent riots on the streets of San Francisco. Governor Ronald Reagan ordered the National Guard to control the situation. Several people were injured, one was killed. After a thirteen day siege the riots were over, the community reclaimed the land and rebuilt the park. *The Berkeley Barb* developed a reputation as a journalistic defender of the people.[70]

The Oracle

The Oracle was a different kind of newspaper altogether – firmly positioned in the psychedelic San Francisco community of Haight-Ashbury (the centre of the hippie world), it was less concerned with reporting political truths and more with communicating within the local hippie scene. Produced bi-monthly, this was truly a community paper reflecting the experiences and actions of the San Francisco hippies.

This was one of the first papers to truly appreciate the potential of offset printing. Without this cheaper alternative, the group would never have been able to afford printing costs. They also made full use of the new opportunity to reproduce exactly what they had designed on the page, including hand drawings, photos and elaborate fonts. Printing processes became less rigid and there was no longer any physical need for neatly ordered layouts. *The Oracle* became famed for using multi-coloured collages, woodcuts and psychedelic paintings, representing exactly the psychedelic style that was first popular within the hippie movement and then infiltrated into popular culture.

Their subject matter reflected these changes. They looked less at the situation throughout the rest of America and more at their own experiences specific to San Francisco. They filled the magazine with quasi-religious Hindu myths, hymns to nature, spiritual introspection and astrological charts alongside radical design. This new material emphasized how counterculture publishing was changing and how people were now feeling the urge to publish whatever suited their individual needs rather than feeling tied to any previous publishing traditions. They were making their own rules while breaking the old ones.

The Diggers

There was another group in Haight that worked to distribute local news through self-made publications – the Diggers. This radical group, shrouded in anonymity, took their name from the English Diggers (1649-50), a group who envisioned a society free from private property and the notion of buying and selling. The Diggers operated similarly, originally as a band of local poets and actors involved in street theatre who provided food and lodging to impoverished like-minded visitors to the city.

Through the foundation of what they called 'The Communication Company', this group distributed news in paper form by hand, or posted it on telegraph poles across Haight. This news would be anything from leads on where to find free food to an announcement of a poetry reading, party or gathering, or a new philosophy or manifesto. Reporters would gather news from the streets then rush to the flat where Chester Anderson,[71] who had previously been a part of the San Francisco beat culture, and his partners Claude and Helene Hayward had a small printing operation of two mimeograph machines. Within a short time, a new leaflet would be produced and distributed.

This was a unique and immediate form of press, with ideas being passed out almost as soon as they were conceived. It was almost like secret messages being passed out in the street, wonderful new ideas which could be transmitted through self-publishing. Of course, leaflets had always been produced and distributed in this way. However, the Diggers' work was very much connected to the time and place; growing directly out of the particular and unique environment of San Francisco – the underground art scene alongside the political attitudes of the New Left. Their activities were short-lived, lasting just two years, but the impact of the Diggers' work can still be seen today. For example, many slogans that they coined in their papers infiltrated the counterculture and remain in use, such as 'Do your own thing' and 'Today is the first day of the rest of your life.'

On the Haight at this time, hippies were almost in control. Everyone knew that was where they lived and so they were accepted. This sense of acceptance meant that the hippie community felt less persecuted and more relaxed. *The Oracle* reflects this sense of communal well being. They celebrated their lives, reflected them with glee across their pages and did not focus on attacking the mainstream. The counterculture was now so widespread it was almost an accepted norm for many. This was not New York in the 50s and editors did not experience the same pressures. They were able to express the positive side of the new culture, which was flooding America. A mass movement seemingly dedicated towards peace, liberal drug use and establishing a supportive community changed the atmosphere of the underground.

UPS: The Collective Approach

The prevalent sense of widespread community in the 60s enabled the editors of self-published newspapers to work together to strengthen their approach to publishing. Sensing the growing importance and readership of the underground press, the editors of the five most prominent papers, *The East Village Other, San Francisco Oracle, Los Angeles Free Press, The Berkeley Barb* and *The Paper of East Lansing, Michigan*, formed the Underground Press Syndicate (UPS). The syndicate was formed in 1967 at a meeting in Washington DC, the day before the march on the Pentagon at a time when political action was at its peak in America. This was the next step in underground news reporting, a truly workable network formed between the major independent newspapers. They could thus exchange information and help each other with access to news stories, legal issues and finances. This was a move beyond the strength fostered by each paper publishing their ideas in isolation, as the founders realized they would have greater strength if they worked together. The Liberation News Service[72] operated similarly as a left-wing news agency which papers could join to share resources.

In the UPS, each member paper shared the copyright on all material and could take anything, from major breaking news stories and features to comic strips, and reprint the item without having to pay. Each edition of a publication would be sent out to everyone else in the syndicate. They worked together to attract advertizing, tackling collectively one of the major problems for underground papers. If another newspaper, not in the syndicate, wanted to reprint an article then they had to pay for it. All the money earned went to a collective fund to benefit all member papers. The original aim for this fund was to raise enough money to set up a telex, teletype and telephoto wire service between San Francisco, Los Angeles, Chicago, New York and London to facilitate the communication of breaking news stories and information.

The UPS's strength came from the numbers of papers involved. Soon it represented over one hundred publications across America including *Rat, Old Mole, The Great Speckled Bird, Liberation, Ramparts, Kaleidoscope, Resist* and *Leviathan*. The larger independent newspapers were supporting the smaller ones in an act of solidarity in the underground press. The idealistic co-operative approach that grew in America in the 1960s had now spread to publishing. Any country could become involved with the UPS. This meant that they could share world-wide news stories and enable the network to achieve a global effect.

The Great British Magazine

It was not just in America that people began working together to publish their own newspapers and magazines, throughout this time Britain had produced many of its own. Whereas America had the beat writers in the 50s, Britain had its own 'Angry Young Men'. A group of writers so called because of their dissatisfaction with their experiences as part of post-war society. As a group they were small but they were emblematic of many of Britain's youth. They were angry about the expectations placed on them to be mature members of society, when many of them had already sacrificed their youth for the greater good during the war. They were angry at the people in charge, at right-wing British politics and at the all-powerful institutions that controlled the country. Towards the end of the 1950s the Campaign for Nuclear Disarmament began and became a cause that would dominate the minds of the young for many years to come, with the advocates of nuclear weapons providing a direct enemy to attack.

It was it in this social climate of social dissent coupled with post-war affluence that youth culture exploded. With the rise of the New Left in the late 1950s young left-wing intellectuals disenchanted with British politics and society felt the need to write about their views. The established newspapers would not print their work as it was far too radical to be read by most of the population over breakfast, so, just like the Americans, they decided to publish magazines and newspapers for their peer group themselves. This was an era mythologized as a time of teenage rebellion and these papers were unashamedly rebellious. Throughout the decade, the rise of rock and roll was momentous and the fact that this music was so different from anything young people had heard before, together with the fact that they were increasingly politically aware, made it likely that something entirely new and exciting would develop from these two passions. However, it was not until the 1960s that newspaper self-publishing really took off in Britain. It was during this decade that rock and roll morphed into rock, and the sense of political and social dissent had grown into a full-on cultural rebellion. By the end of the 60s, during May 1968, the protests that occurred in Paris and the rest of France had an immediate impact on youth culture. This was the first televized urban uprising and was witnessed by a generation concerned about its political rights, thus further fuelling the growth of the independent press and the influence it had begun to exercize.

The International Times

In October 1966, *The International Times* was launched. This fortnightly publication was not welcomed by everyone, least of all by *The Times* who threatened legal action if the editors did not change their name to something less similar to their own. *The International Times* became knows as *IT*. Much of its importance lies in the simple fact that it was the first of its kind in England. The editorial team expressed their political ideals, a revolutionary stance. They were reflecting the shift in attitudes that they saw across the country.

OZ

After *IT*, others began to see the potential of self-publishing. The next major impact on the British underground was provided by *Oz* magazine. This was a visual as well as print experiment, the magazine becoming famed for its psychedelic style and often controversial content.

The magazine lived two separate lives, one in Sydney, Australia and then in London. This first Australian incarnation of the magazine was produced by university students Richard Neville, Richard Walsh, Martin Sharp and Peter Grose. This editorial team was influenced by the magazines *New Statesman* and *Private Eye,* who wanted to create an alternative to express their sense of dissatisfaction, a satirical protest in print.

It offered a detailed look at the counterculture movement, though contributors did not just write about what was happening as passive observers, they tried to express this new way of living to their readers as a call for action. The writers believed that these changes taking place in society were a form of cultural shift and that they were pioneers of a new youth experience. They were trying to push the boundaries of what journalism could be. They were influenced as writers by what influenced them as individuals and the magazine subsequently covered controversial issues such as censorship, police brutality, the Vietnam war and civil rights: the very same issues that the American underground press addressed. The writers used the magazine as a platform from which to tackle issues of particular concern to their own country, they attacked the government's racist White Australia Policy and regularly satirized public figures. They did not shy away from causing controversy, willing to print whatever they felt would make their readers think. These included Mark Sharp's satirical poem about Sydney's youth culture titled, 'The World Flashed Around the Arms,' and the cover of Issue 6 which featured Neville and others pretending to urinate into a fountain which had recently been unveiled by the Prime Minister.

At the time, such attacks on figures of authority and power were considered highly controversial and the editors twice faced obscenity charges. During the second trial Neville, Walsh and Sharp were tried, found guilty and sentenced to six months hard labour. The verdict and the harsh sentences caused a major outcry but after a highly publicized appeal, the verdict was overturned.

Sharp and Neville both decided to move to London, far from the controversy they caused in Sydney. Walsh returned to university, attempting to resurrect *Oz*, which he published in a reduced form until 1969.

It wasn't until 1967, that Sharp and Neville, reunited in Britain, decided that it was time for them to try and restart a new version of the same magazine. Fellow Australian Jim Anderson joined them and together they founded the London version of *Oz*. In 1968, Anderson decided to leave the paper and young Londoner Felix Dennis replaced him. This marked the beginning of a new phase in the life of

Oz, which would prove to be even more controversial than the last. As the magazine had attracted the criticism that it had lost touch with youth, one of the first decisions its new editorial team made was to invite a group of secondary school students to edit a special edition titled *Schoolkids Oz,* entirely devoted to new youth culture.

Many felt that the Obscene Publications Squad had been waiting for a chance to shut down *Oz* and used this issue as an opportunity to try and prosecute them. As with previous editions of *Oz* magazine, and as with many American underground magazines of the time, the offense Neville, Anderson and Dennis were charged with was obscenity.

The trial began in June 1971 and with great media attention from the mainstream the three were both vilified and championed. Despite the efforts of their defence team all three editors were found guilty and given long prison sentences with hard labour. Dennis was given a lesser sentence because the judge, Justice Michael Argyle, claimed that Dennis was 'very much less intelligent' than Neville and Anderson. The verdict was subsequently overturned on appeal, with the appeal judges finding that Argyle had seriously misdirected the jury on numerous occasions.

This trial brought the magazine to wider public attention than ever before. Everyone knew about *Oz* as it had emerged from the underground to gain mass attention. Many supported the editors, including celebrities such as John Lennon and Yoko Ono who joined the protest march against the prosecution. They also organized the recording of 'God Save Oz' by the Elastic Oz Band, released on Apple Records, to raise money and awareness of the case.

Oz continued with diminishing success until 1973. After the trial, and the burst of publicity that followed, it had lost its momentum.

Red Mole

Other British publications felt that they needed to speak directly about the political state of the country. Published by the International Marxist Group, the *Red Mole* was one of those publications which focused its attention on political and social issues. Its editors, Tariq Ali and Robin Blackburn, were eager to document the revolution. The shift from rock and roll as the force of social change, with The Beatles seen by many as the populist emblem of this, to more politically aware rock music is best illustrated by John Lennon's own move towards focusing on political issues. *Red Mole* interviewed John Lennon and Yoko Ono in January 1971 and Lennon discussed frankly his sense that he had always been political. He claimed, 'I've always been politically minded, you know, and against the status quo. It's pretty basic when you're brought up, like I was, to hate and fear the police as a natural enemy and to despise the army as something that takes everybody away and leaves them dead somewhere.' He explains his position as a young working class musician at the start of his career, '[the bourgeois class] own all the newspapers and they control all distribution and promotion. When we came along there was only Decca, Philips and EMI who could really produce a record for you. You had to go through the whole bureaucracy to get into the recording studio.'[73] By considering such issues in print, *Red Mole* began to explore what a generation was experiencing.

The End of the Underground Press?

By the early 70s, the underground press in America was at breaking point. Readership figures had peaked and were now in rapid decline. According to the Underground Press Syndicate in 1971, four hundred underground newspapers existed in America. By 1978, this had dropped to only sixty-five.[74] The situation was mirrored in Britain. There were three main reasons why the sudden decline happened at this time. As the issues and events that they were collectively fighting against ended, such as the Vietnam War for example, the sense of the immediate need to protest was reduced. Without this sense of immediate rebellion, it was difficult to attract new readers.

The second reason lay in the actions and motivations of the editors and writers themselves, as the underground began to lose its coherence towards the early 70s. It is difficult for a community to support itself indefinitely, particularly if it is as idealistic as those which were behind many of the underground publications. Founding members move on to other projects or are forced to abandon plans due to the financial pressures of everyday life. There were several traits which existed in many of the independent publications that were both part of their success as well as their decline. The inexperience of the editors and writers, which added to the appeal of their publications, meant that many mistakes were made, often stemming from political naïvete and a tendency towards self-indulgent writing. The inflated sense of self-importance felt by some of the writers lead to arguments and in-fighting of the kind that could potentially destroy a community. These personal issues began to affect the publications, both in the way they were being produced and in the way they were viewed by society at large.

The third and much more controversial reason, in the US in particular, was the interference by the government in the activities of the underground press. (Indeed, with such pressures, it became increasingly difficult for the newspapers to survive and many folded.) Acknowledging the success of the underground press with its high readership figures, and the subsequent power of the printed word in this field, the US government saw cause for concern. It was felt that the growing numbers of self-published newspapers should be monitored, to determine whether or not they posed any threat to national security or to the moral state of the country. The newspapers of the underground operated differently from the mainstream press and so they were viewed with suspicion. Most importantly, the sources from which they gathered their news were different, causing concern over the possibility that they might relay sensitive information to the general public. Established media outlets were typically supplied with information directly from government sources whereas the underground relied on the Liberation News Service and Underground Press Syndicate for their information.[75]

The power of the underground press lay in its determination to print the truth. These publications did not simply reprint the information they were fed by government sources but looked for their own news stories to report and worked hard to expose corruption in the country.

The government viewed this approach to news reporting with extreme suspicion. They observed that emergent political groups were becoming more powerful as they became organized; that those individuals dissatisfied with the government were working together; moreover, that those involved with the underground press who supported civil rights movements often directed their efforts away from the printed page and worked with various charities to bring about real social change. This was one of the first times that such a huge group of people began to work together for a similar cause and the FBI soon instigated an intense investigation into small press activities. Many writers reported that they were being interrogated and pressured to stop what they were doing.

As US policy is designed to protect freedom of speech and the newspapers could not be directly charged with what they were printing, the government had to think of other charges designed almost to sabotage their actions. Government paranoia following the bombing of Haiphong in 1972 resulted in 'incitement to riot' charges being brought against many underground newspapers. Four writers from the *Columbus Free Press* were charged with causing a riot that they had simply reported on. Street vendors selling the papers in question were often arrested and charged with loitering – an offense that was extremely difficult to define. Even though the charges would rarely stick, they created enough disruption to make things very difficult for the editors. There were rumours that printers and advertizers were being intimidated. Many newspapers reported that they were under surveillance and experienced raids, as well as misinformation being circulated in attempts to sabotage their work.

One newspaper which was hit particularly hard by the efforts of the FBI was the *Black Panther Party Paper*. The Black Panthers were at the centre of the black liberation movement during the 60s. It was reported that the FBI were increasingly suspicious of the group's actions, kept writers under surveillance and started a sabotage campaign, which included disrupting meetings and forging defamatory letters. The feminist magazine, *Off Our Backs* was also allegedly under investigation as part of a wider investigation into the action of the women's liberation movement.

Such investigations and trials obviously outraged editors as they felt that their own civil rights were being attacked. In a statement to the commission on obscenity and pornography in Washington DC in 1970, Thomas King Forcade of the Underground Press Syndicate exclaimed, 'We are the solution to America's problems. We are the revolution, these papers are our lives, and nobody shall take our lives away with your goddamned laws. We are tomorrow, not you.' Attacking what he considered to be unconstitutional disruption, writers like him were angry at a government who tried to silence them using the strength of the law.

Mother Jones

Not everything was over by the mid-70s; one American independent newspaper was just starting out. *Mother Jones* (named after a labour organizer who worked on behalf of coal miners, steel workers and children working in textile factories) was launched in 1976 as a non-profit magazine. This publication aimed at championing social justice through well-written investigative reporting, exposing corporate and political corruption.

Although the 60s were over, the memory of the political activities of the civil rights and anti-war movement still remained. People had realized that they could effect change. They were influenced by the positive aspirations of the 60s and were not yet willing to give up. The political agenda had changed, however there were many new causes to fight for – environmental issues and increased women's rights for example. Richard Reynolds, current communications director for *Mother Jones*, explains the links that the magazine had with 60s counterculture. 'Some of the people who founded *Mother Jones* had been involved with *Ramparts*, a progressive magazine that was based in the San Francisco Bay Area and was published between 1962 and 1975.'[76]

America was still undergoing a process of change and the

new activists were the frontrunners. Just as papers such as *The Village Voice* had used investigative reporting to find out what was really happening in the country, so did *Mother Jones*. This was the time when investigative journalism really became an important force in newspaper reporting. In 1974, two young reporters from *The Washington Post* uncovered the Watergate scandal and the world began to realize that this form of journalism was powerful and influential. *Mother Jones* used this style of journalism, though instead of focusing on exposing corruption in politics it geared its attention towards multinational corporations, which were rapidly growing in strength.

The editorial team of *Mother Jones* worked hard to run the magazine in a professional manner – with first rate writers, designers and photographers working together. They wanted to reach a wider audience than the radical magazines of the 60s, infiltrating mainstream culture whilst remaining an independent magazine. Reynolds explains the original aim of the magazine. 'The idea was to create a "glossy" magazine that had attractive graphics and published articles written for a general audience, so as to reach a wider audience than other left/liberal American publications, which tended at the time to be printed on newsprint and reach a fairly limited audience.'[76]

Even though this was almost a decade on from the difficulties the independent newspapers of the 60s had faced when they attacked authority, many were still wary of what they felt to be subversive interference. After *Mother Jones* printed a number of stories which antagonized state officials in Washington, the Internal Revenue Service launched an investigation into the magazine's non-profit status. They claimed that, even though the paper was losing money each year, it owed taxes on the income received from sources such as advertizing; a claim that was seen by the editors as a vendetta against their work. Reynolds explains the event: 'The IRS initiated a routine audit in 1979. In 1980, not long after Ronald Reagan took office, the IRS came back to the magazine and said they did not see that *Mother Jones* was significantly distinguishable from a magazine operating for profit. We appealed the case to the Washington office of the IRS, and the threat to the magazines non-profit status got a good deal of press attention. Eventually the national office of the IRS overturned the decision and reinstated the magazines non-profit status. The decision pointed to the fact that the magazine regularly published articles that alienated potential advertizers and to the widespread use of *Mother Jones* articles in classrooms and other educational settings.'

In a similar situation to that which occurred during the *Oz* trial in Britain, with the authorities attacking an independent publication, many mainstream papers realized that the situation was unfair and objected in print. This shows how things were changing – such support from the established media would have been unheard of in the 50s.

The History of Political Zines

The history of zine-making is heavily connected to a tradition of individuals expressing their own views and these views are often strongly political. With the freedom to write almost anything – one of the benefits of operating outside of the mainstream media – many have seized the opportunity to produce overtly political zines.

This tradition is not new, political groups have always published their own pamphlets to let others know about their ideas and activities. As editor of the zine review publication *Factsheet Five* during the 90s, R Seth Friedman pointed out in his interview on zine culture for *Time* magazine in 1994,[77] even Benjamin Franklin produced zines. These were political broadsheets produced by printing press and then distributed during the American revolution; similar in many ways to the zines that have been produced since. This early method of self-publishing in America has continued ever since.

Similarities to the political zine can also be seen in the Russian revolutionary practice of self-publishing by post-Stalin dissidents during the existence of the Soviet Union. This practice was called '*samizdat*', which literally means 'self-publishers'. This was so named as a parody of terms such as '*gosizdat*,' meaning state publishers. This was a means to circulate nonconformist material privately, away from government control. Although most later zine publishers were not facing such censorship of their views, the action of publishing and circulating personal ideals and political viewpoints remains prevalent.

Underground publications have always covered topics that the mainstream media has shied away from, such as civil rights, class, feminism, war, government corruption, corporate power, animal rights, sexual freedom and alternative lifestyles. The importance of their attention to these issues lies in the fact that today they are addressed in the mainstream media: their efforts have brought about change.

There are many individuals and organizations operating today, which use both print and the internet to spread their ideas. SchNEWS is one of many independent publications produced today with a political agenda, started by Brighton's Direct Action Collective as a part of their campaign against the Criminal Justice Act of 1994. The group saw a need for a paper to report the news of direct actions – a means of protest which typically causes disruption to force change. SchNEWS' roots lie in this direct action network and so it is provided with first hand information on activities including anti-road protests and Reclaim the Streets events. The paper is produced weekly and given out for free. This idea of independently publishing news aimed directly at a specific community echoes the work of the Diggers in 60s San Francisco. But while the Diggers kept their focus on the Haight, SchNEWS wants to help effect change on a global scale. As the notion of direct action has begun to shift its focus from the local to the global so SchNEWS has moved alongside the changes. When it first began, the newsletter was distributed around Brighton and sent for distribution in other towns across the country, but by developing a website the group can reach more people with their news. Including hits on the website, the current readership is estimated at around 25,000.

Interview with **John Hodge** of SchNEWS on political zines and the motivation behind SchNEWS.

Could you outline briefly your role at SchNEWS?
'There is a range of media which SchNEWS is involved in from researching and writing articles, to doing graphics and web work, to running info-stalls at festivals and events to producing and projecting videos to performing political satire live. Most of those activities I'm involved in as well as keeping the network of computers going which mostly come from skip-bins.'

What were the original aims of Schnews? Do you feel that these have been achieved?

'The original members of SchNEWS have mostly gone, and the audience has changed a lot as well, so why it was going then, and why it's going now are two different things. SchNEWS emerged initially as a national-based newsletter against the Criminal Justice Act in 1994, but it quickly became the national newsletter of the direct action movement, which was in full swing in the mid-90s with all the big anti-road protests etc like the M11, Newbury and the Reclaim The Streets street parties across Britain. In the later 90s through to now a lot of these political currents turned their attention more towards international politics, globalization and international issues like GM food and climate change. A key catalyst was of course the rise of the internet and SchNEWS changed function: it joined an international network, and wrote about global issues more.

Back to the question – the aims of its initial period were met well – and since then it's been able to change in the ways it's needed to. But you have to keep on your toes and not become irrelevant!'

When did you realize the potential of self-publishing? What was your earliest influence? Were you influenced by any of the independent newspapers of the 1960s?
'For me it all started as a reaction to the mainstream media, and knowing that people were mostly being fed rubbish. It's just so easy to do your own media now, with computers, internet etc. And I'd much rather work with people who are not doing it for a CV or a promotion, but doing it cos they believe in it, or cos it needs doing.

I come from a background of writing satire, so my early influences were things like "Monty Python" or *Private Eye* and TV satire. Growing up I was very influenced by a lot of things going on in the 60s: music and politics and 60s graphics like Martin Sharp, but I never saw copies of *Oz* or *IT* until recently. These days however I'm a bit wary of anything which came out of that well-heeled London avant-garde elite in the 60s (like the Indica Gallery etc) which I'd be suspect of if it was going today.'

How important is the SchNEWS website?
'Initially the website was an add-on for the weekly newssheet. Now the numbers who get SchNEWS are far greater on the web – it's got to the point that some people think we're primarily a website. Because we have articles on various subjects our site is full of key-words, which appear on google searches, which means that a whole range of readers world-wide are available to us, thus changing our readership base and influencing the sort of material we cover. So the website is important because it's transformed the publication.'

How connected is zine writing to political situations ie at times of political or social unrest do you think people turn to independent publishing?
'How many millions saw Michael Moore's *Fahrenheit 9/11* (even though Bush allegedly still got in)? I think people are turning to independent media, yes, but I wouldn't say that zines are a big part of that these days. There's still a lot of zines produced, but at the same time a lot of people have got into having independent websites, and blogs, which I imagine replace zines in many ways.

I think there's a growing appetite for information which is not tarnished by the spin from corporations and governments, whether blatantly in *The Sun*, or more implicitly in the BBC or *Guardian*.

The trouble is that whether or not independent media

gets better, the mainstream brings in more PR and marketing techniques (and outright lying) to maintain the spectacle. I mean what does it matter if there's a decent documentary on Abu Ghraib prison on one channel if the millions were tuning into "Celebrity Big Brother" on the other? People going to RAF Fairford in Gloucestershire to protest against the B52s taking off on bombing missions to Iraq can be dealt with if the mainstream media either maintain a black out, or else find some way of trivializing it. If the protest doesn't permeate the spectacle it doesn't exist for a lot of the population, or else it's just something the weirdy-beardy people do. SchNEWS is part of a range of independent medias which try to attack that spectacle, how ever they can.'

Do you think that independent publishing is a political act in itself?
'Independent publishing is an autonomous, libertarian activity, whether the politics it's peddling is left-wing, right-wing or whatever. For me it's a political act, I have decided to devote part of my time to working for social and environmental change, and as it happens my skills are around writing, and I am not very good at chaining myself to bulldozers. It takes people with a range of skills to work for social change.

In a period where a lot of things are getting privatized and commodified, information being one, it's important to maintain a media which is directly opposed to this commodification. A good example of information technology which is succeeding in this is the world of open source software and Linux and copyleft, publishing like the wikipedia.'

There is certainly a correlation between the political climate of an era and the focus and numbers of independent publications being produced. It is when times are difficult due to social and political pressures that most publications are produced – the most passionate calling for change. Brent Ritzel, editor of *Zine Guide*, sees this trend and explains his predictions for the next wave of punk self-publishing. 'I think we'll also see a new explosion of punk music because, in the last few years, people have gotten complacent. That's why we have Bush as president now, 'cause people got a little fatter in the pocketbook and forgot the rage. People forgot how bad things were in the Reaganomics era. And the Reagan era was the last great period for zines. I think we'll see a return to anger in zines.'[78] It is this anger that fuels self-publishing.

However, it is not just this overtly political form of the zine which has the potential to bring about change, but also every zine that is working away from mainstream culture. Strengthening the networks and relationships within underground communities means that ideas for political change have a platform. The self-published publication has been used to talk about sci-fi, art and music and the development of these traditions has slowly built a strong independent media network. The very fact that the zine exists independently of the established media forms and commercial culture is a subversive element, and ultimately can be a political action.

Guerrilla News Reporting
One recent development, which can be seen as stemming directly from zine origins, is the concept of participatory media: media which helps individuals to tell their stories and amplify their voices in an unprecedented way. The

impact of the internet has obviously been immense on this practice of individuals gathering news, which has come to be known as 'guerilla newsreporting'.

Dissatisfied with their allotted role as culturally passive consumers, many continue to feel resentful of the process of 'receiving' news, as a form of product, as this involves placing trust in reporters and media organizations. They want to be involved in gathering and presenting news themselves and the rise of the internet makes this new form of control possible: it is now possible for the news to be presented in an unfiltered fashion, without interpretation. To achieve this, those people actually involved in the news stories – the eyewitnesses to the events – are encouraged to participate. During a war, isn't it more valuable to hear news reports from someone who actually lives within the conflict rather than a detached news reporter who is reporting for a government controlled media source?

The Independent Media Center movement, for example, allows individuals to be involved in news reporting and news gathering by offering a network on which to broadcast. Established in 1999, it is run as a network of collectively run media outlets working together to provide unbiased coverage of world news. They provide information, photos and footage to journalists. They also run their own newspaper distributed throughout Seattle and to other cities via the internet. Making use of both print media and the internet, they are making the best of both mediums. Realizing that it is communication between activists, the media and the readers that is vital, in much the same way the independent newspaper editors of the 60s, they have worked to set up independent media centres in every continent as a part of the overall network.

There are many other similar organizations, such as

Alternative Press Center, INK, British Independent News Collective and Guerrilla News.

The realization by the founders of Guerrilla News that such media organizations were much needed came in 2000 when Josh Shore and Stephen Marshall, both working for MTV, found that their vision of important, socially aware television programmes would never be accepted on mainstream networks. They realized that they would have to not only produce their own programmes but also their own networks.

Guerrilla News runs two separate branches. The Guerrilla News Network which is an underground news organization aiming to expose people to global issues through guerrilla programming on the web and on television. Guerrilla NewsVideo produces music videos: mini-documentaries with tracks from top recording artists and interviews with leading experts about important issues they feel are underexposed by the big media outlets. Recent examples are 'The Diamond Life' (examining the role of the gem trade in Sierra Leone's brutal civil war) and 'AfterMath', a major documentary investigating the unanswered questions surrounding 9/11.

As with many companies based on the internet, commercial or otherwise, Guerrilla News has grown rapidly. The two founders have been joined by renowned journalist Anthony Lappé and investment banker turned producer Ian Inaba. They have made use of new technologies, working with San Francisco-based Switch Technologies, to develop a unique open-source web publishing system. This has enabled syndicate writers to self-publish their articles and videos without the need for HTML coders. Making use of new technology means that they are kept at the cutting edge of media production.

Their efforts have been wide reaching. Their audience swelled from an initial three hundred site visitors per day to over 25,000 per day during the Iraq war.

Such use of new technology by independent media production agencies has meant that they can really achieve their ambitions and effect substantial change. They have followed on from the ideas of the 60s independent newspapers and magazines and moved away from relying on costly production and managing to avoid the difficulties of finding wide scale distribution.

Although in theory it seems a perfect solution to news reporting – to get those involved to participate in news gathering – in reality, things as always are a little less clear. Placing trust in any media organization is always a complex process. Even the most allegedly independent papers or websites will have personal or political biases or agendas. Chip Rowe, zine writer and author of *Book of Zines*, explains his own attitude, 'I don't trust them anymore than I would trust any news site. That's not because I think people are deliberately misleading anyone, but just because the truth lies somewhere in the middle, and it takes a lot of work to find.' This is important to bear in mind, that independence does not necessarily equal honesty.

Adbusters

Based in Vancouver, Canada, Adbusters Media Foundation is a global network of individuals who have realized that the information age has brought with it the opportunity for social change. They make use of this technology and the network that it can allow to advance the new social activist movement. The group publishes *Adbusters* magazine, operates a website and offers its creative services through PowerShift, an advocacy advertizing agency, which helps groups with similar ideas to achieve their aims.

They do not limit their actions to just writing about events or building a community, though they do realize that these are important stages, instead their ambition is to radically change the way that society operates. They aim to achieve these ambitious by addressing issues such as genetically modified food, the impact of mass media, ecological damage and injustices in the global economy. They also support direct actions such as 'Buy Nothing Day' and 'TV Turnoff Week'.

Connected to Adbusters, CultureJammers is the physical action-wing of the operation. As a global collective of individuals, this group works towards advancing the new social activist movement of the information age. Realizing that information and the transmission of this information equates with power and that those who have it and those who do not experience life very differently, they feel that by trying to change the way that information flows – by setting up their own media networks as well as sabotaging others – they will be able to shift the balance. Their activities of sabotage also include the subversion of existing advertizing campaigns. They are moving one stage on from just producing their own media and actually working to disrupt the mainstream media.

With the same ambitions as the radical papers of the 60s, papers, websites, individuals and activist groups now have access to the immense potential offered by the new technology available. It brings not only a new media to work with but also the ability to quickly form communities and transmit ideas with ease. Throughout the history of the independent underground press, people have worked with the technology available to them to produce extraordinary results. Contemporary independent publishers will almost certainly work with the new technology, as each group before them has done.

Music Zines

Rock Zines

As many writers recognized the importance of the rock music that appeared in the 1960s, in terms of its potential as a political tool as well as being a cultural phenomenon of vast proportions, music played an important part in marking the territory of the underground. With their editors keenly aware of developments in youth culture, underground publications were among the first to realize the changes that were taking place in popular music and were just as quick to write about it.

Beginning as a British edition of American music magazine *Rolling Stone, Friends* appeared three years after *IT* in November 1969 (changing its name to *Frendz* by Issue 29 in May 1971). From its beginnings as an offshoot of *Rolling Stone,* it consciously developed into an independent alternative paper with ideas of its own; focusing primarily on the new music that was emerging.

During this era, many people who had previously been writing sci-fi zines turned their attention to producing music zines. These two groups of fans have always been close in terms of their self-imposed status as 'fans' and in terms of their enthusiasm. Indeed, many were passionate about both sci-fi and music. This explains why what we may recognize today as some of the earliest music zines, produced in the 1960s, were created by sci-fi fans who were familiar with the zine medium, as sci-fi zines had been produced since the 1930s.

Paul Williams' *Crawdaddy* and Greg Shaw's *Mojo*

Navigator Rock n' Roll News, both published in 1966, were the first of their kind. Both writers were involved with science fiction fandom, having previously published sci-fi zines, and took what they had learnt about self-publishing and used to it write about music. Their enthusiasm for music was different from the commercial magazines in print. As they were not restricted by commercial pressures, as they didn't have to worry about selling records, attracting advertizers or discovering the 'next big thing', they were free to write about whatever they wanted. They subsequently wrote about bands that would never have been featured in the mainstream magazines, enabling new and unknown bands to achieve a degree of media coverage. This helped new bands to gain momentum and began a tradition, with zine writers taking on an influential role in the promotion of new bands. These zines placed great importance on the new rock music. Their writers celebrated the style and content as creating a power capable of revolutionary change. This outlook may have been a little naïve. However, their identification of the integral link between music and counterculture – and their vocalization of its importance – was a valid contribution to the underground movement and our understanding of it.

Punk
The explosion of dissident publications that appeared in the late 70s was fuelled by the rise of the underground press in the 60s. People had realized how easy it was to print their own media and so continued what had fast become a core activity of the underground. The early 70s was a bleak time for zines with stadium rock so popular, glorifying slick professionalism. Punk was different, celebrating the amateur approach and championing the

idea that anyone could create anything, and it is this key ethic that has echoed throughout underground culture ever since. Punk's zines were an embodiment of the ideal: the perfect emblem of the DIY attitude and a suitably anarchic celebration of lo-fi techniques.

The roots of punk can be traced initially to various musicians based in New York City during the mid-1960s. The influence of bands such as The Velvet Underground, The Ramones and The New York Dolls instigated a new direction in music, a move away from the earlier rock and roll roots of the 50s and folk which had risen in popularity during the 60s, and away from the stadium rock bands of the early 70s. This new sound was quite different from any heard previously. The Velvet Underground had offered a darker and more experimental alternative to the prevalent 60s pop, and from this edgier sound the speed-fuelled frenzy of fast-paced punk arguably developed, with British bands such as The Sex Pistols proving that you didn't have to know how to play the guitar in order to pick one up and start a band – it was the attitude that counted. So The Sex Pistols, who certainly weren't lacking in attitude, became better known than their US contemporaries and London took over as the city of punk.

Punk, in both America and Britain, offered young people a chance to establish some sense of control over their own lives, which given the political and social climate of the time was a challenge. In the beginning it wasn't so concerned with artistic development as other underground movements (though the zines would later focus on the music); it was less about the music or the entertainment and more about developing a community for the nations' disaffected youth, a means to express their sense of anger and frustration – an attempt to break the stranglehold of contemporary society. Punk zines were often rants against this control. They were seen as the ideal means to distribute information. They provided a network in the music scene, tying localized scenes and ideas into a more cohesive whole. Those involved quickly realized that this was a music scene that needed to forge a tight community to survive against the mainstream.

These new punks were generally opposed to the earlier hippie movement and raged against their assertions of peace and love as ideals to be followed. The punks were angry and this anger was reflected in their music and their zines. Their take on the zine did not look directly to the radical papers of the decade before for inspiration but to the art zines which existed earlier in the century. Many of the aesthetics typical to the punk zine, such as the handmade collages, use of slogans, appropriation of mainstream adverts and angry ranting articles, are all techniques seen before in the zines of the dada movement. It is often thought that these punk zines were the first stage in zine history, that they were an original invention. However, just as the punk band did not invent rock music, the zine was also in existence before this time. What punk did do was to use elements of its own aesthetic style to adapt the medium and make the zine its own.

As the readership figures of independent newspapers dwindled, the number of punk zines in print began to rise. Zine output dramatically increased during the late 70s, not just because of the new bands emerging to fill their pages but also due to the technological improvements that made it much easier and cheaper to print copies. One of the main reasons why people do not produce their own newspapers and magazines on a wide scale is the cost. When the cost dropped significantly at this time, many people made good use of the opportunity to self-publish.

Though the look of the punk zine can be compared to the dada zine, the style of these punk zines is also similar to the radical underground newspapers, which reached their peak in the previous decade. This was true of both the passion and the energy found within their pages and the feeling that this was an alternative space forged away from the mainstream. Where they differed was their attitude. The punk zine was far less idealistic, this was the cynical side of self-publishing.

Punk Zine

In New York *Punk* zine chronicled the early punk scene. It was set up in 1976 by John Holmstrom and Ged Dunn, with Eddie McNeil – nicknamed 'Legs' – as their self-proclaimed resident eccentric punk.

They basically wanted a magazine to appeal to people like themselves. Holmstrom, School of Visual Arts graduate and main force behind the zine, explains, 'So I thought the magazine should be for other fuck-ups like us. Kids who grew up believing only in the Three Stooges. Kids that had parties when their parents were away and destroyed the house. You know, kids that stole cars and had fun.' [79]

They decided to call their magazine *Punk*, as Holmstrom explains: 'The word "punk" seemed to sum up the threat that connected everything we liked – drunk, obnoxious, smart but not pretentious, absurd, funny, ironic and things that appealed to the darker side.' As their own form of DIY advertizing, they began to cover the city with posters that read: 'WATCH OUT! PUNK IS COMING!' 'Legs' McNeil recalls that, 'Everyone who saw these posters asked, "Punk? What's punk?" John and I were laughing. We were like, "Ohhh, you'll find out!"' [80]

As with Mark Perry in London, who would start the infamous punk zine *Sniffin' Glue*, Holstrom, Dunn and McNeil were inspired by the music they were hearing and the community it had created. They wanted to document the 70s New York punk scene that they felt represented their experiences. 'Legs' McNeil envisioned the magazine as a Dictators' album come to life. On the inside sleeve of their record was a picture of The Dictators hanging out at White Castle, dressed in leather jackets. This was whom the editors wanted to emulate. You can imagine them running ragged across town, passionate about what they were experiencing and cynically ranting against everything which was not a part of their world. Holmstrom explains that the original aim of the magazine was to, '...reflect the music I loved – hard, driving rock and roll with a sense of humour. I wanted it to be wild, unpredictable and something that would influence the culture somehow. I wanted to publish interviews that truly reflected what it was like to meet and hang out with someone. But most of all I wanted it to be funny.'

Like so many of their generation, the editors of *Punk* were tired of the hippie culture and tired of the 'peace and love' slogans of the previous decade. Their attitude was less optimistic, far more antagonistic. They wanted to enrage and they wanted to have fun. Holmstrom explains that the magazine was a reaction against both mainstream society and popular culture of the time. 'We hated Jimmy Carter and the hippies and the disco scene and the bad fashion and everything around us. So we embraced fast food culture, cartoons, TV, B-movies, violence, alcohol and rejected "being cool", "do your own thing", peace, love, left-wing politics, pot, protests and everything else that was popular. We heard rumours that the CIA used to bribe underground newspapers to run certain stories in the 1960s so we'd openly publicize that we'd accept any bribe from them. But they never took us up on our offer. Anyhow, we became SO hated. We were despicable. We were the worst. But it's always more fun to play the villain. And wow, did we have fun!'

The zine reflected the attitude of many others and became one of the most important and widely read chroniclers of the downtown Manhattan bar CBGB's scene, of bands like The Ramones, Patti Smith, Television, Talking Heads and Blondie. The editors became pioneers of many characteristics of the punk zine, which survive today in the DIY zine. John Holstrom recalls that: 'Once *Punk* was published, all these kids started sending me fanzines that looked a bit like *Punk* – bad spelling, hand-lettering, shocking content, weird photos and cartoons... I honestly think that *Punk* kicked off the fanzine explosion that started in the late 1970s and ended in the 1990s. We made it look so easy!'

Sniffin' Glue

In contrast to the group effort of the radical papers of the 60s, where a whole editorial team would work together, punk zines were often created by just one disaffected youth. The first, and probably most well known British punk zine, was *Sniffin' Glue*; produced solely by Deptford punk fan Mark Perry. The legend goes that Perry was working as a bank clerk in 1976 and one evening went to see US punk band The Ramones. This band had such an effect on him that he immediately decided to start a zine to begin to chronicle the changes that he judged were about to occur on the music scene, and express the passion that he was feeling for this music and lifestyle. Within a few months he had left his job and *Sniffin' Glue* became his life and an essential part of the British punk scene. He wrote about emerging bands such as The Sex Pistols, The Clash and The Damned. *Sniffin' Glue* ran for twelve issues between 1976 and 1977 and in that time gained an immense following. This zine was a mess of hand printing and mis-typed interviews – representing in print the values of punk. It was gloriously unprofessional and looked as though it had been produced in such a state of frenzied excitement that there hadn't been time to worry about presentation. Perry became one of the most well known figures in the scene and was often asked to comment on punk to the mainstream media. He was viewed as a spokesman of sorts, because of his zine and his passion for communicating what punk meant to him.

Although this is often regarded as the first punk zine, Mark Perry acknowledges that he was influenced by other zines such as Brian Hogg's *Bam Balam*, which was on its fourth issue by the time Perry began to write *Sniffin' Glue*. Although the subject matter was different (Hogg was fascinated by 60s music) the principle ideas of zine-making were there; once again proving zines to be an ideal format that can be reused and reinvented for different subjects and with different agendas.

Jon Savage, author of *England's Dreaming: Anarchy, Sex Pistols, Punk Rock and Beyond*, began writing his own zine in London during the early punk era. He explains the roots of his zine, *London Outrage*, which was launched in December 1976 with just fifty copies (photocopies) and then rising to one thousand copies in early 1977. 'It contained about twenty A4 pages with montages and text. I was influenced by *Sniffin' Glue* but also by other rock fanzines like *Who Put The Bomp?* and Brian Hogg's *Bam Balam*.' He explains his impulse to create the zine, to take

part in then punk community, which was rapidly growing
at that time: 'The aim was for me to put down my thoughts
and feelings on experiencing punk rock for the first time
that autumn. After seeing The Clash and The Sex Pistols I
was so fired up that I felt I could do what I wanted to do,
which was to write.' For him, it was this sense of potential
that fuelled the punk scene and its zines, 'The whole idea
was to do whatever you wanted, to communicate in a
totally pure form without any other mediation/editorial
intervention. A great ideal!' [81]

Search and Destroy

London and New York were not the only places where
music fans were turning to self-publishing and writing
about the new punk scene. Writers all across America and
Britain were creating their own forms of media,
documenting the new bands and writing their impassioned
opinions.

In San Francisco, that Mecca for the counterculture
during the 50s and 60s, V Vale was writing a zine which he
named *Search and Destroy*, after both an Iggy Pop song and,
as this was during the Vietnam War, the dangerous search
and destroy missions that soldiers would be sent on.

Vale was already involved in alternative culture. His first
job was working at Lawrence Ferlinghetti's City Lights
Bookstore in the early 70s at the age of twenty-one, where
he came into contact with not just Ferlinghetti, but also
Allen Ginsberg and others who had been involved in the
San Francisco beat scene in the 50s. Again, the influence of
underground culture can be traced directly back to the 50s
beat writers. Though certainly influential on him, it was the
growth of punk which gave Vale the real motivation to start
his zine. The punk scene introduced him to the DIY ethic,

which provided him with both the inspiration and the means to take part.

Not only was Vale inspired by these earlier beat writers but the first issue of the zine was funded in part by Ginsberg and Ferlinghetti who both, upon hearing of his plans, immediately wrote him a cheque for $100. This support meant that *Search and Destroy* could go into production and Vale borrowed the format from Andy Warhol's *Interview,* which was a magazine consisting only of interviews.

At this time, punk was just beginning to creep up on San Francisco. It was when The Ramones played, in August 1976, that it really hit the city, and the impact was immense. For some, punk awakened the realization that it was possible for them to produce their own music, that anyone could play an instrument; for others it was instead the realization that they could publish their own work. It was this first wave of punk in San Francisco that Vale documented, the scene which grew around the Mabuhay – the only club in town which positively encouraged punk music. He became well known for his interviews with punk bands and issues of his zine are important documents of the people involved, their actions recounted in their own words.

Vale's interest in self-publishing did not end with this zine, which he produced from 1977 to 1978 while the influence of punk was at its peak. He went on to start his own publishers, RE/Search, in 1982, with the ambition to publish voices that would not usually be heard – taking the best from the cultural underground and presenting it in book form. This approach is similar to Ferlinghetti's City Lights, the publishing wing to his bookstore. Vale wanted to give everyone the opportunity to read what those operating outside the mainstream had to say. He produced books about contemporary tattooing and body piercing, about people who produced zines, collections of interviews with women in rock music, a collected edition of all the issues of *Search and Destroy.* He made the decision to make the books appear as professional as possible, investing in a printing press and moving away from the typical and enduring belief that an independent publication should look unprofessional, as though produced on a low budget.

Through each zine he wrote, and each book he now publishes, Vale has been trying to record what he calls 'primary sources' – those people who are more original than others and have something vital to say. Vale acknowledges that his influence stretches beyond music and literary culture to the art world. He has always been influenced by Duchamp as well as the work of the surrealists. To him, the idea that everyone is born an artist, with an imagination, that anyone can create and it is not the privilege or talent of a few, is fundamental. From there, it is just a case of finding the means to distribute your ideas to your audience.

The Impact of the Punk Zine

The punk zine did not need to appeal to a wide market. As their publications could be sold at gigs and in record shops, unlike the editors of underground newspaper editors, punk zine founders were rarely concerned with widescale distribution. In fact, they were only really interested in reaching fellow punks. This meant that they did not need to tone down their attitudes to court the mainstream, and such disregard is evident in the dominant style, which was rough and angry looking. The sloppy style seemed to be a badge of authenticity. If a zine wasn't slick in appearance or perfect in terms in presentation, and was not interested in reaching a mass audience, then the content was seen as truthful and therefore something to believe in. The rough style intentionally emphasized the unprofessional nature of the zine and asserted its independence from the mainstream. The punks did not aim to please anyone else or sell their zines to anyone who wasn't already a part of their world.

Music was generally the primary focus of the punk zine. It was this angry new sound that brought young punks-in-the-making together and it was this that was most celebrated. Zine pages were filled with reviews of gigs and records as well as interviews with bands. But this was different from the representation of music in mainstream magazines. This was media written by people who were positioned inside the music scene rather than impartial critical observers on the outside. New bands were written about almost as soon as they were formed, long before the mainstream music magazines such as the *NME* knew about them. This was a music scene documenting itself, caused in part by the lack of early coverage of punk in the mainstream music magazines, who failed to recognize its worth as a valid music scene. That they were so slow on the uptake meant punks were at first forced to write about themselves, and their antipathy towards the music industry meant that they were happy to do so. This set the punk scene apart from other previous music scenes. It was founded on DIY principles and these became its strength. The zine was a medium over which the creator had ultimate control. The punk ethos could be transmitted without any interference from the mainstream press, or the music press.

As Jon Savage explains, 'Although the British music magazine, the *NME*, is always presented as the champion of punk, that was not actually so. Because of the *NME's* collective ego, it hung back before it could give its "imprimatur" to the movement.' Other British music magazines, *Sounds* (John Ingham, Giovanni Dadamo) and *Melody Maker* (Caroline Coon) were much more off the mark in 1976. (I never saw Tony Parsons or Julie Burchill as being as representative or as influential as they, and many others, would now have it.)'

When the British music press caught up with the new punk music that the zines were writing about, it revitalized them. Savage explains, 'Punk made the UK music press, suiting form (black and white, broadsheet/tabloid) with content that you could not find anywhere else (unlike today's pop saturated mass media). Sales were about 15 000 to 25 000 per week, readership up to five times that. It was massive.'

While the mainstream press took a more calculated approach to writing about punk, the zine writers took more immediate action. New bands were forming all the time and new zines quickly followed, springing up to write about the music. This rapid pace of zine production meant that they were immediate, writing about what was happening at that very moment. The enthusiasm was infectious and more zines joined them. Savage explains his own impulse to produce his zine, *London Outrage* at speed: 'In the lunch hour, I sit on the bog attacking bits of paper with Pritt glue in a very real fever – got to do it now, now!' It was this need to do it 'now' that fuelled the scene and spread the DIY spirit like wildfire.

Almost overnight, a large number of fans of a genre felt sufficiently empowered to self-publish – punk gave them the drive and the now long history of self-publishing gave them the means. Writing a zine gave an individual an identity; they were not just a fan of the music, they could also take part in producing something themselves. Although those who produce zines might describe themselves as 'fans' of a particular style of music or cultural scene, the zine is viewed slightly differently to the fanzine. The concept of being a 'fan' has firm roots in mainstream popular culture. To be a fan you consume a cultural product, you are the target audience being sold a form of entertainment. DIY culture consciously worked against this premise. In this idealized world, everyone was encouraged to create. The prevailing attitude was that everyone has a valuable contribution to make. There should be no bands to revere and no one you could not approach as an equal.

Fans became creators and in producing and distributing their zines were valued as an important feature of the musical climate. They could interview the bands and artists they admired, write about their own opinions and experiences and then sell the finished product at gigs and in record shops – thus exercizing a direct influence upon the scene themselves. Though not overtly political, at least not in the same way as the independent publications of the 60s, punk zines did express the views of a generation of young people. In Britain, this was the voice of the angry working class youth, angry at their sense of alienation in their own country. Although within their pages they celebrated their music with interviews and features, they also printed more personal manifestos and articles explaining the punk attitude. Zines fast became a way to continue the musical impact of the punk band. The whole cultural climate was up for debate. Ranting articles addressed the social situation at the time, books were heatedly discussed and knowledge was shared through the zines with music as the continuous backdrop.

Punk was over quickly for the music press and mainstream media, a short burst of musical activity, but in its underground roots it managed to retain a stronghold.

Punk did not die. The mainstream embraced its surface fashions – the dyed hair, leather jackets and angry lyrics – but at the heart of punk lay the DIY ethic. Punk developed into an underground community, which then developed, reshaping and evolving into many different strands. The punk explosion lead to an upsurge of interest in zines as an alternative to mainstream media. People realized that they could produce their own versions of the media and find an audience. The punk movement was vital in establishing DIY as a valid means of working. They proved that it is possible to establish and support a scene through the DIY approach. As Lemmy Caution, founder of contemporary punk zine, *Fun in the UK* says. 'Punk ignited the whole DIY scene, it gave everyone the determination not to settle for any of the crap the music press feeds you, or accept anything less than 100% exciting. Publications like *Sniffin' Glue* showed us all that we could do it too – and this ethic prevails. Listen to Billy Childish: *Punk rock ist nicht tot!*'[82]

Post-punk

Post-punk bought experimentation with the punk musical style, a reworking of earlier influences and the grasping of new ones, and zines continued to document this growing scene. During the last years of the 1980s and the early 90s, there was a second wave of punk youth culture. Those born in the 60s and 70s who were now reaching maturity were a readymade market to be cornered by corporate America. A new demographic was realized, dubbed 'Generation X'. With Seattle, Washington as its epicentre, this new youth culture, 'grunge', found itself in the media spotlight. Although this was quickly moulded into a trend for the mainstream media to grasp hold of, grunge grew from the DIY culture with its roots in the punk ethic of a decade earlier.

It was during this period that zine culture again flourished. Before grunge became a mainstream phenomenon it began – as with punk – with people who did not see their lives represented in the pages of everyday magazines. Their lives and activities were also similar to the earlier punks, they formed bands, made their own art, organized their own events. They needed their own form of media to document this and to help find others to form a community, and looked to the punk zines of the 70s and the hippie publications of the 60s for ideas. This was another conservative era, and became the third time that such a DIY culture would thrive. It is often when faced with a restrictive cultural and social experience that people feel the strongest urge to create their own experiences and find others with similar attitudes. Many in the late 80s felt that there was a cultural void. Those who had been a part of punk knew of one solution, which was to initiate their own form of culture.

They developed a particular approach to self-publishing that combined practices and influences from the immediate past. Stephen Duncombe recognizes this culmination of independent media traditions in the 90s zine, 'I think there are a couple of influential forms. The first is the long history of underground publications from Diggers' manifestos to American Revolutionary pamphlets to Abolition newspapers to the underground press publications of the 1960s. Then there was punk rock, which actualized the ideal that anyone can (and should) be a producer of culture regardless of training or expertize.'[83]

In many ways, the post-punks modelled themselves on the culture of beat writers of the 1950s. They wrote about being set apart from a rigid society, not following the ideals of the time but instead focusing on art, music and literature.

The zines they produced were more cynical than those of the 60s. They realized that money controlled the mainstream media, that there was corruption rife in society and social injustices were a part of everyday life. They realized that they could do little to change this and so attempted to create their own alternative away from it. These publications could not be called eager, idealistic or naïve. Realizing that there was little chance of them changing anything, the founders of the zine appearing at this time were aiming to set themselves apart, creating the stereotype of the 'slacker'. This was often presented as a façade of detached cool. This served to set them apart from the culture around them and eventually found itself feeding into it when it found popularity. They followed a bohemian ideal rather than a political one. Celebrating the artist, the musician and the menial job which left time and brain-space for formulating new ideas and community building. This was reflection rather than action.

Of course, the zine writers of this period also took ideas from the punk zines of the previous decade. This was their closest link. In fact, many of the people producing zines in the late 80s and early 90s were those same individuals who had been producing them during the punk era. To an extent, the initial communities and networks were still in place and so grunge culture developed along similar routes. The style of the new zines echoed the punk aesthetic and collages, cut n'paste and hand-written articles were most common. As with punk, many of the zines focused on music. There were so many new bands emerging that zines became essential tools to publicize them.

Though the zine had been an underground phenomenon of the late 70s it seemed even more relevant in the 90s. It was at this point that the zine found its ideal audience. Most people now had access to a photocopier and networks were already in place, and at last the rest of society began to understand what the word 'zine' meant. By the 1990s, along with the rise of grunge in the mainstream media world, the zine was finally gaining the recognition it deserved.

However, there were many mainstream publications that referred to zines as though they were a new development. Often assuming that they had come from nowhere, they sent reporters out to investigate their emergence within the literary underground. In 1995, even *The Wall Street Journal* ran a front-page story on the 'zine revolution' in America, demonstrating just how popular zine culture was at the time. In this same year, R Seth Friedman, editor of *Factsheet Five,* estimated that there were 20,000 to 50,000 zine titles in print in America. Zine-making was sweeping the country.

In spite of this striking popularity, some zine writers believed that there was a need for music magazines with a more professional look and approach. They aimed to remain independent whilst fashioning themselves more like the mainstream magazines. With the new music that was emerging they had a market, and wanted to be the ones writing about the scene and reaching its target audience. The Berkeley, CA based *Maximumrocknroll,* along with other fanzines such as *Flipside, Your Flesh Chemical Imbalance* and *Punk Planet,* proved itself able to attain a suitably slick level of presentation and sufficient circulation to make an impact on the independent music scene, and its underground subcultures, without compromize.

These zine writers were not the only ones who realized that there was a new market to be targeted. Businesses realized the potential of this new youth movement, which was in fact 'a neglected $125 billion dollar market.' Stephen Duncombe realized that mainstream culture lacked 'authenticity'. This is the very same thing that the underground realized at this time, as the same ideas were marketed back to them, packaged as a new and authentic experience. The original principals were diluted and zines were manufactured by businesses as marketing campaigns, as the corporate world suddenly realized the power of the underground.

Maximumrocknroll

Maximumrocknroll is one of the biggest and longest running music zines ever created. With the intention of supporting the underground punk scene, it started its life as a radio show in the Bay Area of San Francisco in 1977. The group behind the show were dedicated to playing the latest punk and hardcore music, and achieved international coverage. They knew that it was important for the music that they loved to be heard by as wide an audience as possible so they started their own magazine.

This was no ordinary zine; it grew to be something extremely special. Appearing in print for the first time in 1982, as a newsprint booklet given away with the *Not So Quiet On the Western Front* compilation LP (released on the Dead Kennedys' label Alternative Tentacles), it soon developed into a monthly magazine, staffed by volunteers and run not-for-profit. One of the reasons for its success was its wide distribution as it reached outside of the immediate community to share the news of new bands with others. Interviews, news from music scenes around the world, reviews and editorial columns meant that readers were kept up-to-date with the underground punk scene wherever they were. Despite its wide appeal, the magazine did not dilute its content or ambitions for a mass market. At its core was the central message of punk – the challenging idea that you can be a part of the culture. In today's media climate where several major conglomerates own most of the current publications, a magazine like *Maximumrocknroll,* which continues to thrive, plays an important role in celebrating the underground roots of many forms of music.

Growing out of the punk scene of the late 70s and being influential during the grunge scene, *Maximumrocknroll* has a new relevance today. It has always tried to combine political visions with the punk culture and so use the impact of the music to stimulate thought and the potential for change. Unlike many other magazines started in the 70s, it remains in print today and its contributors worked hard to highlight the relevance of punk music in an increasingly difficult political climate.

In the second half of the 90s, many books devoted to the zine and anthologies of popular zines began to appear. A variety of titles were published, such as *Factsheet Five Reader*, *Book of Zines* and a collection of Pagan Kennedy's zine *Pagan's Head* entitled *Zine*. Academic interest in zine culture began to develop, and definitions of the word 'zine' appeared in dictionaries for the first time.

A wider audience embraced zines as a form of self-publishing, finding them a refreshing break from commercial art and culture. Stephen Duncombe explains that, 'By this point in the mid-90s, you did have more people move from being zine writers into more respectable writing professions, as zines became considered legitimate training grounds. This was a shift from the previous decade. As Mike Gunderloy, founder of *Factsheet Five* once told me about zine culture and mainstream culture in the 80s: "It's hard to sell out when no one is buying." '84

However, those underground publications that had begun

to resemble the mainstream press – in visual style and content – were viewed by much of the community as less authentic and many *were* accused of 'selling out', of betraying their origins to become part of mainstream culture. Duncombe explains that 'Back in the 80s and 90s there was a strong suspicion of any zine that appeared too "slick". The irony was that this was the time in which it got easier and easier to produce something that looked slick without being commercial via home computers and desktop publishing. So you had this odd phenomenon of people using publishing software and then going back over it with pen or photo-shopping pictures so they looked as if they had been pasted in by hand. Sort of a simulacra of authenticity.'

This may seem a somewhat ridiculous idea, but shows that many individuals remain deeply committed to the zine aesthetic. The history of DIY publishing has been seen to include pioneers of many forms of self-publishing, but this practice of sitting in your bedroom with a pair of scissors, some text and some glue is one that looks unlikely to die out any time soon. Few zines will reach the levels of circulation that publications like *Maximumrocknroll* have achieved. However, zine-making on any level is a valid contribution to the DIY culture: you don't need access to a printing press or a computer to do-it-yourself.

SAMPLE ARTWORK FROM DIY
PRODUCTIONS

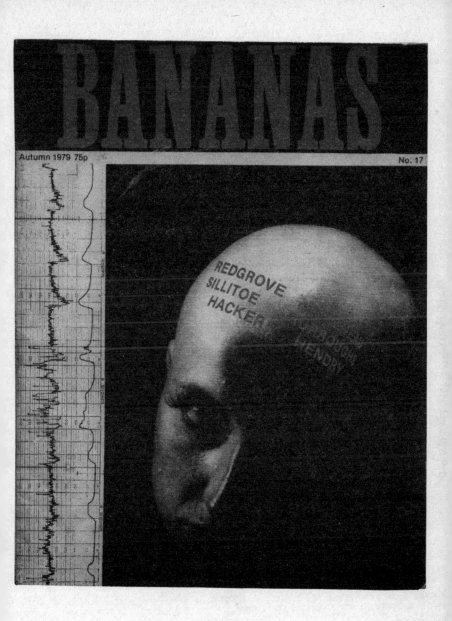

Fiction and poetry zine *Bananas*, Autumn 1979

Sample page from *Red Hanky Panky* by R.House

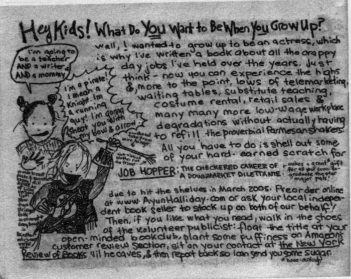

The East Village Inky by Ayun Halliday

i'm not impressed at all. not like i used to be. you're in the little dark room— telling me how much you wanted to see me. whatever. i could be with my ⟨xx⟩ friends. i could be stealing apples. i am so out of place in here. and we don't even have that in common any more. ⟨gx⟩ it used to be that i didn't even know your name; we stood on the street. in a city we'd never been before — and not say a word. but now ⟨xxxxxx⟩ there is just nothing to say. i've got ink on the back of my hands and i want ⟨x⟩ to go. there's this whole ⟨xxx⟩ town and places to sit, but you just want to breath the smoke.   oh really? do you like my hair like this? is that the point of view i'm going to get out of you? cos didn't you know that's enough? now i'm so flattered i'm ⟨xxx⟩ seeing the smiles on your face. it's like you talk about the weather. but what i'm really talking about is vapour-trails and the colour of the sky.

i sit at work and i write these things down on a piece of paper in my pocket.

you keep asking me what i'm going to get out of it. and it's so hard to explain. because what's so important to you means nothing to me. maybe i'm going to stick my fingers in your wolf-whistle.

are you going to paint me a picture? are you going to ⟨xxx⟩ write me a story? you told me you were going to write me a story. make it a long story. and don't correct the ⟨xxxx⟩ spellings— that's not what's important. tell me about the way you feel. write me back. you are what i am going to get out of this. and not the sound of kids just standing around.

by • **michal**

* ⟨· · · · · · · · · · · ·⟩

I've always hated writing.Its something I've always found difficult and when things aren't easy I ⟨·xx⟩ give up before I even try.When Michal(the supreme⟨xxxx⟩ writer)suggested that I write something for this,my reply was probably"cool".This is something that I⟨x⟩ say a lot.I'm not very good with words/conversation so⟨x⟩ I often stick to saying meaningl⟨⟩ phrases.I thought yeah I'll wri⟨t⟩ something,it'll be"cool".It did⟨r⟩ really occur to me that I'd jus⟨t⟩ said I'll do something I've nev⟨⟩ liked.Gradually it became more r⟨⟩ and I started to dread putting ⟨⟩ to paper,but I thought I'll sti⟨⟩ with it and not just give in.I ⟨⟩ want to sound like some cheasy Hollywood actor talking about t⟨⟩ therapy,but thats what this⟨xxx⟩ ⟨xxxx⟩(Spazoom,Headfall,everyth⟨⟩ we do)is about to me.Its about

t gtaking the easy option of
ing up.and this is the proof.
s may not be the best bit of
ting,but I did it.Doing Spazoom
helped me do things that
ore would of made me throw
ngs around and scream about how
less I am.I still find it
ficult but IxRxperserver instead
just running away.

This goes out to Lisa&Mike for
being the worlds grea test and to
everyone I owe letters to(expect to
hear from me soon).

by

. george .

by

. lisa .

DO I HAVE TO FIND THE RIGHT

form TO CONNECT WITH

YOU — MORE THAN JUST THE

WORDS TO SAY WHAT I MEAN?

Style is great   and style makes me sick (style) vs (substance)

SOMETHING THAT CAN LEAD US

TO EACHOTHER BUT IT IS A

PATHWAY **not** A DESTINATION

DON'T GET LOST, SO CLOSE

BUT NO EXCHANGE JUST THE

AFFIRMATION OF ITSELF

similar music doesn't necessarily mean that we kxx have

SIMILAR **ideals** LIKING

WHAT MOST PEOPLE SEE AS

IMPERFECTION CAN SEEM FALSE

BUT YOU HAVE TO FOLLOW YOUR

HEART IF ITS WHAT INSPIRES YOU.

Sample spread from *Spazoom* by Michal Cupid

Flyer for *JDs* compilation tape

Kathleen Hanna playing live with Bikini Kill at
The Garage, London, 1996

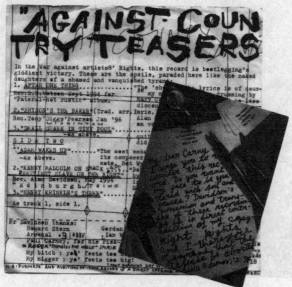

Cover artwork from The Country Teasers and
The Yummy Fur 7" releases from Guided Missile

Huggy Bear press shot from Wiiija Records

Cover artwork from 7" Slampt compilation
by Rachel Holborow

Cut n' paste artwork from Youth Club Tape Club's compilation for
the Ladyfest tour 2001.

PART III: THE RISE OF LO-FI MUSIC

The Skiffle Legacy

The 'do-it-yourself' approach to music making is all about producing your own music using whatever resources are available to you. Those using guitars and cheap 4-track recorders to make and record their own music have epitomized this approach for decades. However, much earlier in the 20th century, musicians were experimenting by going one stage further and making or improvizing their own instruments. Throughout history, feeling the urge to produce music, people have often needed to make their own instruments. The interesting thing about the period in which skiffle emerged was that even though professionally produced instruments were available, some still made a point of preferring to create their own. In fact, the most celebrated example of this approach was skiffle itself: a style of folk music with a jazz or blues influence.

This was a democratic form of music, which almost anyone could produce, usually played on home-made or improvized instruments. The tea-chest with a broom handle attached became a bass, the simple washboard played with a thimble was the percussion; and both could be played along with the jug, kazoo, cigar-box fiddle and comb and paper. These domestic instruments were cheap and accessible and, as always, it is accessibility which enables new music to flourish. So began the tradition of lo-fi music, the concept of not trying to seek out new technology to produce your music. This was based on the realization that you don't need the most expensive instruments or the most high tech recording equipment to make good music, but can instead celebrate what resources you have.

Although the term 'skiffle' refers to the form of grass roots music produced in the first half of the 20th century, it also goes by other names depending on the specific location.

In America, a kind of skiffle was played by 'spasm bands' of the late 1890s, bands which were often heard playing in the streets using instruments like kazoos, whistles, jugs, mandolins and harmonicas. In the early 1900s, 'jug bands' also appeared, producing similar music in Louisville, Kentucky. These bands played a mix of different styles including country, blues and jazz, and the resulting hybrid became almost instantly popular, peaking in the early 30s. 'Rent party' bands, playing a similar style of music, originated in the 30s and 40s (the 'rent party' being a party thrown by tenants to raise money to pay their landlord). Each variant style is seen culminating in the jazz band explosion of the 40s and 50s. In 20s Britain, 'skiffle' referred to the replacement of traditional jazz instruments by improvized instruments, such as the washboard and tea-chest bass. In the 50s, skiffle enjoyed a boom in popularity among a young British audience as they developed a new style of music combining American folk, jazz, country and blues, and this could soon be heard playing in coffee shops, jazz clubs and concert halls across the country. Although there have been different divisions of the same genre throughout its history, 'skiffle' always refers to a simple yet rhythmic style of music using home-made or improvized instruments.

Though skiffle did mark, for some professional musicians, a break away from a rigid means of producing music, the style is not original. Skiffle has strong roots in African-American folk music, where musicians imitated traditional

African instruments by using household implements. This necessity of improvization meant that they needed to be resourceful and imaginative and this became the principle of skiffle music: the use of everyday items (such as kitchen utensils) to create music. This appropriation of music from African and African-American sources has always been a feature of popular culture, particularly spreading from skiffle into the rock and roll of the 50s.

Slightly predating rock and roll, which would soon take both Britain and America by storm, skiffle was its first incarnation. Post-war economics meant that this was the age of the teenager, and skiffle hit the first generation of post-war youth who had more money in their pockets, more freedom and a gnawing sense of rebellion. The media and entertainment industry grew out of post-war conditions as mass production was both economically and technologically viable. There was now a means of production for skiffle recordings as well as a new audience.

Skiffle was primarily a simple style of music, so although the first musicians to play it were typically professional jazz musicians, it soon attracted other amateur musicians. With its emphasis on the live element, the skiffle style soon spread and by the mid-50s had captured the imagination of Britain's youth also, who took inspiration from the earlier American bands.

The man at the centre of the British skiffle movement was Lonnie Donegan. Born Anthony Donegan in Glasgow, Scotland, in 1931, he changed his name as a tribute to blues musician Lonnie Johnson. He was a great admirer of blues as well as American country and folk music and became an influential member of the pop music scene in Britain of the 50s and 60s. He joined Ken Colyer's and Chris Barber's Jazz Band in the early 50s.[86] Ken Colyer, a traditional jazz musician, claimed to have discovered skiffle music on a field trip to New Orleans in 1952, when he was collecting folklore and other material from the birthplace of jazz. Donegan's own musical style began to move away from that of the other band members, who typically focused on Dixieland renditions. Between songs, Donegan would take to the stage with just a washboard, tea-chest bass, and Spanish guitar and play a short set. This short skiffle session soon became an audience favourite. British listeners responded immediately to this novel music style, which, although having a long heritage, appeared fresh and new. Part of the appeal was the simple nature of the instruments, which suggested that anyone could make music with a little imagination and spontaneity.

Donegan's success with this new skiffle sound led him to leave the band and start his own. Inspired by musicians such as Leadbelly and Woody Guthrie, he dedicated himself to skiffle. He was not just popular in a niche market. In fact, between 1958 and 1963 he had more than thirty songs in the top thirty UK charts.

In 1956, Donegan and the Chris Barber Jazz Band had achieved international success with a cover version of Leadbelly's 'Rock Island Line'. Donegan went on to further success with the novelty song, 'Does Your Chewing Gum Lose It's [sic] Flavour on the Bedpost Over Night?' in 1959, 'Cumberland Gap', 'Gambling Man' and 'My Old Man's A Dustman'. The skiffle trend spread across Britain during the 50s, and musicians such as Chas McDevitt[87] also began creating skiffle music, as did bands such as The Vipers and The Gin Mill Skiffle Group.

Chas McDevitt explains how his band achieved their sound with improvized instruments, 'As for the instruments used, we did not use a tea-chest bass, but we did have the finest washboard player in the country, Marc Sharratt. At the end of a session his knuckles were raw. He had a standing order with Timothy Whites, the hardware store, for the metal inserts to the washboard, he used to beat one flat in a week!'[88]

Clubs playing this kind of music began to spring up across the UK, and the young people that gathered in them created a social network around the new music. One such club, one of the first to realize the growing popularity of skiffle, was The Cavern in Liverpool, which would later be famed as the place were The Beatles played their first gigs.

The increasing popularity of skiffle was reflected on the BBC on the television show '6-5 Special'. Presented by Pete Murray and Josephine Douglas, this program was aimed at young people and featured an audience dancing to music being played live in the studio (a format similar to the long-running 'Top of the Pops'). Bands from all over Britain auditioned for a chance to appear on the program. It developed a strong association with the new skiffle craze and Lonnie Donegan, Chas McDevitt and another musician called Willie McCormick all made regular appearances.

The fact that musicians on mainstream television were seen to be making music from little more than household implements made skiffle even more influential in terms of encouraging young people to do this themselves. It gave them the inspiration and all important self-confidence to start their own bands. Many realized that they did not have to have expensive instruments in order to create their own music, and neither did they need experience – the instruments often being so simple to play.

Thousands of kids started playing the washboard, guitar and tea-chest bass in their own skiffle bands and some of these would later become prominent figures in the music world. The Quarry Men, for example, were an unknown skiffle group formed around Liverpool in March 1957 by sixteen year old John Lennon. Although his interest in popular music had begun with Elvis Presley's 1956 hit, 'Heartbreak Hotel', it was skiffle that inspired Lennon to form a band himself. Moreover, he was ideally placed in Liverpool to hear about American music from the American sailors who used the city as a base. Playing initially with a school friend as The Black Jacks, the group quickly renamed themselves The Quarry Men, after a line in the school song of the Quarry Bank High School, which both boys attended. Joined by an ever-changing line-up of friends, the band performed at parties and skiffle contests around Liverpool, drawing inspiration from Donegan and covering a selection of his songs. Lennon met Paul McCartney in July 1957 and by October he had also joined the band. This band later began playing as The Beatles and, as is well-known, achieved iconic fame.

Van Morrison was just ten years old in 1956 when Donegan's song 'Rock Island Line' was in the top ten. He knew the song because his father had been playing Leadbelly songs to him for years. The following year he formed his first band, directly influenced by skiffle, using home-made instruments and taking inspiration from Donegan and Chas McDevitt. They called themselves The Sputniks after the newly-launched Russian satellite, and began to play at local events.

Surprizingly enough, Mick Jagger's musical career also started with skiffle roots. Although he has claimed that he was not really a fan of the musical genre, he was a member of the Barber-Colyer Skiffle Band playing at the time.

The skiffle music of the 50s was in many ways influential on both 50s rock and roll and the British rock scene of the

60s. This introduction to rock music through the use of simple instruments removed some of the mystery of the technical production of rock music, thus making it more accessible and attracting people who might have otherwise been too intimidated to take part themselves. This stage in DIY music making was crucial. Music enthusiasts would later become accustomed to the idea of forming their own bands and producing their own records, but this early introduction to DIY music was pivotal in popularizing the idea that you didn't need a 'professional' band to produce your own music.

The association which would later emerge between lo-fi music production and left-wing political movements also had its roots within the skiffle movement. The skiffle boom, as well as that of traditional jazz, was connected to a rise in political activity such as the Campaign for Nuclear Disarmament. Those who could find no place for themselves in popular music looked elsewhere and developed their own musical cultures and these people were often also involved in left-wing politics.

The original skiffle style is still popular in certain music scenes today. Chas McDevitt notes the enduring nature of the skiffle trend, 'There are many young groups around today that play this music enthusiastically, The K.C. Moaners from Leeds, The London Philharmonic Skiffle Orchestra and the fabulous Werner Brothers from Finland.' Skiffle still retains its original quality of drawing people together by its accessible form. McDevitt explains how the skiffle community relies on events and conventions to sustain itself, 'Each year there is a Skiffle Festival in Hankasalmi in Finland. They call it "Kihveli Soikoon", which roughly translated means "dustpan and broom"! They have workshops for all, young and old, showing how to make a tea-chest bass and encouraging the invention of unusual instruments. In fact they have a small museum there where various noise-making implements are displayed for all to play, which really encourages the young to participate in making music.'

Sadly, skiffle is now sometimes dismissed as just a crude forerunner to British rock and roll with a rustic and old-fashioned style. It is true that it did set many of the trends that emerged in rock and roll, but in the history of DIY music it played a much more important role; not because of the type of the music but because of the way it was created. Though in Britain skiffle remained popular in mainstream culture until the late 50s when it began to be seen as somewhat old-fashioned and twee, it was the resourcefulness and imaginative approach to music making that ensured the principles of the skiffle movement would endure in the musical underground. However, it was not until the emergence of the punk movement that the DIY ethic found a suitably 'gung-ho' genre within which to continue these principles.

Punk

Everyone knows what 70s punk involved: angry kids wearing leather jackets, safety pins through noses, graffiti on walls and violent rants against conservative society; forming bands such as The Sex Pistols, The Ramones and The Clash to vent their frustrations. Seen by some as abrasive, violent and immature and by others as an important social and cultural movement, punk was certainly a form of music, media and style which revolved around the do-it-yourself ethic. You certainly didn't have to be an accomplished musician to be in a punk band: you just had to have something to say.

Punk carried a simple message, which has been played over by generation after generation: the rejection of existing rules, the assertion of the need for change and the desperate call to be yourself. It took many of its primary elements from the early days of rock music, celebrating youth rebellion and individuality above all else. It included in this the idea that there should be no sense of elitism in music. Like skiffle music before it, punk was a simple musical style but it was a powerful one. In comparison, skiffle can be seen as optimistic and naïve, with its musicians singing about relationships and everyday life, whereas punk was far angrier as dissatisfied youths sung caustic songs about their own lives. It was its energy and passion that made it attractive to so many. It was making a similar statement that music should be accessible to all: that it can be easy to play and the audience should not just be stuck in the role of listener, of consumer, but should be empowered to create their own music. They wanted the boundary between musician and audience broken down. There was no reason why the fans could not create their own music and so there was often little sense that the musicians were figures to be idolized from a distance.

Punk was, in part, a reaction to the era of supergroups, glam rock bands and disco. Popular music at this time, which was predominately hard rock and disco, was seen by many as uninspired. Many people were looking for something different. Rock star mentality was taking over in the 70s. Musicians seemed untouchable to ordinary people, their lives and behaviour wildly different. Playing huge arenas established a barrier between them and their fans. The rock star lifestyle had taken over and rock music was typified by the figure of the distant star appearing to play convoluted guitar solos on huge stadium tours. Even bands such as The Rolling Stones and The Who, who were regarded as rebel icons in the 60s, were seen by many as distant and inaccessible because of their success.

There was a new audience looking for a type of music to call their own. Those who passionately listened to rock music in the 60s were growing up, and by the 70s were settling into adulthood. Many were less interested in struggling towards the establishment of an alternative cultural movement. This demographic, dubbed the 'baby boom generation', had been the largest record-buying group that rock music had seen. Now that they were moving away from being passionately involved in music, as thousands of them had been, there was room for a new alternative music movement. There was a new generation, in both America and Britain, angry at the social conditions they were facing and the increasingly corporate music industry. While rock music of the 60s had claimed to be about striving towards a widespread revolution it had not widely succeeded and the revolution was still a long way off.

Punk was something different. It was a break away from what mainstream rock music had developed into by this point. It was a direct attack on the music industry, which was increasingly profit driven and seemingly manipulative of both musicians and audiences. To the punks, well-rehearsed performance and technically advanced production were not standards to aspire to but rather something to rebel against. This set their attitudes directly against those of the music industry, who made use of the ever-improving music technology. Many punk musicians were notoriously amateur in their approach to music making; often claiming that they did not even know how to play their instruments before starting their bands. Using cheap, basic equipment, they simply improvized as they went along. This epitomized the punk attitude and was the first time since skiffle that such a shambolic approach was celebrated. The prevailing attitude was that they didn't know what they were doing but were doing it anyway. Talent and technical musical knowledge were not the most important things. They were passionate about music, and the potential to express themselves through its form. The three-chord song became the ideal way to do this, it was direct and to the point. More importantly, it established the idea that you could create your own musical style that was different from the mainstream. There was no sense of mystery in what they were doing, this was simple and straightforward and anyone could do it.

Many people did. Richard Hell from the band Television considered punk to be 'secret teenage news'.[89] It certainly was a form of teenage rebellion, more extreme and enraged than any that had been seen before. Those who took part were a new rock generation, with a very different attitude to that of the hippie movement of the 60s. Whereas the hippies were determined towards a new peaceful existence, celebrating a liberated form of culture, the early punks were angry, abrasive and intentionally offensive. This was a generational clash, as always youth culture was rebelling against the attitudes and ideals of what had gone before, struggling to be different. Punk began like a secret club, a gang of like-minded people. The experience was almost tribal. This was an entirely new group who consciously tried to shock society around them.

The word 'punk', originally meant 'rotten' or 'worthless', and was also a prison slang term for a person who is sexually submissive. The first use of the term in connection with the movement was in 1970s essay, 'The Punk Muse: The True Story of Protopathic Spiff Including the Lowdown on the Trouble-Making Five Percent of America's Youth,' by journalist Nick Tosches in the music magazine *Fusion*. Tosches described it as a music that was a 'visionary expiation, a cry into the abyss of one's own mordant bullshit,' its 'poetry is puked, not plotted.' This is the early punk attitude and one which has been longstanding. So punk encapsulates an emotional artistic response, a means for an individual to assert a sense of their own identity in what they see to be a constrictive society. But punk was never just about one thing, not just about screamed lyrics, noisy guitars or any particular clothing style. It was a culmination of factors and influences which caused it to grow first in New York and then move to Britain.

Although punk soon became a part of the musical mainstream, with record companies scrabbling to sign the next big punk stars and almost all of the best known punk bands releasing records on major labels, its roots have always been in its early days where people were looking for a way to express themselves and build their own communities. They adopted many methods which were already a part of DIY culture – making your own music independently, releasing your own records, organizing your own concerts and producing your own magazines. Although the initial shock of punk soon died down, its influence has remained in the underground and is still relevant in the process of creating your own cultural alternative.

Punk Beginnings

Early punk centred around New York City but many claim that the origins of punk lay in the American rock scene of the 60s where musicians used their early rock and roll influences to produce a heavier, harder rock sound. Many musicians were opting for this sound, creating primitive music with loud guitars, bass and drums. It is almost impossible to determine who the first punk band were or what made them different from the other rock bands which had been forming.

Early 60s bands which held some of the qualities later defined as punk – the rebellious spirit and lo-fi approach – were Mouse and The Traps[90], Question Mark and The Mysterians[91], The 13th Floor Elevators[92] and The Chocolate Watchband[93]. Early garage bands from Milwaukee, Detroit and Minneapolis contained many elements that would later be associated with punk. In 1968, James Newell Osterberg, soon to be known as Iggy Pop, decided to form a rock band in his home town of Ann Arbor, Michigan. Following the lead of Lou Reed from the 60s band The Velvet Underground, along with Jim Morrison from The Doors, he took on the role as frontman. Together, Iggy and his band The Stooges pioneered a new Detroit sound, with loud and abrasive performances that may have been the inspiration for the antics of later punk bands. In time Iggy Pop's body contortions, self-mutilation and dives into the audience became a notorious part of the live punk show. Much of what inspired their musical and performance style as well as the impetus for starting a band was boredom – boredom with both the music scene and with their own lives. Much like the punk bands which would follow, this 'pre-punk' band used this boredom as a means by which to create their own entertainment and fuel their band. Although The Stooges set out with the aim of producing music from almost nothing, to create music from their enthusiasm rather than previously learned skills, they were soon signed to the major record label, Elektra. Other bands soon joined this new Detroit music scene, among them MC5, who, although more vocally political than The Stooges, were also first signed to Elektra, who had realized the growing popularity of this new hard rock style.

The Blank Generation

The music being made in early 70s New York City was different from the American mainstream, different from what was being heard on the radio and on the records that teenagers had been listening to in their bedrooms. It was a new form of aggressive 70s rock mixed with the influence of rock's earlier roots. The reworking of earlier influences, which has always been a feature of rock music, was at the heart of early New York punk.

New York punks took much of their rebellious attitude from the city itself. Punk was originally known as 'street rock', because of its original links with street culture, and only later came to be known as 'punk', as those who came to use the name often tried to emulate tough hoodlums and New York street gangs. This was the beginning of the punk aesthetic and the leather jackets, ripped jeans, ragged clothes which would become so synonymous with punk. Although they adopted the style of street hoodlums, the typical New York punk was, in reality, far removed from thug culture. Early punks were intellectualizing what they were doing, satirizing popular American culture and reworking earlier styles for this new audience.

Those who took part in the early years of the New York punk scene were influenced by generations of previous artistic movements. Early punk was primarily concerned with music, revolving around forming bands, making and performing music. But the genre did not come from nowhere. The most obvious influence upon punk was the early days of rock and roll. Punks were similar to teenagers of the 1950s, discovering rock and roll and realizing that this was a means through which they could express themselves. Punk took traditional elements of rock and roll (which itself took influences from African-American sources) and reworked these influences to produce a new sound. Borrowing simple guitar riffs, chords and structure, punks adapted these elements by playing at ear-splitting volume, in an intensely aggressive fashion and with lyrics screamed instead of sung in tune. Bands like The Ramones did not feel tied to the traditions which had existed up to this point. Performances for the punks were not expected to be perfect, this was not what was now valued. Music just needed to be loud and confrontational. Obnoxious behaviour was actively encouraged as dancing became 'slam dancing', with audience members almost causing fights in front of the stage.

New York punks did not just look to the past for musical influences to rework or subvert but also for inspiration and guidance on how to form their own cultural alternatives. They aspired to be the new bohemians, seeking to develop a culture centred around music. They styled themselves in part after the French bohemians of the late 1800s, who felt that the only way to distance themselves from the confines of the French middle classes, and achieve social and cultural freedom, was to set themselves apart. They believed that their youth was their freedom and celebrating this was, in part, asserting their independence. Punk worked similarly as it celebrated the excitement of youth through high voltage hedonism.

Some bands, such as The New York Dolls and Television, found inspiration in the French romantic poets. The New

York Dolls' David JoHansen used the influence of the poet Rimbaud, and wrote songs about urban decay. Television's Tom Verlaine went so far as naming himself after 19th century French symbolist poet Paul Verlaine. Such New York bands used a poetic style to craft their lyrics, offering cryptic lyrics to their listeners, addressing similar themes to those addressed by the much earlier French poets.

The early punk movement during the mid-1970s also found influence in the lives and work of the beat writers, who had challenged contemporary American culture of the 40s and 50s through their writing, and used this to forge a new genre of rock music and youth culture. The beat writers had themselves found influence in an earlier American cultural movement. They mirrored themselves on the 'lost' generation of the 1930s, who, in the aftermath of World War I, exiled themselves from the familiarity of their homes in America and travelled to Europe where they lived as literary expatriates.

Richard Meyers was just one of many people who left their hometowns to move to New York City in the early 70s. Changing his name to Richard Hell, he formed the band Television. He wrote the song '(I Belong to) The Blank Generation', asserting that his generation was lost, much like those American writers of the 30s and the beat writers who carried many similar ideals in to the 50s.

Subcultures often have to search for their place in the world, with participants moving away from their hometowns and forming communities in unfamiliar environments. In the 40s and 50s, restless youths moved to New York and San Francisco from smaller suburban or rural communities, looking to find themselves and like-minded comrades in the big cities. Fifty years later, people were experiencing a similar sense of alienation and dissatisfaction and the action once again centred on New York City, which had been the scene for much of the beat activities. The early punk musicians, and other artists who worked alongside them, followed this artistic tradition of building a new creative community within an existing urban structure but separate in its ideas and aspirations. New York was their territory, the place where so many previous art movements had grown. Many punks moved from the suburbs looking for excitement and validation of their identity. Here punk was set in the middle classes, with middle class youth from the suburbs looking for an escape route from a life they felt to be dull and predictable.

In America, this pattern of rebellion had already been set, with social and political conditions repeating themselves in cycles over the years, and a distinct group of each new generation feeling that they need to opt out of the rigid social network and do something different. A strong sense of cultural ancestry has always existed in America, with people looking to the past for influence. Such an attitude spurs the underground to also look back at the past and offers its members the privilege of reworking previous ideas and so grasping some sense of validation for what they are doing – hoping to build on what has gone before. Punk probably would have never existed if it was not for previous counterculture movements like the beats, and without them it would certainly have been far more shocking and unexpected. Richard Hell agrees with the idea that punk was directly influenced by the decades of youth movements which preceded it. He explains that they were all influenced by, '...the beats and hippies (even if it was also a reaction against them), by motorcycle gangs and surrealist poets, by 50s rock and roll style, etc, etc. All the "disaffected youth" movements are the same. Which isn't to say that they aren't great and real and true – because the established order will be corrupt and oppressive and needs to be exposed and fought.'[94]

This was a rebellious style of music and New York punks, despite having a rich heritage of independent cultural sources to gather inspiration from, were typically financially poor. Although they were often middle class kids relocating to the big city from the suburbs, New York in the early 70s was a difficult place to live. The country was in economic recession, most people had little money. The prosperity of the post-war era was over and New York was in decay, crime-ridden and grim in the poor neighbourhoods. However, rent was cheap and so young people could survive relatively easily. Many kids were looking to alleviate their sense of boredom and the punk movement grew as people with little better to do started to form bands. They were looking for a cultural movement that they could call their own

Punks were uninspired by mainstream music. This was the height of the disco era in New York and rock musicians and their fans were dissatisfied. They were looking for something similar to early rock and roll. To begin with, there was a loosely connected group of bands with different musical styles, tied together by the sense of community, and the belief that these bands were in control. Even those who were signed to record labels gave the impression that they were doing this themselves and calling for others to follow them.

The history of punk did not run one smooth course, starting with one innovative band and then with others following their lead until there was a definitive type of punk band. Early punk contained a number of pioneer bands like The New York Dolls, Talking Heads, Television and The Dictators, all of whom – although forming an integral part of punk's early years – were developing their own sounds. It was their attitude that linked them together. They encouraged their audiences to start their own bands and follow their lead. They made a statement that they were not above their audience and so the audience felt that they knew these people, they were just like them, they could be their friends.

One of the bands which came to seen as almost the definitive punk band was The Ramones. They epitomized the sound that would later be defined as classically punk. They weren't interested in being original or technically accomplished, instead just raging against what they considered to be boring in most of the mainstream bands of the time. They celebrated the amateur approach, they did not aim to be great musicians, just to create an alternative. They songs were typically based on just a few chords, with lyrics that were often repetitions of short phrases, mixing early rock and roll with aggression and unconventional lyrics.

Punk was not just about music however. It was the community that grew up around the pioneer bands that gave the movement its initial strength. Clubs like CBGB's in New York provided a place to play and an enthusiastic audience. CBGB's was certainly the place to go for New York's punk population. This old decrepit bar was originally named The Palace Bar, ironically situated underneath the largest flophouse on the Bowery. By 1974, there were few places that welcomed rock music, no club would let you play original rock unless you had a recording contract. Obviously this greatly limited the bands that could play live. CBGB's recognized this and adopted the bold policy that you could only play at the club if you performed your own music. Originality was seen as more important than technical knowledge. They wanted inventiveness and excitement, not stale cover versions.

The new music did not achieve widespread appeal, to begin with it received no airplay and there were no hit records. American punk was peaking in 1972, but American pop charts certainly did not reflect this trend. The number one song in America in 1973 was 'Tie A Yellow Ribbon' by Tony Orlando and Dawn. Popular music was far removed from punk, which made little impact on the charts.

This sense of community, which existed in the New York punk scene, is explained by Richard Hell. 'The society of the bands and music clubs of "punk" in its earliest years in New York was definitely distinct, and its members conceived of themselves as separate from and opposed to the straight, adult world. People had a lot of different kinds of personal values, though. If there were shared beliefs, maybe they were that the straight world was hypocritical and otherwise dishonest and exploitative and that therefore we'd try to be as completely opposite those things as possible. That's pretty general, and could basically be said of any "youth rebellion" movement, but maybe a difference is that we acknowledged that honesty is pretty complicated, too; more complicated than the overly romantic, deluded, immediately previous "youth rebellions" – hippies and beats – seemed to understand.'

To begin with punk music existed solely in the underground but its impact soon spread. The New York scene did not develop into mass culture. It did, however, have impact on similarly dissatisfied kids across the country, and in other countries, as a similar type of scene began to develop in other cities.

Anarchy in the UK
Though Punk began in New York, it caught on with much greater force in England. British youths began to discover

American punk bands which provided an exhilarating alternative to the stagnant mainstream UK music scene. They soon formed their own bands, such as The Sex Pistols, The Clash, The Damned, The Buzzcocks and The Slits, taking inspiration from their American counterparts. The popularity of New York punk hit its peak in the early to mid-70s, while in Britain, 1976 was the year of crucial uprising.

Punk hit home harder in Britain than it had in the USA, as new punk bands from the British scene shaped their influences into a greater force, one which came to be identified as the driving force of punk culture across the globe. Most British punk bands did use elements of New York punk to shape their own scene, influenced by the aesthetics of the New York punk figureheads, adopting the fashions and above all continuing the simple spirit of rebellion.

While New York punk acknowledged and often celebrated influences from an eclectic range of musicians and artists of the past, British punks saw punk as a brand new force which would change rock music. British punks were influenced by American trends but adapted them to fit the social and political climate that existed in the UK. In Britain, it was about more than music, it was about the social conditions that young people were experiencing. British punks were affected by their immediate situation and the situation for many was grim. In 1975, they were facing the highest unemployment rates since World War II. It was a conservative time, with the BBC strictly controlling both radio and television and a conservative government in power, under the leadership of Margaret Thatcher. This was the era of strikes, three-day working weeks and power cuts. This generation of working class British youth was leaving school and struggling to find jobs. Some turned to music to vent their feelings of frustration, and it was characteristically aggressive, a violent assault on society. Fast, loud music and angry lyrics helped them express their anger, as did the bands names they came up with, like 'The Sex Pistols' and 'The Clash'. It made for uncomfortable listening. British punk launched a direct attack on society and the lagging economy, demanding immediate change. Bands were singing about the issues that affected their lives: unemployment, poverty and the class divide. They believed what they were singing about was the heartfelt truth – that their country was failing them.

Unlike the punks of New York the British punk was most often working class and struggling to find a job. Disgusted with society, their response was to be as disgusting as possible; often using shock tactics to get their message across. Bands were almost vicious on stage, with the audience spitting on band members and band members lashing out violently at their audience. This was a total shift from the usual revering of the band as hero figures. The punk gig was a means for young people to vent their frustration, with the band almost conducting their responses, it was a highly physical event. The audience members intentionally started fights with one another and the band, and the 'mosh pit', which gathered at the front of the stage, was the place where most of this action took place as the audience was driven into frenzy. 'Fight back!' was the message. If someone pushes you, push them back, if they hit you, hit them back. This was the practical element of punk, and many of those involved were the kids who were pushed around at school. Punk provided them with a mask to hide behind and a way to feel better.

Their clothing expressed this sense of anger also. They went beyond the initial style of the New York punks to develop an even more extreme fashion involving ripped clothing often held together with safety pins, studded leather jackets, spiked hair dyed in bright colours, tattoos and multiple body piercings. At first, punk fashion took its lead almost entirely from Malcolm McLaren's London clothing shops – most notably SEX on the King's Road. Along with designer Vivienne Westwood, he drew influence directly from what American punks were wearing, and adapted these styles to create a high impact visual confrontation. Mixing fetish wear with T-shirts bearing controversial slogans, McLaren and Westwood reworked the visuals of punk, which would become the elements that made the punks stand apart from the rest of British society. This, of course, was their intention. They did not feel part of the constrictive society in which they lived and so vented their bitterness in any way that they could.

This anger was exemplified by such songs as The Sex Pistols' 'No Future' (later to become 'God Save The Queen') and The Clash's 'London's Burning', both of which expressed the sentiments of an entire generation. When he sang 'Pretty Vacant', Johnny Rotten claimed the right not to work, and the right to deny all the values that traditionally went with working life. These were new voices expressing the almost apocalyptic vision that there was no future for Britain's youth.

Their anger was particularly directed at the Queen's Silver Jubilee celebrations of 1977. In a society so divided by class, where unemployment was so high for the working classes, it seemed to many distasteful to celebrate the monarch so publicly when much of the country was struggling.

Writer Jon Savage, who was involved in early British punk through the writing of his zine *London Outrage* explains how the British punk scene, which was initially concerned with music and style, later became more socially and politically aware. 'The Sex Pistols had older people involved with them who had a sure news sense (like Jamie Reid and Malcolm McLaren) and the whole thing reached its peak with the Queen's Jubilee Weekend and "God Save The Queen" reaching or not reaching Number 1. That was when the world's media, come to the UK to cover the Jubilee, found its perfect anti-story and punk, from being a tiny elite youth culture style, became a global news phenomenon.'[95]

British punk gained more media attention than the earlier New York bands because its message was more direct and reached an audience who were experiencing the same things as its leaders. It was very different from the New York ambition of forging an idealistic version of bohemian culture. As British youth struggled with the demoralizing effects of welfare and unemployment, American youth involved with punk *chose* the bohemian lifestyle. Economic conditions were not so difficult for the young Americans who formed punk bands.

Punk style began to be seen as British, as the UK claimed the punk rock movement for itself and sold it back to the US (much like early British rock bands exported American blues back to American audiences). As with the American punk scene, which began in New York City before spreading across the country, so was London seen as the epicentre of the early British punk movement. This was where the key bands were located and the clubs which were willing to have them perform.

Jamie Reid, underground publisher, school friend and business partner of Malcolm McLaren, explained how vital the punk attitude was for Britain's angry youth. 'It was perfect timing, with that first generation of kids coming out of school, particularly working class kids, who'd been given loads of promises but had nothing to do, whether jobs or opportunities. It was all about that "do-it yourself fuck-all-that-fucking-corporate-glam-rock-shit" that was going on in the music business. We did our own artwork, produced our own music and the whole thing was inspirational.'[96]

Punk grew to be an extremely influential force in Britain and though this is much disputed Malcom McLaren likes to claim responsibility for much of the movement. He acknowledged that rock music was intrinsically linked to youth culture, that through it people were most receptive to radical ideas, and realized that there was money to be made. He saw American punk almost as a product, borrowing the original punk aesthetic and then selling it to British youth who were desperate for such an experience. His eye was caught by a band called The Swankers – soon to change their name to The Sex Pistols – and he began promoting them, with the intention of them becoming Britain's premier punk band. For him, The Sex Pistols were a commercial proposition from the start, an investment and a product.

McLaren discovered rock and roll at an early age, like many kids listening to Elvis Presley in 1957. His early teenage years were spent exploring the youth culture that was sweeping Britain, chasing whatever was deemed to be cool. He found that he had a talent for recognizing new trends, discovering what would become popular and grasping it before his friends. After a few years at art school, enjoying the London youth culture that centred around the clubs and coffee bars of Soho, he decided to turn this skill into a business, and opened a fashion boutique on the King's Road with partner Vivienne Westwood. They at first catered for the 'teddy boy' market, a movement slowly dying out in London.[97] On a trip to New York in 1973 for New York's annual National Boutique Show sourcing stock for their shop, they discovered a new trend perfect for London. In America, youth culture was strong and gaining further strength. Punk introduced itself to McLaren in the form of the New York Dolls, the extravagant cult punk band, as two of its members were selling their multi-coloured hand-knitted sweaters at the National Boutique Show. McLaren was intrigued by the buzz of New York and when he returned to the depressing state of London he decided to change the focus of his shop, moving away from targeting teddy boys and instead looking for a new biker market who would buy into emulating the Marlon Brando era of American cool. However, this was still not enough for McLaren, who become hooked on the new punk style that he had witnessed in New York. In 1974, he changed the name of the shop from 'Let It Rock' to 'SEX' and Londoners first gained exposure to this new style for themselves. They began to create and sell a new subversive form of fashion – T-shirts with obscene slogans, customized bondage trousers, reinvented fetish wear. Mixing these trends with the music of American punk bands touring Britain, they helped punk hit London town. When McLaren encouraged The Swankers to become The Sex Pistols, which was the name of a New York street gang, it was a carefully crafted move, shifting them to the forefront of a new generation of musical rebellion.

McLaren realized that times were changing in the music world. He explained, 'Groups became like an aristocracy; it was something you worshipped, something you paid a lot of money for, to see a group no bigger than a sixpence on the stage. That wasn't rock and roll. In my opinion, rock and roll was getting up there, stepping out and creating the greatest possible imperfection. The music wasn't important. It was just a declaration of intent and an attitude. If you got that, that's what it was all about.'[98] The Sex Pistols were orchestrated by McLaren to be the band that would embody his vision. They would be the band with the attitude, who would embrace the lo-fi ethic and amateurism to produce truly passionate music. Johnny Rotten half-sang and half-screamed the lyrics over crackling PA systems, their songs savagely attacking the status quo. McLaren also understood the value of shock and encouraged the band to be as shocking as possible, both in their fashion, attitudes and behaviour. After a series of shambolic gigs and being banned from venues across London they began to gather fans and press interest.

Jamie Reid is amongst those who argued that McLaren was not the most important force in the popularity of British punk. 'The most important people are always the punters – I know it's a cliché but it's about the people on the streets. Because that's where real life is and where all the real ideas always come from. He was just in a position to put the ideas out.'[99]

The aesthetic of 70s British punk shared many similarities with that of earlier art movements such as dada and situationism. The situationists celebrated making art from the materials of everyday life. Punk came to harbour similar views. Both shared the belief that modern consumer society was alienating people and that they needed to fight back. The means to do this was not just through the lyrics of the punk band but by their whole attitude and look. In Britain, this was due in part to the situationist imagery that Malcolm McLaren used in SEX shop designs and the marketing of The Sex Pistols. From the situationist-type slogans on T-shirts, the playing with language and the appropriation of visual styles, in the UK punk became an art style as well as a radical music movement.

British punk reached its peak during the sweltering summer of 1976. The nation was suffering, authority was losing its grip, the labour government was battling with the trade unions and on the King's Road dissatisfied punks were parading the streets with their anger written all over them.

Adopting a rebel music for commercial purpose has its problems. McLaren felt that punk needed a wider audience, moving it from the underground into the mainstream mass media. It can be argued that the public reaction against punk began in 1976 when The Sex Pistols were interviewed on the 'Today' show on Thames Weekend Television by Bill Grundy, where they unleashed their opinions on a still largely unsuspecting British public and became infamous. Grundy was ill-prepared for such guests and to them he represented the middle-aged establishment. Ever ready to attack the establishment and be as controversial as possible, also goaded by Grundy's questions, the Pistols swore profusely at their host. This was the first experience of punk for many members of the British public. The next morning newspaper headlines such as 'THE NIGHT OF THE NASTIES: FOUR-LETTER PUNK GROUP IN TV STORM!' (Daily Mail) and 'PUNK FILTH' (Daily Express), expressed the disgust of the majority. Their record label, EMI, was furious but controversy sells records and this foul-mouthed, obnoxious, scruffy version of punk became infamous almost overnight. Punk reached its widest ever audience, with many people horrified at what the British youth could become. Punk was judged by the responses it provoked and the response from most people was shock and horror. The Sex Pistols were largely responsible for the vilification of punk. Their behaviour on and off stage caused much controversy as did the lyrics of their songs. In their single, 'Anarchy in the UK' they made anarchist claims, and in Britain at that time the word 'anarchist' had the same connotations that 'communist' once had in America; there was widespread fear of a covert but dangerous force in society. So their shock value not only brought the Pistols fame at the time, but also secured their place in music history as the most recognizable band of the punk era. Many believed that punk rock began with the Pistols. Those taking a more hardcore attitude, however, believed that the commercial potential of The Sex Pistols made punk into a novelty and signified the beginning of the end.

For a culture which had previously existed in the underground, this attention from the mainstream had its price. The Sex Pistols became almost a cartoon version of punk, their image became mass-produced, copied and diluted for a wider audience. By 1977, punk was everywhere. That summer, *Time* and *Newsweek* informed their readers of the punk subculture that had emerged in America and Britain. They were scathing towards what they saw to be an ugly style, with this trend of men and women dying their hair unnatural colours and piercing their flesh with safety pins. Punk was being noticed by the mainstream though they were assuming that its most obvious aesthetics held the most meaning, and ignored its origins, which were rooted in the independent culture of decades before.

The original do-it-yourself ethos of early punk became obscured as record companies began to manipulate and exploit punk as a mass product. Soon every record label had its quota of punk bands. By the mid-1980s, the face of punk had become publicly acceptable, but this was a sterilized version of the original punk rock approach, retaining few of its unique characteristics. It had moved far away from its roots as a movement for the youth to express their situation and more about selling as many records as possible to anyone who would buy them. Even Johnny Rotten of The Sex Pistols realized that punk had become a mangled version of its original ideals. At the end of the last Sex Pistols' tour, he asked 'Have you ever felt you've been cheated?' Later he would form a band sarcastically called 'Public Image Limited', whose album's title song describes a bitter embrace of success seen through the eyes of the quintessential punk.

The superficial image of punk became well known, the dyed hair and leather jackets, and not the do-it-yourself ethos from where it began. The accessibility of punk, the attitude that anyone could create music, was, in the end, part of its curse. It was seen as commercially viable and the whole attitude was packaged, marketed and sold back to young people. This is not to say that punk is dead. Despite the treatment of early punk, the original do-it-yourself attitude has lived on as a powerful movement in both music and wider alternative culture, with the punk aesthetic continuing to influence bands, zines and other artistic ventures across the globe today.

Punk Heroines

To many, punk appeared to be a male-dominated music scene, hostile to those women who wanted to take part. It followed the earlier rock and roll tradition of being fiercely anti-domestic, a world full of young men avoiding social and domestic responsibility, instead touring the country alongside their bandmates. Punk celebrated these activities but did so with a pervasive anti-social sense of anger and dissatisfaction. For a female musician to break into this environment seemed a daunting task.

In her essay in Roger Sabin's book *Punk Rock: So What?*

(1999), writer Lucy O'Brien explains that punk helped to shift gender boundaries in music[100]. Until the 60s, women had rarely been seen in the role of 'musician' within the industry. Instead they were generally singers – performing songs written for them by someone else. Of course there were exceptions, but generally women were regarded as secondary figures, occupying limited roles. They could be adoring fans, glamourous or sensitive singers, but were rarely seen performing at the front of the stage with an electric guitar. Punk challenged these preconceptions in the 70s, with the arrival of The Slits, Siouxsie and the Banshees, The Raincoats, X-Ray Spex, Delta 5, The Au Pairs and The Adverts among others.

In the 70s the realization that women could indeed be a creative force in music followed many of the ideals set by the hippie movement in the previous decade; that women could demand a place in society equal to the male. Punk was critical of many of these assertions, viewing them as naïve, and pointing out that as sexual liberation was difficult to achieve women would have to fight to make any kind of headway.

As punks called for revolution, a rejection of authority and an assertion of freedom of self-expression, it was never clearly stated where women stood in this revolution. Male bands did not seem to acknowledge their position. Were they equal participants? Were they intended to be part of this revolution? Although championing an alternative set of values, male punk bands were often still singing about female stereotypes.

But those women taking part in punk, both in Britain and America, were actively breaking stereotypes. Their femininity was far from passive or docile, it was aggressive and often shocking, far removed from the image of feminine beauty of the hippie age. Traditional images of beauty were subverted. Women wore many of the same clothes as the male punks, sporting leather jackets and ripped clothes with garish makeup, tattoos and piercings or developing their own style quite different to that previously expected of a female performer. Punk gave women a license to rage, to be brutal and confrontational and this was often reflected in their appearance. Female sexuality was portrayed differently; it could be ambiguous, aggressive and violent. Women were interpreting punk differently from men, using it to express their own experiences and visions and in doing so were challenging societal expectations.

It was the lo-fi aspect of punk music that encouraged many women to take part. Like their male counterparts, they realized that you did not need to be an accomplished musician to be seen as a great punk musician. This is not to say that women of the punk movement were not accomplished musicians, but the DIY musicianship made the scene appear more accessible and many women felt able to enter a world from which they had been previously excluded. Record labels and the music-buying public began to sit up and take notice. Geoff Travis explains: 'Women were relatively empowered by punk. I don't think I'd ever seen a band like The Slits before – I think punk gave them the impetus. We just had respect for women. We didn't see any reason why women couldn't be equally good at making music as their male counterparts. We were very open to it at Rough Trade.'[101]

Female punk bands began appearing in the late 70s, but in total the numbers of female punk musicians were far less than the number of male musicians. Many of these female musicians and their fans were vocal in calling for more women to join them in the scene, feeling that with its emphasis on the do-it-yourself ethos, everyone should take part. One zine writer, Lucy Toothpaste, a 1977 issue of her zine *The Jolt* asked, 'Well, why aren't there any real girl punk musicians around?'[102] She then went on to explain, 'But it's not really surprising if girls are still a bit uncertain about how to bust into rock. The very fact that rock, the so-called rebel culture, has always been completely male-dominated just goes to show that if there's one person more oppressed than a teenage boy it's a teenage girl. Girls've been so squashed that we haven't even dared complain. And now we've woken up at last, we haven't just got to cope with the total lack of encouragement and having no precedent, but also with the gawping and sniggering of the male music establishment.' These angry assertions that the music industry was dominated by men, and was therefore a hostile environment for female musicians, pre-dates the riot grrrl movement of the early 90s, where hundreds of girls would make similar claims. In her article, Lucy continues passionately to call other girls to action, emphasizing punk's do-it-yourself roots, 'But NOW's the time for us to get going, it doesn't matter if we don't know how to play the guitar yet, we can soon learn to play as well as any other punk band, and I think the punk public is just waiting for more girl bands to appear. I am, anyway.'

Punk Politics
Punk was not just a musical or cultural movement, it also had roots in the political. It took elements of the anarchist spirit; the social philosophy arguing that people have the potential to live without governmental control. It is often asked whether punk achieved anything. Punks were certainly angry, as seen through their music and behaviour. But who was this anger directed towards? They publicly raged against the popular musicians and the stars of the

previous decade (such as The Who and The Rolling Stones), at their record labels and even against their own fans. The Sex Pistols, for example, became famed for spitting on their audience during live performances. Some feel punk's anger was misdirected, just a protracted and obnoxious rant against mainstream culture. They did not have a firm political focus, they were more likely to be seen swearing and ranting against authority than working constructively to change it. British punks were angry about social conditions and the treatment of the nation's youth but did little to address the issues constructively or make practical suggestions for change.

British punk in the 70s has been regarded as more political than in America. British youths were seen to be reacting against their circumstances whereas American youths were primarily re-enacting and celebrating influences from the past and raging against the values of their parents' generation. John Holmstrom from *Punk* magazine explains his view that American punk was apolitical, 'It was apathetic. I don't remember having many political discussions back then. Whenever someone would start, we'd just sort of tune them out...'[103] In America, young dissidents did not have the dramatic political events of the generation before, such as the Vietnam War, to protest against. The peak of the punk movement occurred during the late presidency of Nixon and early Carter, but the anger of its members was never sufficiently well channelled. The call for social change was not prevalent in the US punk movement. This is not to say that, despite their apathy, American punks weren't in their own way continuing the activism of the 60s into the 70s. It was just different. Punk was a reaction against the harmonious ideals of the 60s, and voiced objections to the hippie movement of the previous decade. The approach here was far more cynical than optimistic.

Counterculture has always been concerned with capitalism, attempting to escape or subvert it, trying to disrupt or shift its power. Punk was no different in its opposition to commercialism. Bands tried to make their gigs and records affordable for everyone, wanting their audience to have access to events at the core of the movement. This continues the debates raised in the 60s, that the sense of a DIY community, in which anyone can participate, is vital and revolutionary. Even though it typically lacked direction and focus, with no clear agenda, punk can be heralded as a new kind of free speech. Although not explicitly politically motivated, punks were claiming the power to say whatever they wanted and at this time they were listened to, mirroring the Free Speech Movement which was active in America in the 60s.

British punk has been recorded as a more political movement than its American counterpart. Some people involved in the early British punk scene did see its distinct potential through which to spread political messages. Jamie Reid, who had been designing pamphlets and posters for the radical Suburban Press, was fascinated by the idea of using music to spread political ideas. Following situationist ideas of spreading messages (as Malcolm McLaren came to do also), he created much of the visual material now so firmly associated with punk. Realizing the power of visual images, the posters he designed for The Sex Pistols are still famous today; he also developed other situationist ideas, such as convincing bands to miss their own gigs as a form of detournement and writing anarchist songs to attract attention to spread political ideals.

Many were certainly vocal in their dislike of the music industry, which they saw as exercising an unfair control over music. Punk had a strange relationship with the music industry as many of the most influential bands, including The Sex Pistols and The Ramones, released records on mainstream record labels, and even attacked the major record companies through the songs they were releasing. It was a new position for the bands to be in, voicing objections to the music industry while at the same time accepting their offers to release their records. It seemed for many that the labels were an easy enemy, but strangely enough, the record labels benefited from this behaviour, which enabled them to market the bands as authentic and angry. While the bands were seen to be venomous towards the major labels they were signed to, they could be presented as part of the original incarnation of punk. The situation resembled kids rebelling against their parents.

It was within this early punk scene that the do-it-yourself attitude really ignited. Although it had been emerging in the counterculture, this was the time when it was vocally, and passionately, addressed. Although many bands soon signed to major record labels and so effectively became part of corporate culture, the original spirit of the early punk bands was to do-it-themselves. Richard Hell explains, 'I'd say the essential thing was a rejection of the readymade corporate means of expression, whether in clothes or advertizing or music or any other form of communication.' It was this sense of rejection of existing mainstream culture that formed the basis of the punk ethos. Although for many people punk will never be seen as a serious form of social protest it was an expression of social dissent and drew attention to a new form of creativity.

A few punk bands took a radically political stance in what they were doing. Among them was the anarchist punk band Crass. Forming in 1978 at Dial House, an Essex farmhouse that housed a large commune, by drummer Penny Rimbaud[104] and singer Steve Ignorant, Crass were part of an already radical community. The music became an extension of their beliefs and the community around them both influenced and became members of the band. Crass held their position as an independent band at the core of their existence. They took the punk ideals seriously and used them as a means for setting up their own punk community, transmitting their ideas through the networks they created. For them, punk was just as much about a chance to express political commitment as it was about screeching guitars and sweaty gigs.

They played their first gig at a squatter's free festival and were approached by Small Wonder Records in January 1979, who were eager to release their first EP. However, a controversial opening track, entitled 'Asylum', meant that no pressing plant would agree to manufacture the record. To release it, the band were forced to remove the song – replacing it instead with a protest of two minutes' silence, the length of the missing track, which they listed as 'Free Speech'. The band were disillusioned by this incident with the independent record label and decided to launch their own Crass label and so bypass any form of external control over their output. As a band they became self-sufficient, turning down a major label record contract in the mid-80s, preferring instead to continue releasing their own records.

The band was outspoken about not only their musical but also their political ideals. Their lyrics were anarchic as well as their actions. They had already decided that the band would end in 1984, as a reference to the novel by George Orwell – a comment on how they felt the government was controlling the country – and each record they released was numbered as countdown to this date. Reflecting their anti-capitalist stance, they sold their own records at little more than cost price, printing a 'Pay no more than…' price label on the records. As well as these efforts, they were part of a wider anarchist society. Their gigs were real community events with poetry, film and performance arts as well as music and included stalls from political organizations. They pioneered the genre of 'anarcho-punk', taking elements of punk but mixing it with anarchist principles. In doing so, they championed the CND movement, bringing it to wider attention. They also launched a graffiti war in central London, spraying slogans on walls. They designed the anarchists' 'A' symbol, which has adorned punks and activists since and has endured as a visual image synonymous with anarchist ideas.

Putting into practice the do-it-yourself values that punk had been preaching, they expressed their ideology through their music and the means by which they released their records. Rimbaud explains: 'I certainly think without Crass, none of what has now looked back as the effects of punk…it would have no affect at all. I mean, the Pistols and that group, those commercial people, lasted for about two years. They were just an extension of the usual music business tactics. They had no sort of political overview whatsoever.'[105]

Whether or not punk was a political youth movement, it was certainly a cure for the sense of boredom and dissatisfaction that was affecting so many young people. For bands such as Crass, it was an extension of their anarchist principles. For many individuals, who didn't want to participate within commercial culture, it offered an escape route. Punk grew from young people's boredom with the current music scene, with being poor and with their being sick of the loneliness they experienced through not fitting in. It grew out of the urge to change your own life, and subsequently the lives of others. The personal became political, and it was this sense of boredom and dissatisfaction, as well as underlying political attitudes, which ultimately ignited the underground scene.

The Punk Legacy

New Wave

One distinct movement that developed after the peak of punk was 'new wave', a genre which moved away from punk's angry cultural response to produce a more artistic one. Journalist and historian Alan Betrock explained in his 1977 *New York Rocker* article that because of the difference between the focus of British and American punk, most of the American bands were calling themselves new wave, leaving punk to the British. New wave developed the artistic and cultural influences that American punks had celebrated. The scene was born in New York City in the late 70s and early 80s, and centred around the popular punk club CBGBs. To start with, the term 'new wave' was interchangeable with 'punk rock' but each soon developed into distinct genres. The term was then applied to any of the bands that followed in the wake of punk without relying on punk's original angry sensibilities and rough style. New wave is seen as a more artistic version of the same idea, blending together many musical styles and attitudes, while preserving the original lo-fi attitude of early punk.

British Post-punk

With the release of The Sex Pistols' album *Never Mind the Bollocks* in 1977, many people involved in punk felt that the demise of their scene had begun. The contents of this album were certainly incendiary and angry but ultimately it was felt by many to be just another hard rock album. It did not hold the same vital spark. The initial impact of punk had been fiery, a vicious rebellion against the over-produced music of disco and big budget stadium rock of the 70s. Punk had started something new but this had now been diluted.

What came next took many of the original ideas of punk, with its often sloppy instrumentation, aggressive lyrics and expressively nihilistic attitude, but modified them. This new direction, beginning to take shape in 1979 after the first blast of punk, became known as 'post-punk'. This term has been a source of much confusion and misunderstanding. If is often used to describe any music that came after punk's peak, following many of its original characteristics but mixing this with more artistic influences. As a rejection against the nihilism of punk, instead of calling for an undefined revolution over sloppy guitars played through screaming amplifiers, post-punk bands wanted to create art. These art rockers were typically marked by their lack of attitude, their determination to build concrete DIY scenes within which to retain their ideals of artistic freedom and mark them outside the corporate music industry within which they could not see a place for themselves.

Although distinct, punk, new wave and post-punk all shared common ground, in that all were energetic reactions to the slick, uninspired mainstream music of the 1970s. Although labelled 'post' punk – indicating that it came after punk – the two existed alongside one another and analysis can be complex, as punk music continues to this day.

Post-punk generally refers to the distinctly creative

period after British punk's peak. The early punk bands had broken new ground, set new standards, and so the bands that followed had the opportunity to be more experimental. It is known for being punk's arty offspring, an innovative style that took elements from punk, the sense of DIY ethics and lo-fi style, and incorporated experimental musicianship.

Post-punk lost some of the confrontational attitude of punk. It was the impulse to make art and explore new ideas that led its enthusiasts to bands and promoters working to create their own networks through which to manufacture and distribute new music. This art rock was far more DIY orientated than previous incarnations. The early post-punk bands were not trying to enter the established music industry but were trying to create their own alternative. They had seen what had happened when the original punk bands were signed to major labels and did not want a similar experience.

One of the earliest indications that this new version of punk was on its way came in 1977. The Sex Pistols' singer John Lydon (Johnny Rotten) began a show on Capital Radio where he showcased the experimental side to his musical tastes. Playing records by Beefheart, Peter Hammill, Can and contemporary Jamaican dub artists like Dr. Alimantado, his audience now saw that he was not a one-dimensional punk, he had other musical influences.

He took these ideas further by forming a new band when he left The Sex Pistols in 1978. Public Image Ltd (PiL) was nothing like his previous band. It expressed the bitterness he felt towards Malcolm McLaren, with whom he found himself in a bitter legal dispute. To avoid any similar problems, this new band managed themselves and produced their own records. It was only by establishing this new post-punk band that Lydon could take control. He was now following the punk ethics that he himself had championed during the rise of punk. Countless kids throughout the 70s had embraced DIY politics at The Sex Pistols' command but only now could he realize this for himself. By now punk was seen by many as a tired cliché and Lydon was doing something different.

As well as operating differently from The Sex Pistols, PiL also sounded very different. Lydon recruited Keith Levene on guitar and Jah Wobble on bass, and with influences ranging from Krautrock[106] and art rock to dub, this new band was what he had wanted The Sex Pistols to sound like. Their adoption of what would later be considered a distinctly post-punk approach was intentional, the aim being to mix a variety of eclectic musical styles. This was more staunchly anti-music-establishment than punk ever was. Whereas The Sex Pistols ranted against the music industry whilst being part of it, PiL was deliberately subverting its ideas. By mixing different musical genres including rock, dance and dub, and continuously reinventing themselves, they refused to play the music industry's game. They could not be pigeon-holed and revelled in this position as outsiders. It was only through this band that Lydon began to really express his own experimental ideas.

The two British groups quickest to respond to the post-punk challenge were Alternative TV and The Pop Group. 'I was disappointed by the lack of musical progress,' says Alternative TV's Mark Perry. 'Punk had brought in the DIY ethos but it didn't take it far enough.'[107] Both bands took political and philosophical influences on board as well as musical. Intellectual influences of The Pop Group included Wilhelm Reich's theories, Antonin Artaud's Theatre of

Cruelty, John Cage's spirituality, situationism and 50s beat poets like Ginsberg and Kerouac.

Some post-punk bands consciously set themselves against the earlier values of punk, seeing their music as a clear critique, and ultimately a rejection of rock traditions. Post-punk was a kind of musical discussion of rock and roll. Songs such as the TV Personalities' 'Part Time Punks', The Fall's 'Repetition', Scritti Politti's 'Messthetics', and The Prefects's 'Going Through The Motions' and 'Faults', were pitted directly against punk's values.

Post-punk sounded different, instruments were used differently. The sound was often harsh and angular, traditional guitar effects were rejected, timing was altered and there were gaps within the music. London-based post-punk band Gang of Four (who have been a huge influence on current bands like The Futureheads) explained how they shunned rock's intuitive composition methods. 'No jamming, everything thought out in advance, plotted'. This was a rejection of how punk saw the amateur approach. For punks, getting up on stage with little rehearsal was admirable. To many post-punk bands it was important to carefully construct a lo-fi sound, which could be just as authentic.

Early punk was seen by many post-punk bands to be a particularly macho, sexist scene. Although it had challenged female musicians to take part, it had soon become a very aggressively masculine culture. Bands like The Gang of Four worked to create a new form of rock that was hard and aggressive but not so oppressively macho. Post-punk not only challenged musical traditions but also social restrictions prevalent within the early punk scene.

Punk had been centred around London, and the visual image of the punk figure came to characterize London of the 70s. In fact, the brightly-coloured 'Mohican' hairstyle and leather jacket still features on postcards throughout London's tourist hotspots today. However, post-punk spread to the provinces as new bands were formed and DIY flourished all over the country. Groups like The Fall and The Passage enabled Manchester, for example, to rise up in opposition against the capital and lay claim to being the centre of the music industry. 'Leave The Capitol,' exhorted a track on *Slates*, The Fall's 1981 10" mini-LP. In their song 'Lon don', Fellow Mancunians The Passage sneered, 'Too many peacocks in one part/they must be very dull in London'.

Sheffield was the home of one band who followed DIY ideals particularly closely – The Cabs. Despite having no manager and without signing to a record label they released their own records via their own 8-track studio, Western Works, so prolifically that they were able to live on the profits. They were experimental, originally using tape loops to create their sound. Their cultural influences were broad and they weaved these into their sound. For them being DIY was about creating a unique style, not following what had come before. They needed to 'do-it-themselves' to be able to produce such music without creative or commercial boundaries.

Along with The Fall and The Cabs, other northern bands such as Cabaret Voltaire made the North a place where post-punk flourished. New city-based scenes emerged in Leeds, Sheffield and Manchester, but much of the music was being created and produced in bedrooms across the country. Amateurism was truly celebrated, and the musicians involved often did not have any ambition to become part of the music industry. They just wanted to make their own kind of music. This became the nature of post-punk – hence its long-running and close association with DIY ethics.

This is not to say that London didn't play an important role in post-punk; its influence particularly centring around Ladbroke Grove's bohemian neighbourhood. This is where Rough Trade, the nearby Better Badges and other numerous venues were located, and many of the musicians and promoters lived in the areas. Vivien Goldman owned a house on Ladbroke Grove itself, where the founder of Rough Trade, Geoff Travis, lived as her flatmate for a while. She explains, 'It was a real bohemia. Lots of squats, and the rents were very cheap too. It was pretty scuzzy, but there really wasn't that much violence. There was about half a dozen places within walking distance where you could go and rave all night – shebeens, blues dances etc.'

Experimental bands could thrive in the late 70s and early 80s away from the British musical mainstream due to the supportive network that was developing across the country. Independent record labels were being started which would release new music, as well as zines which would spread the word about it. This was seen as the main flaw of punk, that it could not quickly develop adequate networks to sustain the scene. After punk's initial spark, post-punk was able to constructively forge such networks.

It is almost impossible to overstate radio DJ John Peel's importance in the post-punk era. The 'John Peel band' almost became the name of a genre as he, enthralled by even the most eccentric of post-punk bands, would give them airtime on his Radio One show. He would play their records and invite his favourites into the studio to record live sessions. Across the country, musicians would tune in regularly to this show to see if their records were played and to hear the offerings of other bands with similar lo-fi ideals.

The British music press was in an extremely powerful position at this time. Apart from Peel, the only other nationally accessible media by which you could find out about post-punk was the weekly music press. Punk had revitalized the British music press, given them exciting new bands to write about and an eager audience who would hungrily devour what they wrote. As it was the primary tool through which to discover new music, the music press at this time was extremely powerful. For most of the 1978-81 period, the *NME* sold over 200,000 copies each week, and at its height reached 270,000; the combined circulation of *NME* and fellow music magazines *Sounds* and *Melody Maker* was in excess of 500,000, its actual readership three times greater.

The Heat was an avant-garde band to whom anything could be an instrument. They amassed an instrumental arsenal of broken instruments and anything that would make a noise. They preceded punk, forming in 1974, and spent their early years building their sound. Using tape loop as an early form of sampling, they developed a uniquely abstract lo-fi style. In 1977, as post-punk emerged from punk, they found a musical climate to appreciate their style, which did not follow previous musical rules. They wanted to be political but in their own way.

Other post-punk bands were commenting on modern society through their lo-fi style. The late 70s and early 80s were a difficult time in Britain. There was a tremendous sense of dread with Thatcher's election, the resurgence of fascist street violence with the National Front, mass unemployment. This sense of doom spread to the music industry: *NME* ran a regular column about nuclear weapons and nuclear power called 'Plutonium Blondes', and both Kate Bush and UB40 had hits with singles about World War III.

No Wave

The 'no wave' scene was connected with post-punk and new wave. It existed for a few short years in the late 70s and early 80s, among downtown New York's avant-garde art crowd, as an offshoot of New York punk. This was a rebellion against form, a rejection of the format of the traditional rock song, with its 'verse–chorus–verse' structure. Instead, no wave artists looked to other influences such as free jazz, and contemporary music like funk and disco. Belonging to no set genre and having no fixed style, musicians consciously declared their experimental nature. No wave was far more experimental than punk, though the new sound embraced the anarchic and amateurish style that punk celebrated, it went further and rejected the formulaic nature of rock and roll altogether. This was a scene consciously trying to reinvent the very concept of the song. So no wave bands bypassed punk, which was considered too predictable, and rejected new wave also (for being a commercial version of punk flourishing in its wake). The very term 'no wave' both references and rejects new wave.

This is not to say that no wave artists completely disowned their musical heritage. They borrowed from punk the idea that the nature of performance was integrally important in music. However, they were more experimental with the nature of performance, developing new and novel ways to play music.

No wave bands also tried to stretch the boundaries of the music that they could produce. It was an exciting new sound but with echoes of older forms, resembling 'noise experiments' of the 60s by Albert Ayler and Sun Ra, The Velvet Underground, Yoko Ono, The Godz and Captain Beefheart. It also incorporated German art rock influences and took elements from this distinct style, blending them with other influences to create something new.

Two prominent bands in the scene were ESG and Liquid Liquid, who exemplified the minimalist funk sound of New York's music underground of 1981. These bands were active at the beginning of the 80s and recorded for Ed Bahlman's 99 Records – a label started as an offshoot from a record shop and releasing some of the music that was being put out by English independent labels such as Rough Trade, Factory and Adrian Sherwood's On-U-Sound. Although no wave is seen as geographically tied to New York, bands were forming with similar ideas in Los Angeles at the same time.

With musicians setting themselves the daunting task of reinventing the nature of rock and roll, it is hardly surprizing that all the bands sound pretty different. Diverse acts such as James Chance and the Contortion, the Talking Heads, Teenage Jesus and The Jerks, Kid Creole and Lydia Lunch illustrate this. Roxy Music's Brian Eno created the illusion that such bands were linked with a common ideal with the release of the compilation album *No New York*. Lydia Lunch explains this perceived sense of community: 'We had a community, but it wasn't based on this "all for one" thing. None of the music sounds the same and none of it has the same repercussions. But we're still on the same side of the line together, and that's it. I think *No New York* was a very representative record of what was happening. The bands on it were doing things that were TOTALLY unlike anything around then. And very original. It was a time of complete diversity, which I have not seen since.'

This new scene, with its experimental reworking of punk, wholeheartedly embraced the notion of lo-fi music. With screams and noises merged with distinct elements of its musical heritage from various sources, no wave took recognizable elements of punk and reworked them. Its key players had mostly been involved in the earlier punk scene but all wanted to develop something new for themselves. Bored with the stale image of the formulaic punk band, they took the elements they liked and experimented with the rest. The result was a new and refreshing form of music, a contrast to what punk had become but retaining the DIY spirit. To celebrate this new genre record labels were launched and new zines written, so that for a short time the early days of punk spirit were replayed.

New York Post-punk

New York post-punk was less politicized than its British equivalent. As with punk era artists, like Patti Smith and Richard Hell, its vision was bohemian, its angst more existential than social. Lyrics emphasized the dark side of human nature, rather than subversion and resistance.

Sonic Youth came together in the New York punk scene of the early 80s. They were clearly influenced by the punk scene but their obsession with avant-garde art and pop culture distanced them from it. Appealing both to the art crowd and to the student crowd, they attracted a very different audience from those attracted to punk. Sonic Youth created walls of sound and noise with lyrics resembling beat poetry, or the lyrics of Jim Morrison.

The post-punk years spanned the three years from 1979 to 1981 though the term 'post-punk' is used today to describe a variety of underground guitar-based music emerging after punk. It was more complex than early punk, not so much about a musical style but about ideas. It was a pioneer genre, encompassing intellectual, political as well as musical influences, laying the path for the late 80s alternative music scenes, which would soon follow.

Olympia

The new generation of punks moved from anarchy and rage to left-wing politics, to some extent emulating the notion of grass roots networks of community action of 60s counterculture. They were not only rebellious but also constructive, realizing that change can only occur through dedicated organization. As post-punk was trailing across America, many of its most interesting activities were taking place in the North-West. Olympia and Seattle in Washington became home to some of the most exciting DIY projects of the time.

Olympia is a small town, dominated in part by the progressive college Evergreen. From the early 80s, it began to cultivate an artistic community, which would redefine the concept of punk as it forged its own DIY politics.

In 1978, the Olympia community radio station, KAOS took one of the first steps which would change the creative output of the town. Music Director John Foster decided that eighty per cent of the music played on the station must be from independent record labels. This meant that small scale labels had a place that would welcome and play their records, and independent bands would get a chance to be heard. The station founded what it called the 'Lost Music Network' (LMN) to play music that was rarely played with the aim of rescuing lost music and finding its audience. In conjunction, they launched *Op* magazine, with similar aims. Each issue featured bands beginning with successive letters of the alphabet, chronicling the independent bands in an ordered approach, taking them and their output seriously, praising their creativity.

At the age of fifteen, Calvin Johnson began to work at KAOS, as part of the station's outreach work and set up his own show playing British groups such as Delta 5, The

Raincoats and The Slits.

When Johnson later returned to Olympia in 1980 from DC to attend Evergreen State College he became a driving force in the Olympia music scene. Meeting fellow student Bruce Pavitt, together the duo worked on *Sub/Pop*, a fanzine that celebrated independent music. Inspired by the earlier *Op*, the publication aimed to promote local bands, given them a chance at a wider audience, and later expanded its output to include a cassette release of the bands it wrote about.

Beat Happening

Johnson had been performing his own music in several Olympia bands, and in 1983, Heather Lewis (who had moved from New York to study at Evergreen College) and Bret Lunsford joined him in Beat Happening. Named after a film that friend and musician Lois Maffeo planned to make called *Beatnik Happening*, they acknowledged that while they disliked the underlying sexist attitude of the beats, they celebrated their bohemian ideals. Their band certainly followed a bohemian set of principles, probably unlike any band previously. They were following the do-it-yourself attitude of early punk and contemporary hardcore bands but making it their own. With cheap instruments they produced a whimsical, twee, retro style, challenging the idea that you needed noise to be punk and celebrating the status of the amateur musician. This certainly was lo-fi music; it broke the preconceptions about what punk had previously been about.

They asked their audience to join them in building a strong community. The ethos behind this community vision was to create a non-competitive, unintimidating atmosphere. Many of those it attracted were women, who had previously felt uncomfortable in the aggressive climate of punk and hardcore. Michael Azerrad, in his book *Our Band Could Be Your Life* explores this shift away from traditional male punk culture, 'Beat happenings...were a major force in widening the idea of a punk rocker from a mohawked guy in a motorcycle jacket to a nerdy girl in a cardigan.'[108]

This scene romanticized a sense of nostalgia for the past. As Azerrad explains, although most participants were in their early twenties, they celebrated the idea of being a teenager, seeing it as a state of naïvete and honesty. To them, being a teenager was a metaphorical state, in which you could remain for as long as you wanted. For many, retro culture took hold as the scene reenacted a version of 50s culture, though the participants were too young to have remembered it themselves. Azerrad describes how people had tea parties and pyjama parties, creating music in a retro style, whilst acting out the wholesome fantasy of a small town community. This contrasted the aggressive nature of the traditional punk and hardcore scenes, but retained many of its DIY elements.

The scene took elements of hippie ideals from the 60s, the working together to develop a supportive community. A community with its own means of cultural production. In such a small town, there was less pressure from the mainstream music industry. Bands could release their own records, book their own shows, their records could be played on local radio stations and people could document this scene in the pages of their zines.

K Records

As a key player in this scene, Johnson was in the perfect position to start his own label, which he called K records and through it developed his vision of an 'International Pop Underground'. Many people have questioned where K

Records got its name. Johnson has claimed that it stands for 'Knowledge', whereas others believe that it is the letter before 'LMN' – The Lost Music Network. Whatever the derivation, first cassettes and then vinyl records with a crayon drawing of a K inside a shield began to appear in record shops across America. To begin with, the medium Johnson chose to release on was also lo-fi – the first recordings were released on cassette tapes. During the year 1983, his label produced its first compilation, titled *Danger Is Their Business*. The cover was a white spray-painted cassette box hand stamped with a carved linoleum block design. Choosing the cassette format over vinyl was a low cost version but it also had roots in the wider DIY community as a medium representing a sense of accessibility. By the end of 1983, the Beat Happening had started to record its own music. The following year, Johnson released a five-song Beat Happening cassette on K Records, his fledgling label. By the end of 1984, K put out its first vinyl single, Beat Happening's 'Our Secret'/ 'What's Important.' From these early releases, the label found its audience, and continues to do so.

K Records was, and still is, about developing a viable underground alternative, about uniting people with similar visions. Johnson wanted to establish a music and art scene in Olympia, a supportive community. Not just at Evergreen College, but in the town where he lived. He did not feel the need to move away to find a sense of excitement in a larger city, he wanted to nurture and grow the community himself.

Calvin Johnson took advantage of Beat Happening's networking in 1987 when K launched the 'International Pop Underground,' a series of 7-inch singles devoted to underground music. By 1991, the Olympia creative community, and the wider cross-country community that had grown around it, was large enough to showcase its talents in a festival – The International Pop Underground Convention. This festival brought together musicians and fans to celebrate the new music and independent community that was rapidly growing.

Kill Rock Stars

K Records was soon joined in Olympia by another independent label when Kill Rock Stars was launched in 1991 by Slim Moon (with financial assistance from Calvin Johnson). It was intended at first to only release spoken word 7" records but this expanded and the team were soon releasing records by such DIY stalwarts as Unwound, Bikini Kill and Huggy Bear. The label firmly embraced DIY ethics, as well as lo-fi ideals. Their primary concern was not to make a profit but to offer a wider choice than mainstream rock stars were offering. The very name of the label expressed this vision that you did not have to be a rock star to produce music. This celebrated the amateur approach to music making: that you did not have to take a professional route but could instead successfully operate on the independent music scene.

Soon enough, Kill Rock Stars was forging its own identity, initially acting as the unofficial home to the riot grrrl movement. This loose collection of feminist-minded punk rock acts was led largely by women. Bratmobile, Bikini Kill and England's Huggy Bear all released records on Kill Rock Stars and earned large amounts of press attention, in part because many of the musicians refused to speak to the mainstream media.

Olympia at this time was a unique creative community. It became the epicentre of riot grrrl and has ever since been seen as a mecca for underground musical activity.

Grunge

During the early 90s, post-punk broke out into mainstream music from Seattle with the branding of grunge as the next new rock genre. This scene adopted many of the elements emerging in nearby Olympia, such as the championing of independent rock and celebration of underground influences.

Though it grew to become a world-wide marketing tool and virtual brand, grunge began as punk did – as an alternative to contemporary American society. The decade in which grunge began, the 80s, was similar in many ways to the 50s when skiffle, and then rock and roll, eased the sense of boredom. Both were greedy conservative money-conscious eras, fertile atmospheres for the development of an underground scene. This put the underground scene in a position of having something to communally fight against and the impetus to start something different. The American indie movement of the late 80s was a reaction to the corporate and commercial mainstream rock which was increasingly dependent on perfectionist aesthetics, expensive technology and slick marketing. It had many links to the early punk scene when punk was a response to a similar sense of inauthenticity and commercialism. Many bands were looking back to punk and celebrating a sense of unpolished rawness and independence from the music industry.

The sound they adopted was lo-fi, taking influences from early rock and roll, punk and post-punk. In this new age of increasingly available technology, bands were deciding whether to ignore or embrace new technology. Some bands stayed lo-fi, retaining the sound of analogue guitar recordings. Rawness was celebrated as bands tried to strip away 80s rock polish and get back to the raw roots of guitar, bass and drums. Despite harking back to an early rock style, musicians made use of cheap technology and 4–

track recorders captured this sound well. Amateurism was almost revered and was mixed with a sense of nostalgia for the past that led to much of the music being released on vinyl rather than the newly available CDs.

The music spread through the post-punk networks, over college station airwaves, small clubs, fanzines, and independent record stores. But if grunge was ever truly a DIY scene, its independent status was short lived. This spirit of independence soon became questioned as money swallowed the culture and the original grunge underground was sold to the world via MTV. The sound soon became marketed as a soundtrack for 'Generation X'. Which was of course in opposition to the whole ethos of the scene, as Kathleen Hanna (of Bikini Kill and Le Tigre) says, 'We weren't doing what we were doing just to gain fame, we were just trying to hook-up with other freaks,' (from Greenblatt, 1996). The impetus for the genuine DIY bands wasn't to sell a new product – grunge – to people via established channels like MTV or the *NME*. They wanted to get music enthusiasts to investigate their culture for themselves. As Niki from Huggy Bear explained, in an interview with Fabian Ironside for *Libeller's Almanac*: 'I don't want to change the fucking world, it's too fucked up anyway. One band is not going to do that. That's what I mean, this British culture doesn't teach you to investigate... I don't give a shit if they hate our music, but kids starting to get investigative again, curious about their own culture... Britain is, like, so rich of people doing stuff but just we're not aware of it, and that's why the *NME* and *Melody Maker* fucks up.'[109] As with punk however, the initial germ of the DIY idea was lost in the attempt to create a product, as the grunge movement really took off.

It was of course Kurt Cobain and his band Nirvana who

burst open the grunge underground, after the release of their second album, *Nevermind,* in the early 90s. Drawing from influences like Sonic Youth and The Pixies they were able to create a sound that was popular both to the mainstream and underground audiences. They became rock stars and their label Subpop became a multi-million dollar operation. Grunge became more about demographics discussed in boardrooms than an underground sound. Bands like The Smashing Pumpkins and Pearl Jam were embraced by the music industry as the commercial face of post-punk. It became a commercialized glorification of teenage angst. The music industry has always looked to the alternative for new trends. Since the 60s, the anti-establishment has been seen as cool, and the celebration of the outsider rebel figure has been a dominant feature in popular culture. This was part of grunge's mainstream attraction and ensured its transition from lo-fi roots into a world-wide fashion. Many of the original elements of early punk were now firmly incorporated into American mass-produced culture. 'Alternative' became the new name for this form of rock music but as boundaries blurred it quickly became unclear what it was meant to be an alternative to.

For many musicians at this time, sticking to the 'real' underground was the preferred option. Some were not willing to lose the sense of credibility and the authentic that DIY culture gave them and so played the game of becoming successful, but not so successful so as to be labelled a 'sell out'. It was not until staunchly independent punk groups like Sonic Youth began to consider signing major label contracts (fed up with their experience of the corporate world on the independent level) that others followed suit. Sonic Youth couldn't see why they should remain impoverished on an independent label when they knew they could be receiving better pay elsewhere. Acutely aware of the effects that the economy was having upon small businesses, and labels, bands began to leave independent labels in droves. This mass movement to major labels sparked several years' worth of intense debate and cries of betrayal within the punk and otherwise bohemian music establishments.

Rock zine *Maximumrocknroll* once discussed this issue concluding that the new punk ideology was that you should write music for yourself and your friends, produce it independently and utilize all the means at your disposal. You did not have to get someone else to manage your own business affairs, but should do this yourself, in order to retain control over the creative and political aspects of your own work. So radical American punk groups such as The Dead Kennedys and Black Flag rejected major label offers as they would not have been able to express their radical political ideas. Instead, they started their own SST and Alternative Tentacles labels and signed other bands to them. Fugazi is another major band that took this ethos on board from the outset. The punk ideology had developed into an ideal that you could support yourself through the underground network by organizing your own means of production and taking control of your art.

Queercore

Queercore Origins
Through the pages of their influential *JDs* zine, Bruce LaBruce and GB Jones were almost militant in their call for a place for queers like themselves in punk culture, and

scathing of their treatment in mainstream gay culture. They tried to articulate their views to the wider punk community in an article for the popular and respected zine *Maximumrocknroll*. The article appeared in February 1989 and simultaneously attacked both punk and gay subcultures for failing to extend the boundaries of sexual politics. They claimed that, the gay 'movement' as it exists now is a big farce, it fails most miserably where it should be the most progressive – in its sexual politics. Specifically there is a segregation of the sexes where unity should exist, a veiled misogyny which privileges fag culture over dyke, and a fear of the expression of femininity which has led to the phenomenon of the 'straight-acting' gay male.' As a man and woman working together, they were critical of a culture which imposed rigid gender segregation while at the same time celebrating gender fluidity. This was their starting point, the idea that there needed to be a queer space within the punk community, where they could be themselves.

Following their article, a queer punk culture did begin to emerge. Bruce LaBruce explains why he thinks this more radical queer community developed at this time, 'Even by the mid-80s, the gay community was heading in an assimilationist direction… Eventually, when a certain amount of social acceptance was gained, the more extreme signifiers were dropped in favour of a less offensive uniform. In the case of gays, it was the clone look, and homos started to hunker down in ghettos in a kind of bunker mentality.' He is critical of this change in the gay community, the idea that a culture with roots in the left-wing of politics needed to adapt to gain acceptance. He explains that during the 80s, a second change occurred in the attitudes and actions of the gay community. 'With the advent of AIDS, the focus of the movement changed, targeting corrupt pharmaceutical companies and the media and a sluggish medical community and indifferent politicians for not taking the disease seriously because it was thought to be a gay disease. The political and aesthetic and philosophical questions raised by the early movement were allowed to atrophy as the focus shifted to a perceived health crisis.'

For many gay activists, this fight against AIDS in the late 80s was connected with the work of New York based ACT-UP, a group of individuals calling for direct action to end the AIDS crisis. Their radical approach spurred many gay people into a vocal political awareness. However, La Bruce notes that this initial energy was short-lived for many of them as, 'After AIDS ceased to be the sole issue for gays in the mid-90s, the movement became about acquiring more and more rights, essentially to become increasingly like the average heterosexual. The gay fight was now for the right to become as bland and boring as the straight community, the very community which once totally despised and rejected homosexuals. The oppressed started to covet the role of the oppressor. The gays started to become much more bourgeois and materialistic (the early underpinnings of the gay, black and feminist movements were decidedly Marxist-based), and thereby much more superficial and reactionary.' It was this sense of atrophy in a culture felt by La Bruce and Jones to be politically active, that led them to call for other like-minded people to join them in a radical queer movement.

Others did soon join them, writing their own zines and forming bands, around which the queercore scene would centre. People like Larry Bob, who started his own zine *Holy Titclamps*, felt that establishing a queer punk community was vitally important. He explains this need for a queer community away from mainstream gay culture. 'I think that mainstream gay culture is alienating. The accepted social activities, like dancing in clubs which are too loud for conversation, don't provide opportunities to interact with creative people.' It was this crossover of creativity and a radical social agenda which the queercore scene epitomized.

Matt Wobensmith, who started his own *Outpunk* zine and record label and has been involved in various forms of the queer music scene, feels that a person's self-identification as gay shouldn't form the basis of their whole personality. Those involved in the punk scene, in independent music, should be able to merge the two identities. He explains his own experience, 'Music gives me somewhere to hide and to find solace when the pressures of urban gay life are too much. Gay people often sacrifice the cultures they come from just to belong to something.' This sacrifice of a radical culture, whether as an artist, punk or anarchist, is what the queercore movement has always battled against.

Wobensmith acknowledges that *Outpunk* was a conscious reaction against the 80s punk and hardcore scene, which was hostile to gay punks. He explains, 'As much as it was a tribute, it was an appropriation. I'm too young to have been a "true"/real/original punk...punk as it was initially conceived was long dead by the time my teenage self discovered it in the mid-80s. By the early 90s, being truly "punk" meant you acknowledged this fact, and that what you were doing was something completely different. There was definitely a tongue-in-cheek attitude behind it.' So, queercore took many elements of punk culture and made them into something new.

Like punk, queercore is firmly rooted in DIY culture, it

has had to be. As Larry Bob states, 'In general, mass entertainment happens because it's profitable. Queercore isn't profitable – people do things because they want to have the sort of experience that queercore offers. It's such a cultural niche that it's only going to happen if people do it themselves.' People involved in the early years of queercore had already gained confidence from operating in the cultural underground, and so realized that this would be an independent cultural experience. They needed to work to find their own channels by which to spread their ideas. La Bruce and Jones had already used the pages of *Maximumrocknroll,* and people soon started to create their own mediums, both on paper and in music.

Homocore Chicago

The early queer zine festival, SPEW, in 1991, intended to create dialogue between those involved in the queercore scene, was successful in allowing like-minded individuals to meet and begin new projects. This was where Mark Freitas, editor of the US queer zine, *P.C. Casualties* met Joanna Brown, who was new to the queercore scene. The zine culture had achieved one of its aims, to bring people together in order for them to create physical spaces where they could meet and collaborate, as together Freitas and Brown decided to organize queer events. They wanted to create a space for queer punks to hang out and listen to live music, mainly queercore and feminist punk. Adopting the new term 'homocore' they named their newly founded organization 'Homocore Chicago'. On November 13th 1992 they presented their first event to a crowd of eager queer punks, a show by GB Jones' own band Fifth Column at the Czar Bar. Homocore shows soon became regular events that held together a loose network of diverse queer musicians by giving them a physical space in which to meet.

In creating their own alternative to the gay culture they saw around them, they could employ their own values concerning gender, money and censorship. As with other individuals working in the queercore scene, they were opposed to the prevailing attitude of mainstream gay culture, which was often seen as sexist as well as bland and opposed to queer punks. To directly distance themselves from this, they designed and made T-shirts with the slogan: 'A lifetime of listening to disco is too high a price to pay for your sexual identity.' They attacked the idea that due to your sexuality you should be offered only one choice of social scene, challenging one particular aspect of gay culture: the idea of separate gay and lesbian bars. Through Homocore events, they aimed to create a space for men and women to be together, as opposed to the sense of gender segregation which was the norm in mainstream gay culture.

The organizers were aware of the importance of the events they were presenting and the support they offered individuals and musicians. The majority of shows they organized were aimed at all-ages, acknowledging that those under twenty-one years old also needed a space where they could be themselves. They also adopted DIY ethics concerning money, with all profits raised from events being paid to the bands. There was no commercial motivation.

The Personal is Political

Although zines were vital in spreading the news about queercore and explaining its relevance and importance in both gay and punk culture, it was the music that passionately conveyed its message. In 1988, the scene was large enough for LaBruce to release *Homocore Hit Parade,* a two-record compilation of the best American and

Canadian queercore bands, and queercore began to reach a wider audience.

Many bands emerged at this time, firmly tied to queercore attitudes and politics but often using different musical approaches to transmit them. Some bands were directly connected to the hardcore punk roots of queercore, whereas others consciously defined themselves as of the queer scene rather than hardcore. Some bands were fiercely political, singing about gay rights, and others focused on relationships. Whatever their viewpoint, countless bands such as Team Dresch, Tribe 8, Fifth Column, Third Sex, Sister George, Pansy Division, The Need, Phranc and God Is My Co-Pilot have been the voices of the scene, and record labels such as Chainsaw, Outpunk, Queercorps and Candyass were set up to make sure that their music reached others.

For these queercore bands, the personal was certainly political. In writing music about their own lives and speaking directly to their audiences they strived to help their audience find a sense of identity for themselves. This was part of the DIY ethic, which has been evident in so many other underground movements, from punk to rave culture: the idea that the performer and audience are not so different from one another.

Donna Dresch stated to write a zine entitled *Chainsaw* in 1988. Inspired by other queer zine writers she used her zine as a tool with which to find individuals with similar attitudes to herself. She explains that she always wanted to be part of an underground network of freaks, queers, radical thinkers and artists and felt that the queercore scene was somewhere that she could find this kind of support. She became a strong force in the emerging scene with her band Team Dresch and in 1991 this continued as *Chainsaw* developed from a zine into a record label. This began simply enough when she made a compilation cassette of her favourite bands and started to sell these while on tour with Fifth Column. However, the label established itself as a vital element of the queercore scene when she moved back to Olympia, Washington, and began to release 7" records and later albums by bands such as Team Dresch, The Vegas Beat and Cypher in the Snow.

Team Dresch took a more personal approach to queercore than most, writing songs about love, growing up, self-defence and homophobia, in contrast to the angrier music of the scene. The band's line-up changed over the years. Members included Donna Dresch, Jody Bleyle and Kaia Wilson but also at various times Melissa York, Marci Martinez and Amanda Kelley. Each had been in many other punk and lo-fi bands. Donna was not the only member of the band to start their own record label. Jody founded Candyass and Kaia later ran Mr. Lady.

Like the other queercore bands, Team Dresch were concerned with creating an alternative to the mainstream gay scene. Members' identities were firmly rooted in the American punk and indie underground. Singer and guitarist Jody explains her lack of connection with mainstream queer culture. 'When I was at Reed,[110] I identified way more with the rockers than I did with the women's centre people,' says Bleyle. 'I went to one women's centre meeting and I felt totally... I think what I felt was total gender dysphoria... I felt like a boy who wasn't supposed to be at the women's centre meeting; I felt like a spy who was going to say something wrong or do something wrong and get kicked out.'[111]

The band felt that their influence and position as a queer band had the potential to reach out to others. They released

DIY: THE RISE OF LO-FI CULTURE

'Free To Right', a record aiming not only to provide entertainment but also – quite uniquely! – to teach self-defence skills to their audience. Jody explains her realization that a band can do more than simply entertain, that it can also interact and support its audience. 'I don't want to just put out records and play in bands that are going to go on tour. I want to do something else. Even if I only do one thing a year, I want it to be something that's really important. I want to use this medium to disseminate information and fuck with the standard idea of going to a rock club and seeing a band. Rock clubs are public space. They're one of the only public spaces there is and we need to use this base as a way to get information to people because not everybody's going to show up at the "Y" to take a self-defence class or whatever, but there has to be a way we can get them a lot of information through records.'

Pansy Division, explicit participants in the queercore scene also recognized this potential in queercore. They made the biggest move into the mainstream to date when, in 1994, they opened a series of arena dates for Green Day. This raised their popularity, introduced queercore to a wider audience, and was one of the few times that the movement was able to break out of the underground; as band members began to realize how important their music was to individuals in the audience. After playing the shows, they received letters from hundreds of young gay people thanking them for being open about their sexuality through their music.

Tribe 8 agree with Pansy Division's attitude that one of the obligations of a queer band is to try and help those individuals who are marginalized in society but do not have a supportive network, to move queercore away from just being accessible to those already part of an underground community. Lynn Breedlove, lead singer in the band, explains, 'We wrote with the intent of bolstering queer egos, creating a feeling of belonging for our audience who until then hadn't had a voice. I love getting letters from kids all over the world saying that we saved their asses because our CD was all they had to keep them sane until they could get to a city where there were some of our kind. We kept some kids alive so they could grow up to be big rad punks, artists and connect with others like them.'[112]

Ponyboy, an organizer of Homoagogo, a queer festival which took place in Olympia, Washington in 2000 and 2004, explains the importance of the presence of openly queer bands. 'Well, I grew up in a small town in the Midwest of the USA, where I was one of the only people of colour in my high school, and the only other queers I knew were my (older) friends. So I held any queer culture I could find very tightly to me. Music was already my lifesaver, so when I discovered queercore, needless to say, I felt like something inside me was going to explode.' [113]

For others, queercore was a chance for them to take part in a physical community. From the Homocore shows in the 80s, New York's Homocorps, Scutterfest in Los Angeles to current events such as Queeruption and Olympia's Homoagogo, people have been given the opportunity to meet in person. Larry Bob explains how queercore affected his life, 'Many of the people that I know I met either through doing my zine or though events like ongoing queer clubs or alternative queer convergences like the SPEW queer zine gatherings, the Dirtybird Queercore festival in 1996, or the Queeruption events. I have managed to get my writing to people who can sympathize with my point of view.'

For London-based writer Charlotte Cooper, attending

the Dirtybird Festival held in San Francisco in 1996 was a pivotal experience. 'Dirtybird was the first time that I had met queer punks or thought of myself as one of them. Until that point I was living a pretty straight life. At twenty-seven years old I felt as though I was starting out in life and I felt that I was already washed up. But the people at Dirtybird made me feel welcome, in fact they encouraged me to take part, to get involved and to see myself as one of them. I thought the people I met were amazing, beautiful and cool. That they were interested in me was nothing less than a personal revolution as far as I was concerned. It was the first time in my life that people treated me as a credible being and a sexual being too, which was very liberating.'[114]

British Queercore

In Britain, the concept of queercore hit several years after it first began in America. The first recorded alternative to the mainstream gay experience, following a similar style to American queercore, was Rock 'n' Doris, a monthly alternative gay club started in Newcastle in May 1989. Its aim was to provide people who were currently unhappy with the city's commercial scene with somewhere else to go.

Adopting similar ideas, Manchester's Homocult existed between 1990 and 1995. Manchester already had a strong gay scene but like those queercore pioneers in America, Homocult were dissatisfied with the standardization of the gay experience and wanted to devise a way to speak out against it. The method they adopted was the creation of radical poster art which they displayed on the streets. These posters were often rude, often funny and managed to criticize both straight and gay culture at the same time.

As Patrick, one of the group, explains to writer Charlotte Cooper in an interview in 1999. 'Homocult began because certain individuals were angered by the gay experience. They were opposed to the attitude of the Stonewall movement which they saw portraying gay people as victims. They were angered by the attitude that being gay was any form of lifestyle choice and their posters reflected this sense of anger. Unlike the American queercore scene, they were not trying to create a sense of wider community, though they did start several indie clubs, but instead tried to use punk and DIY methods to express the idea that there should be no need for any form of queer community. They claimed to be anti-political though they labelled themselves as firmly working class and were clearly angered by the different ways a gay person is portrayed according to their financial situation. They celebrated their working class roots and their attitudes mixed their working class and gay experiences.'

The group were among the first in Britain to reclaim the terms 'queer' and 'homo' from being used as insults. Their coupling of such language and queer graphics was seen as shocking at the time, but in retrospect is considered a valuable effort towards normalizing such words and images.

Mike Wyeld, a member of one of the British queercore bands, Mouthfull, ran Up To The Elbow, one of the first queercore clubs in London. Wyeld explains that this club was an important place in the DIY community, not only giving bands, such as Mouthfull and Sister George a place to play but also providing a space for other DIY mediums. 'At the club, we always had a table where people could leave their zines to sell or give away, and we let people sell their singles or CDs, whatever. A few times people would drop zines on the table anonymously while no one was looking – and those were the most vitriolic, most hurt, most wounded by what they saw around them. That is the brilliant part, people really have a voice with a zine or a DIY record.'[115]

In the spring of 1995, friends Mel, Neil, Phil and Sarit launched their gay indie club Vaseline. Taking place monthly, this club quickly became popular with the London indie crowd who wanted a queer alternative. The club was soon renamed Club V and ran for five and a half years, as a non-profit operation, making a name for itself as independent. It prided itself on playing music that would not generally be played in other gay or straight clubs and booked countless bands to perform live. They did not limit themselves to only asking bands with queer members to perform, but any band that they felt deserved an audience. This moved some distance away from the attitude begun by American clubs such as Homocore, but was firmly rooted in the supportive DIY indie scene. Instead of trying to find their place in the hardcore scene, these organizers were finding a place within the British indie scene. With the arrival of Britpop, it was indie that dominated the contemporary music scene, with bands such as Oasis, Blur and Pulp ruling the charts. Wyeld explains that in London queercore and indie were connected. His club attracted attention from London's Britpop scene, 'Lots of the Britpop mob were homos or homo friendly, or just liked the bands that played, so we used to get loads of them in the club.'

Independent queer culture still remains in London, with the establishment in 2002 of Homocrime, a DIY club 'for queers of all sexualities'. This club, supportive of queer punk musicians and artists, is strongly connected to the DIY spirit. Many of its organizers have worked on other projects, launching their own record labels, organizing festivals, all firmly rooted in independent culture.

Queercore Activism

To some, queercore is firmly rooted in political action.

Music is a distinct part of this, as a means to convey its message, but not the main focus. Some groups have returned to the political gay climate of the early 80s and by combining their radical political identity and sexuality, address social and political issues through queer spaces. This is evident in Gay Shame, starting in New York in 1998, and Queeruption festivals, which began the same year in London at the squatted 121 centre in Brixton – since spreading to other countries around the world. People in Britain in particular, have returned to activism, recognizing the political relevance of community-building. Independent gay culture has moved from being focused on music to being used as part of bringing people together to discuss wider issues. European queer culture has become particularly focused on addressing global political issues with direct activism, as well as the politics of queer identities.

In America, queercore has also expanded its focus. Recent events, such as Olympia's Homoagogo festival, have used music and art to draw people to the festival where they can discuss queer issues. Entertainment is part of the festival, but more important to many is the dialogue it instigates. Organizer Ponyboy explains in the programme of the 2000 festival, the need for such an event. 'For me, the excitement and driving force to make HAGG happen was there because we/I wanted an underground queer fest that highlights DIY (including grass roots organizers, union workers, folks that fuck shit up in their "mainstream" scenes, etc.), radical queers. What better way to get amazing folks you know/have heard of to come together? Our various queer communities should be organizers; pool talents and resources together and form coalitions and solidarity and teach each other!' So, drawing from similar events like YoYo A GoGo, Ladyfest, and the general

Olympia spirit, HAGG was born. 'My vision of HAGG includes people coming to a place that is anti-oppression. What about people who don't have access to money and who can't go to lots of performances/movie screenings? What about queers of colour who often don't have a community in the indie rock/punk world? What about sex workers who don't "fit the mould" of body types? Where's the space for them to share their experiences, to feel heard, to meet each other? I want HAGG to be a place where these things are possible.'

People still feel the need to organize their own independent queer spaces, where they can discuss issues relevant to their own lives, that aren't represented anywhere else. Connected to a strong queer musical heritage, events such as Homoagogo bring people together in a physical space and promote an even stronger sense of community. Trans and gender issues have found a strong place in independent queer culture, and such occasions celebrate all aspects of the queer experience.

For some, the concept of queercore will remain specific to the early to mid-90s. Matt Wobensmith's now defunct record label, Outpunk, paved the way for gay punk's emergence as a viable genre that has spawned such relative mainstream successes as Sleater-Kinney and Pansy Division. In 1998, Wobensmith started the Queercorps label, which was devoted largely to recording gay hip hop music. Claiming at the time that, 'In 1998, rock music is shit. It's boring and formulaic and predictable,' he was looking for a sense of independent queer ethos in other musical genres. However, the label released just two albums before Wobensmith, disillusioned with the whole state of queercore, decided to abandon the scene. Turning his back on what he considered to be the increasingly stale state of punk, Wobensmith now sees the same sense of excitement of early punk in hip hop. He explains his sense of revelation on attending PeaceOUT homohop festival in Oakland, California. 'I was blown away. I had sworn off music for four years prior and the shows rekindled my interest in gay hip hop. People came up to me to tell me how much my releases meant to them, and that they – to some extent – were the inspiration for a lot of the artists at the show!'[116] His excitement led to him to want to launch a new label A.C.R.O.N.Y.M. in 2003 to concentrate on releasing queer hip hop. 'I will say that right now, gay hip hop is very much like the formative days of the queercore punk scene. There is a renaissance of music, lyrics, styles and ideas, and it's all incredibly optimistic. Also, it's too early for bitterness and apathy, or for the music to become stagnant. I've been saying – since 1995 – that queercore is more than queer punk. My vision includes other styles of music, other mediums, and other communities. We're just starting to see something that truly delivers on that theory. Queerpunk and gay hip hop are forming the foundation for new gay culture(s).'

The independent queer music scene has certainly changed since its first incarnation in the 80s. It has blurred the line between music and activism and in many ways followed changes in the queer community. Larry Bob points out that the limitation of the queer music scene has always been its sense of exclusivity. 'I think that queercore shouldn't make itself too secret. It should make sure that people know that there's an alternate way of doing things. The word needs to get out about queercore, whether it's through zines, websites, stickers, flyers, word of mouth or coverage in the media.' The internet has certainly offered many advantages to the queer music scene, possibly above all mediums. It has allowed access to those people who would otherwise never have heard about it and promoted cross-cultural discussion – vital for the scene to develop. La Bruce explains that, 'Today there is more need than ever for an alternative to the gay status quo. Even in the mid-80s we thought the homosexual scene was stagnant, politically conservative, and aesthetically impoverished. So you can imagine how bad it's gotten now.'

Riot Grrrl

Much like those who began the queercore movement, many young women in America did not see themselves represented in either mainstream music or the underground in the early 90s. Female musicians felt the sense of alienation at the rising corporate ideals of mainstream music and began to follow the anti-corporate DIY ethic. There had been successful female punk bands, such as The Raincoats, The Slits and The Au Pairs, but male rock had always been dominant. Therefore for some, punk became associated with the empowerment of female musicians. The amateurish ethos of punk culture appeared to give women the confidence to perform. The Raincoats' Gina Birch, in an interview in 1999, explains her view of her position as a women in a band, 'We wanted things to be different. We didn't want to have to wear short skirts and have fab legs in order to have people think what we did was great. Not that I've got anything against that either, but we wanted to be what we wanted to be.'[117] This refusal to take part unless it was on their own terms was a part of the female punk experience which was revived in the 90s. Many bands at the time seemed to glorify the macho attitude and the grunge scene was soon centred on all-male bands. Women already working in the indie underground began to work together to start their own bands and called on others to join their supportive network. Thus the specific genre we know as 'riot grrrl' was born.

Strangely, few people compared riot grrrl to punk, where its origins clearly lay. The media defined riot grrrl as simply a genre of women in rock but did not consider the influences that the riot grrrls themselves claimed to have, such as female post-punk bands of the late 70s and early 80s.

The movement was unique because it involved adolescent girls, a group which had not usually been included in musical subcultures. It challenged the prevalent notion that girls could not have a place in political or cultural activism. They wanted to break away from the preconceived stereotypes of female sexuality in rock music. To do so, they needed the confidence to act.

Pioneer bands such as Bikini Kill and Bratmobile led the way and so from the outset were presumed to be spokespeople for the scene, a role that they quickly rejected. This gave a limited perspective to a scene with its roots very much in the underground lo-fi scene, with labels like Kill Rock Stars and K Records with their DIY ideals. The probing gaze of the mass media was directed here by other popular, particularly male, rock bands, which meant that riot grrrl was seen by many as simply one chapter in a wider rock narrative. This limited riot grrrl by framing it solely in the context of this small area of American activity – when the political implications were far wider reaching. For many, the object was to form communities with a strongly feminist bent, that aimed to challenge all that riot grrrls felt to be wrong within society. Pioneer riot grrrl Kathleen Hanna explained the political agenda in *Bust* 2000: 'I also see (feminism) as a broad-based, political movement that's bent on challenging hierarchies of all kinds in our society, including racism and classism, and able-bodyism etc etc.'

Although originating in Olympia, riot grrrl quickly spread throughout America and then all over the world. In London it became particularly prevalent in 1993, when Huggy Bear fast became one of the most influential lo-fi bands of the time (though they never really broke from their intense cult following). With their dramatically uncompromising approach (Huggy Bear famously told Nude records they'd only ever join the label if it dropped Suede), they burst out of the London fanzine scene, ignited a music press debate and disappeared. Reluctant to be associated with the 'fashion' that riot grrrl became for many Huggy Bear nevertheless pioneered its feminist ideals, though never to the exclusion of male band members. In an interview first featured in *Libeller's Almanac*, band member Chris declared: 'I am a Riot Boy... People would say, "Are you a Riot Grrrl?" and they expect you to say Riot Grrrl's finished. But, it's like it's only a phrase and the things it stands for are the coolest things ever, and if I'm associated with that in a productive way then, yeah, I'm a Riot Grrrl.'

Although focusing around music, riot grrrl has always maintained that this is not all that it is concerned with. Adopting the method of zine writing as well as social events and workshops, it asserted itself as both a social and cultural movement. Adapting theories of third wave feminism into every day life, they attempted to work within an underground community to bring about change. DIY ethics were used to develop new ideas about society and culture.

Karen from Huggy Bear explains her association with the movement: 'It depends what your perception of Riot

Grrrl is, if you see it as a fashion, no, if you see it as a...a load of ideas which provoke you to action, yes, I'm a Riot Grrrl, definitely...' This accords with band member Chris's call for action, 'All you can do is exist, in your own gang or in your own space and cause as much trouble, in terms of provoking things, provoking yourself, as possible. And keep on doing it, don't get lazy. Like pick up on stuff, stir stuff up all the time... If we're trying to achieve anything, it's the destruction of apathy, even if it's only for ourselves.'

For many, the position of riot grrrls working within the established DIY community was one of privilege. It has been criticized as not a movement of feminist pioneers but a group of predominantly white, straight, middle class girls with access to the ideas and established resources that enable them to do-it-themselves. For many, this was seen as nothing new. It was simply women following the existing DIY trail and incorporating a feminist agenda.

Though riot grrrl still exists today in various forms, for many people this initial wave of the riot grrrl movement ended fairly quickly. It was passionate, exciting but did it change anything on a wider scale or was it a missed opportunity? The movement did not shake the music industry, this is true, but it did place women in a stronger position in the DIY community. It spread new ideas, which did change the lives of many of the disenfranchised and alienated that it reached. Arguably as a result of riot grrrl, women came to enjoy a greater deal of respect within the music industry. Musicians such as Courtney Love and Sleater-Kinney broke through the underground post-grunge and found a place for themselves within the music industry. As for its social ideals, riot grrrls original energy fizzled out before their many aims and ideals could be fully achieved.

Many similar ideals re-emerged over the decade since as

part of the musical mainstream. The original call for girl power was appropriated by the British pop group the Spice Girls in the mid-90s, taking elements of the riot grrrl ethos but removing it from its original DIY context.[118]

DIY Radio

Pirate Radio

At its initial stage, British radio was entirely governmentally controlled. Judged to be a powerful means of mass communication, capable of spreading messages and opinions over a considerable physical distance, radio was seen by the government as just too dangerous to let out of their control. This tight management was achieved through the establishment of the British Broadcasting Corporation (BBC) in January 1922. Raising revenue from charging a license fee to every home with a radio, the Corporation provided government approved programmes only. The popularity of the radio grew and by 1930, there were five million radio sets in Britain, all unavoidably tuned to the BBC. Despite the popularity of BBC programmes, there was demand for an alternative. Many people wanted more choice, more daring programming.

As the BBC was the only organization permitted to broadcast in the UK, the only way around these strict regulations was for other radio stations to set up operation overseas. This was legal, as the regulations only restricted the use of radio waves from within the UK. A private company, The International Broadcasting Company, was set up to hire airtime from overseas stations and transmit programmes aimed at the UK market. The British population began to tune into Radio Lyon or Normandy,

Radio Athlone, Mediterranean and Radio Luxembourg.

Although the government was hostile to these stations, as their broadcasts were legal officially it could do nothing to prevent them from broadcasting. This didn't stop it from trying, however, and there were many alleged attempts to disrupt operations. The government put pressure on British newspapers not to print the programming schedules of these overseas stations, to drive away listeners. It also tried to persuade royalty organizations to overcharge them for permission to play recorded material so that they wouldn't be able to afford the high costs of running their stations. In a further move towards sabotage, it has been claimed that the BBC were encouraged not to employ artists or presenters who had previously worked on a continental station. It appeared that the British government was keen to preserve their control, to suppress such mass media communication. Despite their efforts for the BBC to hold a total monopoly over the airwaves, the overseas stations flourished, attracting high audience numbers.

The outbreak of the Second World War in 1939 meant that all commercial broadcasting was abandoned. After the war, the BBC reasserted its dominance over the airwaves and with careful programming tried to boost the morale of the population. In hindsight this can be seen as a patronizing use of this media form but in those depressed post-war years it was seen as an important use of the country's technological resources.

Things soon began to change. Improvements in the 50s soon overtook the hardships of the 40s. The cultural influence of the more economically prosperous America grew. For the first time, British youth began to see what was happening in America through imported cinema. They watched the emergence of a new social group: the teenager, with its own new music and style. This American sound and style sparked the beginnings of a teenage cultural revolution in Britain. The huge number of young people that were the result of the post-war baby boom, were no longer content to listen to the same music as their parents' generation, they wanted something of their own and began to modify the American style. With this change in taste and demands came the need for teen-orientated radio stations, to play the new musicians that they wanted to hear. They didn't want cosy radio dramas and adults their parents' age reading stale news, they wanted excitement.

Opportunities for hearing new music on BBC radio was limited to a Sunday afternoon chart review and a Saturday morning programme 'The Saturday Skiffle Club', both hosted by established BBC presenters. This wasn't enough for most teenagers, they didn't want their exposure to new music limited to these rigid time slots.

One station that – to an extent – provided a young and newly-excited audience with an alternative to BBC Radio was Radio Luxembourg, which had started up its operations again after the war. However, its broadcasts were limited. For one thing, the radio signal could only reach the UK after dark when the signal characteristics changed. This added to the feeling of subversive pleasure but meant that impact was limited. Also, although it focused on playing music, Radio Luxembourg was still a commercial station. It was not controlled by the government but it did serve the music industry. Major record labels, such as Decca, Capitol, EMI and Parlophone, booked time for their shows. They were limited to booking only fifteen to twenty minute slots, so their shows were a rapid showcase of their signed and recorded artists. DJs would play only one minute of each new release, linking these together with a quick introduction. This meant that unsigned or lesser known bands were not given a chance to be heard by their eager public. The BBC held the state monopoly but Radio Luxembourg had the commercial hold.

By the early 60s, there were hundreds of British bands keen to be heard by the willing audience that the new teenage generation provided, but many simply could not get airplay on either the BBC or commercial radio. The potential for a DIY music movement was rife. It had already been acknowledged that you could transmit programmes to Britain from overseas, a costly and complex option. Then some bright spark realized you did not have to go to another country, you just had to transmit from outside British territorial waters. In effect this meant that new radio stations could be set up, broadcasting whatever they wanted, without having to answer to anyone, as long as they were transmitting from moored boats on international waters. In such a position no law was relevant other than that defined by the flag states of ships. If the law of the flag state had no objection to international marine broadcasting then the ship could make broadcasts which were not illegal and could not be stopped. This new idea, the idea of pirate radio stations transmitting radical new programmes directly from the seas, changed what the British teenager could expect to hear on their radio and opened a truly pivotal and exciting new era in broadcasting history.

Radio Caroline

Ronan O'Rahilly, the rebellious son of a well known and wealthy Irish family, found himself in the London of the early 60s, looking for adventure, or at least some excitement to help pass the time. He became involved in the new music scene and started to manage young musicians. Naïve but determined, he soon became frustrated with the inaccessibility of the music industry. He worked at getting them live gigs at small venues but nobody would sign or even record his artists and he could not get airtime for their music. He soon realized that if he wanted his bands to be heard then he would have to do something himself.

He couldn't get airplay for his bands if they didn't have any recordings to play. He began by creating his own record label, paying for his own acetates, which he then presented to the BBC in the hope of them being played. He soon realized that this approach would not work, as they had a policy of only playing established bands. Even at Radio Luxembourg, the most alternative station the airwaves had to offer at this time, he faced a similar reaction. They explained how they only served major labels who could afford to book time for their artists. If no existing radio station would play music by his bands, O'Rahilly realized that the next logical step was for him to start his own radio station. He had already produced records for his bands and promoted them all over town, how difficult could this next step be?

He began to research his options. At a party soon afterwards, a girl told him about the radio station called 'Voice of America', which had been transmitting at sea from the MV Courier, an official American vessel. After travelling to visit Jack Kotschack, the owner of the marine station, as well as visiting Radio Nord and the owners of Radio Veronica, a Dutch offshore radio station, he realized that the idea of an offshore pirate radio was ingenious – and exactly what he needed.

Radio Caroline was named after John F Kennedy's daughter. On a fund-raising trip to the USA O'Rahilly was captivated by a photograph showing President Kennedy's daughter Caroline, playing in the Oval Office of the White House and disrupting the serious business of government. This was exactly the image he wanted for his station, which went on to become one of the most successful pirate stations of all time.

Before long, the British airwaves were taken over by stations broadcasting from boats moored outside British territorial waters. In December 1964, the American backed and styled Radio London arrived on the vessel Galaxy. Radio London delivered highly professional American programming which temporarily at least captured much of the audience of Caroline South requiring Radio Caroline to quickly adapt its own style and format.

Later two more American influenced stations – Britain Radio and Swinging Radio England – were broadcast from the same ship. Radio 270 started off the Norfolk coast, while Radio Scotland operated on board the old lightship Comet anchored off the Scottish East coast. In the Thames Estuary were various marine structures which had been wartime sea forts. Abandoned by the military they made excellent and stable transmitting platforms and were quickly boarded and claimed by further radio entrepreneurs. Soon Radio 390, an easy-listening station and the most powerful of all the 60s offshore broadcasters was on air; while from other structures Radio Essex and Radio King started transmissions.

This change in the country, brought about by the DIY ethos that people could be in charge of their own music and their own media, spread to other forms of production. People began to release their own records, start their own record labels and move away from the stranglehold of the four major records labels (EMI, Decca, Pye and Phillips), which until this point controlled almost all music production. Many people, spurred on by the success of pirate radio and the new music culture that it instigated, now felt the confidence to create something for themselves. The new independent radio stations, with their locations away from British shores, also worked to shift the emphasis of the music scene away from London. Some stations often consciously worked to promote the music of the provinces, giving airtime to new bands from these regions. This helped to fuel the creative culture of the time and inspired the formation of hundreds of new bands.

Music radio broadcasting began to change in response to the popularity of the pirate stations. Seeing how many listeners were tuning in to these independent stations, other radio shows realized that they would need to compete. Not only did they adapt their format but also recruited several pirate DJs and well-known pirate station DJs made the move from independent to commercial stations.

Pirate stations attracted DJs who felt that they did not have a place within restrictive mainstream radio. Having read in the music press that Radio Caroline South was looking for DJs, Tony Blackburn immediately applied and there began his broadcasting career. He made his first radio appearance on 28th July 1964. In 1966, he moved to Radio London and became famed for introducing the first ever soul programme to British audiences. This illustrates the benefits of independent radio – new styles could be introduced without the strict commercial pressures that limited other stations. New music could at last be played.

In the Spring of 1967, a new DJ, John Peel, joined Radio London. He had just returned to London from America where he had spent a few years working as a DJ. Beatlemania had hit America and listeners enjoyed the novelty of a British voice on their radios. On Radio

London, he took over the midnight to 2am slot with his show 'The Perfumed Garden'. The show allowed him to play the music that he had heard in America, focusing on the emerging West Coast Rock, and he introduced Captain Beefheart, Frank Zappa, Mothers of Invention and The Velvet Underground to British listeners. He played all the music that no one else would – Jefferson Airplane, Marc Bolan, Lightnin' Hopkins. He also championed a new breed of British underground acts, such as Pink Floyd, Soft Machine and The Incredible String Band. He viewed his show as an opportunity to play to his audience the music that he loved most, without any hint of commercial motivation. It was a display of his own leftfield tastes and was directed at the 60s 'flower power' generation who were looking for something new. Peel recognized the audience as participating in the cultural experience and between songs he would rave about the music and announce various underground events, as well as reading aloud letters sent in by his many listeners.

The British government, angered by the broadcasting legal loophole that the pirate radio stations were exploiting, threatened Radio Caroline but no serious action was taken. Soon other independent radio stations joined them and twenty million people were listening to stations other than the BBC. The government couldn't legislate against this activity, though it complained about the possibility of cross channel interference. The radio stations enjoyed their position as accepted rebels and continued to broadcast.

It was not until the late 60s that the British government decided that it would make a firm move to stop broadcasts. A government agency unit, the Radio Agency, was set up and they did all they could to silence the pirates. They had the power to seize equipment when stations were raided and adopted the underhand tactic of trying to gain public support for their actions, such as claiming that pirate services interfered with radio signals used by the emergency services.

Through spring and summer of 1967, the offshore stations campaigned against the proposed Marine Broadcasting Offenses Act. Having previously embraced the term 'pirate radio' they now wished to be known as 'free radio' stations. Most outspoken on the subject of freedom of the individual against the system was Radio Caroline. It protested against the Marine Offenses Act but after battling for many months finally closed operation in 1968, though it defiantly started broadcasting again several years later.

Though controversial, Radio Caroline and the other pirates changed not only independent but also mainstream broadcasting. These stations marked a new approach to radio, enabling new independent music to find a place on the airwaves, young bands to reach their awaiting audience and freeing UK radio from the dictates of state control. At the time, this was a rebellious new idea which gripped the nation's youth.

When, in August 1967, the Marine Offenses Act outlawed offshore broadcasting and effectively closed the pirates down, many of its DJs were forced to move to mainstream stations to continue broadcasting. Peel was one of several who made the move to Radio One – the new BBC station designed as an alternative for the listeners of the now illegal pirate stations. Through his Sunday afternoon show 'Top Gear', and later through his late night show, he continued to promote new music.

In the now infamous 'John Peel Sessions', Peel recorded many acts that would otherwise not be played on mainstream radio. Many of the obscure acts he showcased through these Top Gear sessions went on to achieve mainstream success, which they owed in part to his support. Tyrannosaurus Rex (Marc Bolan was a close friend), Rod Stewart and the Faces, and of course The Undertones ('Teenage Kicks' was John Peel's favourite record), were just a few of the bands that he lent his support to. Now that many of the pirate stations were no longer broadcasting, Peel carried their most appealing qualities across with him to the BBC. One listener remembers the experience of listening to Peel's (later) Radio One show, 'It was the highlight of the day! Finish work, get home, have dinner, put John Peel on…and be introduced to anything from the Glaswegian artrockers Male Nurse to urban progmasters like Nought. The best thing about Peel was that you were introduced to music you would never otherwise have bothered with…odd rave tunes played alongside seminal punk records and so on. He also created communities. Really bought people together. Lots of my friends were met through gigs we'd all heard about through John Peel. His influence on the growth of independent music was pivotal.'[119] Peel retained the sense of support and accessibility that has always been so vital in underground media. Throughout his life he worked tirelessly to promote new music, even setting up his own record label – Dandelion Records.

The 60s were the decade of pirate radio at its most innovative. In the 70s, pirate radio came ashore in cities like London, Birmingham, Bristol and Manchester. This new generation of underground radio stations did not try to work around the law, they were willing to break it. Seeing that the pirate stations had failed even though they were legal, they were less concerned with lawlessness. Usually setting up operations in high-rise tower blocks, they would increase their transmission capabilities by erecting aerials as high as possible from the rooftops. They wanted to reach as many people as they could. Although no longer pirate in the original sense, they took the early sea-bound audio pioneers as their inspiration. Without the high costs and commitment involved in buying and outfitting a ship, this new wave of pirate stations were more accessible and became widespread.

Self-published magazines supported the pirate radio culture. Featuring information about radio station frequencies and schedules and articles offering guidance on how to set up your own station, they were a valuable means of spreading the news of this growing underground movement. *Newswave Magazine,* produced by those on the south coast who followed independent radio, was one such publication – printing articles and advice in a passionate and committed manner. Pirate radio came to be about the community it served, as much as the people whose voices were heard on the airwaves.

Several of the pirate stations made the decision, after their start in illegal broadcasting, to apply for a license and broadcast legally. London's Kiss FM started as a pirate station dedicated to new music before the broadcasters involved decided to turn it into a commercial venture and full-time operation. Radio Jackie in South West London, started as a pirate station that supported its local community. First broadcasting in March 1969, and remaining on air illegally each Sunday until 1985, it was a long running station dedicated to promoting community events and working hard to raise funds for good causes. After being turned down for a broadcasting license, they closed down, only to begin again in 2003 when they reapplied for a license and reformed to run their station officially as a legal voice for local people. Other stations chose to remain on the illegal side of broadcasting. Many, feeling that the application to apply for the broadcasting license would inevitably threaten the station, decided to remain underground. To them, pirate radio needed to be immediate and accessible and remain so.

The pirate radio station movement continues to thrive today. Modern pirate radio stations, still run illegally, usually cater for the local community and underground music fans. Those whose tastes and interests are still ignored by the larger corporate radio stations have a chance to tune in to a station of their own preference. Now a regular feature of urban airwaves, there are so many pirate stations that hundreds compete for signals. The UK's urban youth use pirate radio as a means to transmit their music to their peers across the city. Some are more rebellious than others – ignoring the etiquette of pirate stations their transmissions sometimes drift over the airwaves designated for legal radio stations and the emergency services. This kind of incident obviously damages the reputation of the pirate station. A long-argued point by official regulators, that pirate stations interfere with other transmissions, is typically a weak and untrue argument. However, the pirate radio movement is still plagued by such complaints, and those stations that do make this mistake, deliberately or otherwise, do not help the situation.

Pirate Politics

Pirate stations are unlicensed and certainly illegal, so those who run them must be prepared to face the consequences – possible fines and prison sentences. In America, broadcasting without a license is a violation of Federal law and can result in fines up to $100,000 and a year in jail.

However, pirate radio stations are often not overtly political in the nature of their broadcasts. Their very existence champions the ideals of free speech, but the majority do not explicitly address political issues. However, they are typically run by those with left-wing political leanings. Many have anarchistic or activist backgrounds, having previously worked on different projects with similar ideals, and this gives them the knowledge, support and confidence to undertake the work of setting up their own station.

These people use direct action as a tool for those who lack financial resources or power. They take risks and undertake civil disobedience to make their voices heard. In getting their message across to their audience, they challenge the system that restricts them from speaking legally. In starting their own radio stations, people were not just transmitting their ideas, their words and music, but also challenging the very nature of the media. This was more than political ranting, but a reclaiming of the tools of free speech.

The risks, and investment in both time and money, seem greater than in other forms of independent media production. Printing your ideas on paper is far cheaper and less dangerous. The motivation behind these radio stations is evidently not money. These stations are self-funded and are rarely able to generate income. This follows anti-capitalist principles and, in its very nature, challenges the commercial stations. Rather than being driven by the possibility of profit, their aim is primarily to build communities, to entertain and to share information.

Most stations structure themselves along anarchist lines. They are typically run by a collective of people, operating in an idealistic non-hierarchical manner. As the operations are illegal, secrecy is often an issue. People often use false names and those on land operate from rented property or squats to make detection from regulators difficult. The individuals running these stations need to be resilient and highly committed to what they are trying to achieve.

The model pirate station, although rooted in the activist world, appeals to a wide section of underground communities. This is evident in the fact that stations span genres — with almost any type of programming appearing on one or more station on the airwaves. The medium is about diversity — anyone can start their own station and broadcast what they like as long as they accept the risks involved.

American Pirates

Pirate broadcasting in America has taken many forms since the advent of federal broadcast regulation in the late 1920s. To start with, illegal broadcasts were typically low-key and amateur. After the end of World War II, short-wave radio pirates came to the forefront of unlicensed radio activity. With the rise of the widespread social unrest in the late 1960s, more unlicensed broadcasters moved to the normal AM and FM bands. Although short-wave pirates were still dominant, few were heard outside their local areas. In the late 1970s, inexpensive and second-hand radio transmitting gear, of a kind suitable for pirate broadcasting, became widely available and people began to realize that they could try to launch their own stations.

The activity of pirate radio stations broadcasting illegally from the seas has been relatively rare in America. One of the first stations to do so was Voice of the Voyager (inspiration for the UK's Radio Caroline), which took to the air early 1978 from a location near Minneapolis, Minnesota. Its broadcasts could be heard throughout America, much further-reaching than any of the British pirate stations. Broadcasting late on a Saturday night, Voice of the Voyager played a stream of rock music, creating a party atmosphere for its listeners. This was certainly a covert operation, with the identity of the broadcasters concealed to avoid being charged by the Federal Communication Commission, an independent government agency, with a direct responsibility to Congress for controlling the airwaves (including radio, television, wire, satellite, and cable.) The FCC soon realized that a pirate station was illegally using the airwaves and by August 1978 the stations office was raided and closed down. They took to the air again on November 5th 1978, for a farewell broadcast that was so well received that they continued broadcasting regularly until January 14th 1979. Sadly, their aging transmission equipment failed at this point and the station was finally silenced.

Micropower

The next phase in illegal broadcasting, one which would shake the idea of the power of radio, was begun in the late 80s by an unlikely hero. This was not a middle class rebel with ideas of mass communication and revolution but a blind African-American man living on welfare in a neglected and troubled housing project in Springfield, Illinois. The predominately African-American neighbourhood was plagued by the oppression of a racist and brutal local police force and twenty-seven year old Mbanna Kantako decided that the only way for things to change was if the community started to communicate with one another and share information.

Lacking money and technical expertize, he set up a tiny low power station. Kantako bought his original one watt transmitter from an electronic mail order from Paradise,

California for a little over $200. With a broadcast radius of about eight city blocks it was enough for WTRA (Tenants' Rights Association) to reach not only the John Hay Public Housing Project but several thousand people in the black neighbourhood of Springfield's segregated east side as well as most of the downtown area.

This was truly radical broadcasting from the first day it took to the airwaves on November 25th 1987, from Kantako's own apartment. He campaigned tirelessly against police brutality and interviewed its victims live on his show. Referring to the ruling social class as 'the class with no class' he directly attacked social injustice from his own home, transmitting his ideas to others through lo-fi technology.

This grass roots citizen's movement was a community effort, with the support of Mike Townsend, a professor of social work at a small college in the town, as well as Kantako's own wife Dia, and later their children, helping to keep the station running.

In America, the FCC (Federal Communications Commission) required licensed AM/FM radio and TV stations to transmit with at least 6000 watts of power. This made the cost of setting up a legal radio station prohibitive to those without money. Non-commercial educational licenses were difficult to get and limited to a small section of the FM band. Applicants are challenged by religious broadcasting networks and well funded radio franchises. After the fees, with lawyers' costs and commissioned studies reaching an estimated $100,000, it was just too expensive for many would-be broadcasters. By operating using only a one-watt transmitter, Kantako was well under what the FCC saw as a legitimate station. They only wanted professionally run stations to have access to the airwaves and such restrictions served to enforce this.

The authorities, both local and federal, wanted to stop Kantako's work, which so directly attacked the police and local authorities. The FCC was wary to charge him as they feared that it would ignite a civil rights movement due to the sensitivity of the situation. Kantako was a legally blind African-American man on welfare speaking out against police brutality. If he was silenced by the authorities, they knew there would be outrage across America. Instead, they issued him fines, which he simply refused to pay. They felt that eventually he would run out of enthusiasm and energy and the station would burn out. They were wrong.

Instead of showing any sign of quitting, he also led marches against police brutality, and organized an alternative tenants' rights association. He expanded his work into outreach projects for his community's youth as he tried to build a sense of identity and pride in the neighbourhood.

When the FCC again tried to silence the station in 1990, they took it as far as federal court. Kantako couldn't get a court-appointed lawyer for a civil case so refused to attend court. In his absence, he was issued a fine and ordered off the air. He refused to pay the fine and instead of shutting down the station, he started to broadcast twenty-four hours a day, seven days a week.

Through his initial idea and actions, Kantako had devised a model of social action which could be used by others. He knew that if other communities started such radio stations then they would experience the same sense of empowerment. He named these low powered stations 'micro radio' – a term applying to any small scale station which is low cost and easy to operate – but did not have either the money or technical resources to provide broadcasting kits for other stations, which would have made it much easier for others daunted by technology. Instead, he realized that the best way to show others the potential of micro radio, and to show them how to run their own, was by publicizing his own station.

Kantako's story was first featured in the *Illinois Times,* but as his personal circumstances and radical action appealed to the media, articles followed in newspapers and magazines across the country. Receiving donations from those impressed by what he was doing, he could now invest in a new 1530 watt transmitter, which could cover a three mile radius. The $600 needed to pay for this was raised by donations from six prominent scholars – Noam Chomsky, Ed Herman, Ben Bagdikian, Herbert Schiller, Michael Parenti and Sidney Willhelm. His efforts had reached far out of Springfield into wider America.

This new idea of micro radio, the simple technology that anyone could use to transmit their ideas, posed the type of threat to authority that is felt whenever people gain access to information concerning what is really happening in the areas in which they live. Kantako posed such a threat and was determined to spread the truth in his local community. In 1995, the Springfield Housing Authority announced that instead of remodelling the John Hay site, where Kantako and his family were housed, it would be demolished. Many believed that this was to get rid of the controversial Kantako. However, the family moved to an apartment still in range of the east side community, and the landlord was the publisher of the *Illinois Times,* the paper that first broke the news of the radio station. Dedicated to transmitting his shows, Kantako had the station in operation just ninety minutes after his family had moved into their new home. This demonstrated the power of the micro radio station: the ease of operation and transmission.

Kantako recovered from this setback and his radio station

grew again. Though on September 29th 2000, the station was raided by the authorities. Nine cars appeared, full of federal marshals, sheriff's deputies, city police and FCC officers. They seized all the broadcast equipment and computers, cut the cables, took down the antenna and shut down the radio station; herding the six family members into a bedroom as they did so. The ever media-conscious family recorded the whole event. Kantako captured the whole forty-five minute raid on his hand held tape recorder while his fourteen year old daughter, Ebony, videotaped the events.

Shortly afterwards, on October 4th, the court issued an injunction banning Kantako from broadcasting on the airwaves. This time, due to his lack of equipment, he was forced to obey. The FCC argued that his signal was interfering with air traffic controls and it could be dangerous. One pilot at the trial reported that he heard kazoo music coming from the direction of Kantako's house as he flew overhead. It was not mentioned that he had been broadcasting for years with no incident, and there had been no reports from the airport. Kantako's radio station had been on air for 4247 days before the forces knocked on his door. A great success for any pirate radio station.

Free Radio Berkeley
Kantako knew that for micro radio to reach its full potential, it would need to be accessible to local communities. He knew that he did not have the technical expertise to make this vision a reality. Stephen Dunifer, a San Francisco activist and electronic engineer, was the sort of expert that Kantako knew any possible micro radio station would need.

Dunifer already felt strongly against the country's mass media. It was the early 90s and he was angry with the media coverage of the Gulf War. He believed that the links between the government and the media (both commercial and public) were just too close and so news reporting could not be trusted. He wanted to liberate the airwaves from the hold the government had on the free flow of ideas and culture and inspired by what Kantako had done before him, knew it was possible. If Kantako, with no experience or technical knowledge, could achieve so much with his own station, then Dunifer could take the idea one stage further and begin a micropower broadcasting movement.

He started with the founding of his own radio station, Free Radio Berkeley. Dunifer began by using radio as a portable form of social protest. He started to transmit from a portable transmitter at a Rainbow Gathering in April 1992 and then at demonstrations all over the area. In December 1992 and January 1993, he broadcasted in front of the local Pacifica station KPFA-FM, as part of a protest over what he considered to be the decline of this progressive non-profit-making station. It was previously viewed as a progressive, radical station but over the past few years, Dunifer and his friends had felt that it was compromizing its original ethics. Free Radio Berkeley began as an alternative to such stations. From the start, Dunifer was determined to set up a radio station for the people. He could most often be found making transmissions from his '64 Volvo station wagon around the Berkeley Hills, setting up his antenna and beaming Free Radio Berkeley into the east San Francisco bay, hoping to reach its inhabitants with his broadcasts.

Dunifer had always felt that his roots were in activism and was a great believer in direct action and civil disobedience. He had been involved in numerous social causes since the 1970s, describing himself as a full-time community activist. What made him different from the majority of other activists was his practical knowledge of communications. His first job, at age seventeen, was as a broadcast engineer at a television station in the Los Angeles area. His interests in community building, protest and the technical side of communications merged in the realization of the radio station. His vision of technology was a tool for electronic civil disobedience.

In 1993, he found a physical location for the station and set up a 40 watt FM station from his apartment. Providing Berkeley and Oakland with an alternative source of community news, discussions and interviews, he was less interested in playing music. In such a creative and dynamic community, it was vital for local people to have their own media source rather than relying on a distorted governmental media. Micro radio stations were the ideal way for people to easily achieve a voice. They could be set up relatively cheaply and could cover a radius of twelve to fifteen miles – enough for most communities.

An FM broadcast station does not need to consist of masses of expensive equipment. Micro power broadcasting uses FM transmitters with a power output in the range of 1/2 to 40 watts. These are small, about the size of a brick, and when combined with audio mixers, audio equipment such as CD player and turntables, a power supply and antennae anyone can put their voice on the air.

Dunifer had designed his own transmitter and began to produce and sell broadcast kits to other aspiring broadcasters. This was what set him apart from other independent stations – he wanted to show others that this was easy and offer them practical encouragement to follow his example. Free Radio Berkeley was there to offer help and guidance, supplying not only cheaply priced kits but also practical workshops and information. Promoting the organization on the internet, from its very early days, helped to get his message out – that anyone could start their very own radio station. It was illegal but, for many, necessary. Dunifer, as many others, felt that the American airwaves should belong to the people and wanted to reclaim them.

The micro radio station movement in America took shape at the end of the 20th century, helped by Free Radio Berkeley's practical influence, but their roots are in the wider free radio movement and the influence of European underground radio of the 60s. It became a national movement of electronic civil disobedience, a melding of free speech and direct action, a protest and a tool. By 1998, it was estimated that there were over one thousand micro stations in America, all reaching into their communities, many producing idiosyncratic broadcasts which could not be heard anywhere else.

Pirate stations were still being run illegally. Risks were involved as those who took part violated FCC regulations and made themselves subject to possible legal action, fines and equipment being seized. However, it was difficult for the FCC to control such a rapidly growing movement. Though claiming unauthorized stations interfered with registered stations and emergency service signals, little proof was found, and such complaints were likely to be a cover for the real issue at stake: pirate radio was disrupting corporate ideals.

Dunifer began to broadcast Free Radio Berkeley from a fixed location, to a regular schedule in Berkeley in the winter of 1993. However, by May that same year, the FCC had located the station and in June, he was issued a notice to stop broadcasting immediately. Dunifer realized that he would have to fight this ruling. It was not just a matter of denying that what he was doing was against the law; he wanted to fight for the freedom of others to start their own stations. This was the first low power station to directly attack the governmental regulations. The movement for low power community radio was relatively low-key until Stephen Dunifer founded Free Radio Berkeley and, significantly, was willing to go to court in its defence.

He was contacted by the Committee for Democratic Communication (part of The National Lawyers Guild, a progressive organization of lawyers committed to social change and the protection of human rights) who worked to democratize the American media. This group, also from San Francisco, shared many of the same ideas as Dunifer: that current media legislation was blocking the individual's right to free speech. They wanted to fight his case in court – challenging not the idea that unregistered radio stations were illegal but the way that the FFC issued broadcasting licenses. People had previously challenged the government's right to control the airwaves but no one had attempted to attack their methods of regulation. They argued that a transmitter under 100 watts could not be licensed, as the FCC only issued licenses for over this amount thereby restricting radio broadcast to the rich. The FCC took no further action when presented with this argument, but Dunifer had not won. In December 1994, the FCC filed to stop further broadcasts and at the court case that followed claimed that the station interfered with existing signals. Free Radio Berkeley would not concede to taking the station off the air and continues today, championing the micro radio station and its power across America.

The San Francisco Radio Movement
It seems almost obvious that the Bay Area would set the scene for the reclamation of technology and assertion of

free speech, for it has long been a centre of rebel activity. From the early 1990s, it provided a base of the micro radio movement, which would later spread across America. As with the Free Speech Movement of the 1960s, where many of the micro radio movement's founders played a part, micro radio began in Berkeley CA, in People's Park in the early 1990s. This piece of land, owned by the University of California, has long been the cause of dispute, conflict and protest in both the history of Berkeley and the wider counterculture movement. In the late 1980s and early 1990s, a conflict arose concerning amplified music used by those organizing concerts at People's Park. Tom Schreiner of Free Radio Santa Cruz, who was living in Berkeley at the time, said that the city had set up a confusing permit procedure that allowed Berkeley police to confiscate amplification equipment. To combat this, it was realized that a half-watt FM transmitter could be installed on the stage and then all the audience would have to do would be to bring a portable radio with them and the music would be broadcasted to them directly. The idea was inventive and, as the half-watt transmitter was legal, an ingenious way of solving the problem. There were technicalities in the regulations which could be used to the advantage of the local community.

Dunifer was not the only one broadcasting in the Bay Area. Other local activists realized the potential of the medium. Richard Edmonson operated Liberation Radio in the San Francisco Area, using a transmitter from Free Radio Berkeley, driving his Volkswagen van to some high ground to broadcast in the evening. Food Not Bombs, a feed-the-poor activist organization, also supported the micro broadcasting movement and was a partial sponsor of Radio Libre, broadcast from San Francisco.

Many members of the San Francisco activist community were involved in the 60s counterculture movement and retained its ideals and aspirations. Having campaigned for free speech, they saw that the concept of free radio was a means by which ordinary people could spread their ideas. Schreiner saw early on the possibilities in micro broadcasting, especially in organizing the new dispossessed class he observed emerging in America. The first station he helped set up was the first one in the Monterey Bay Area – a Spanish station located in the city of Salinas. His next project was Free Radio Santa Cruz. This was different to Free Radio Berkeley, in the sense that it was deliberately provocative. Whereas Dunifer's station generally followed the FCC content regulations, Free Radio Santa Cruz deliberately violated these by using obscene language. Their argument was that they were simply mirroring the discourse of the local community and that it could not be blamed if the community used such language. The station angrily defended their right to free speech irrespective of what they wanted to say.

The new stations did not just operate in the Bay Area, but all over America. Susan Carpenter started her station KPBJ in San Francisco in the summer of 1995 and moved it with her to Los Angeles in October of the same year, renaming it KBLT. She wrote a book called *40 Watts From Nowhere,* about her experiences in pirate radio, documenting her '24-hour station with almost one hundred DJs coming to [her] apartment each week. Hundreds of bands had visited, played live, DJ'd or been interviewed on the station, including the Red Hot Chilli Peppers, Flaming Lips, etc.'[120] Although both stations were run illegally, at first Carpenter didn't regard what she was doing as a form of activism. She just wanted to broadcast music. 'I considered myself more of a regular person just wanting to hear some good stuff on the radio. In retrospect, I don't think there's anything more activist than squatting on a $200 million piece of FM real estate.'

Others adapted the nature and style of this model of independent radio. Steal This Radio, for example, operated from New York's Lower East Side. As a collective, in September 1995, they began to acquire equipment and technical skills to launch their own micro power station. This station was a mouthpiece for the members of the neighbourhood, a means through which they could organize their community. Moving to a different location each week, the station broadcast not just live music but also poetry, fiction and drama.

Low Power Stations

In 2000, in the face of the multitude of micro radio stations springing up nationwide, the FCC made the decision to create a Low Power Service to allow smaller stations to apply for licenses. Licenses began to be issued in January 2002 and small scale local stations did not have to operate illegally. Now organizations such as church groups, schools, civil rights organizations and environmental activists could start their radio stations away from the risk of prosecution. The FCC realized that it could not realistically continue to ban such small scale stations and by issuing licenses could start to raise revenue from them.

The success of these tiny stations that began to be founded after the FCC ruling was not measured by audience figures or how far their signal reached. The most important thing was that they could reach their local neighbourhood. People who would never get their voices heard, those in marginalized groups and those on low incomes, could now legally start their own stations. One particularly successful example is in South Bend, Indiana, a Spanish language station broadcasting to an Hispanic community. Since its origins in September 2002, members of the community could hear traditional and contemporary Hispanic music and also receive English language vocabulary lessons during the breaks. Relying entirely on volunteer staff and donations, this is a community effort. It would not have been possible without the strong history of the pirate radio which preceded it. The pressure of the illegal stations allowed such marginalized communities to find their voices and bring about practical change in their communities.

Internet Radio

As the internet became increasingly prevalent in everyday life, it was realized that it could be used as a means to transmit radio programmes. This became an alternative to pirate radio – an option with the added advantage of being legal. Radio shows are typically prerecorded before being broadcast over the internet. This means that it soon became possible to access stations from all over the world with ease. Such stations have grown from the pirate and free radio tradition. Though perfectly legal and reaching out of an immediate geographical community, they are able to achieve much more. The choice of stations is almost endless and there are no longer time restrictions as programmes are not often live and are stored in archives which can be accessed and listened to at anytime. Such flexibility allows broadcasters to produce programmes for niche interests. As they are not restricted to specific locations, those with particular interests can find the perfect radio station for them.

The first internet radio station was started in 1993 by

Carl Malumud. He founded the internet Multicasting Service, a non-profit group through which he developed 'Internet Talk Radio', which was credited as being the first of its kind. By February 1995, the first full-time internet only radio station, Radio HK, began to broadcast the music of independent artists from Marina del Rey, California.

These pioneers started a new phase in broadcasting. People no longer needed specialist audio equipment, they just needed a computer and some software. This has meant that almost anyone can become a desktop broadcaster. Radio has moved away from being corporately controlled, you can set up a web station with little money and need have no advertisers or promoters to answer to. No wonder so many thousands of people are now broadcasting their own stations over the internet. Some will just broadcast one show and others with achieve longevity but all are contributing to the history of independent radio – that DIY approach which has long been a rebellious part of broadcasting history.

The Birth of Independents: Release It Yourself

Total freedom for the musician only comes with artist-driven, independent record labels. Often these labels are run by artists themselves, who release their own music and distribute it via networks where they do not have to compromise their ideals. After the first wave of punk, by the late 70s, many performers realized that the idea of starting their own record labels needn't be intimidating. Punk challenged its audience to create their own music for themselves. Many decided that they needed to go one stage further and release their own records. To them, it was not enough to just sing about rebellion and distance themselves from mainstream culture, they wanted to actually do these things. All they needed was the money to press their singles and a belief in themselves. Not only was this sometimes the only way a band could actually get their music released, it also continued the access aesthetic promoted in zines – that anyone could produce their own media. The news began to spread; that it was surprisingly easy to gain access to cheap recording studios and pressing plants, where your records would be manufactured. The demystification of the industry had begun; there was no big secret, the process of releasing records wasn't difficult to understand or achieve. The increase in affordable technology at this time meant that such activities were no longer so far out of reach, and countless people took this opportunity.

Crass were one such 70s punk band who soon began releasing their own records. As band member, G Sus, explains, 'None of us ever believed that you could sign with a big company and think you could play it your own way… We always felt that we'd never, ever allow anyone else to dictate how we were going to do it, when were were going to do it, and for how long.'[121]

This was taking the original ideas of punk one stage further. If punk had begun with the aim of demystifying the process of performance, inviting anyone to get up on stage and play music so that the distinction between artist and audience was not important, then the idea of releasing your own music demystified the process of production. The punk legacy was about more than starting a band: it was about writing your own songs, pressing your own records, starting a label, establishing distribution channels, touring, taking control. Of course the creative freedom that this entailed was complete.

For many people, punk lost its sense of the revolution in the late 70s when it became more about manufacturing and marketing than true rebellion. Bands were signing to major record labels and many felt that this sense of revolution was being tamed.

In this post-punk era, underground bands wishing to remain true to their ideas began to release their own records. They were typically 7" records with enough room for about four songs, often all the songs the band had written. In the mid-to-late 70s, there was a boom in the number of 7" singles released. This increase was a direct response to the established practices of the music industry. Now that people were releasing their own records they had control and could change things, starting with changing the way that music was bought. By releasing primarily 7" records they were reacting against the trend of releasing LPs, which were seen as too expensive for a typical working class kid to buy. As these kids were the primary audience for the punk scene, particularly in Britain, the need to release their music in a format that was both cheaper to produce and buy was vital.

Everything about these self-released records was lo-fi: from the photocopied paper sleeves and rubber-stamped label to the cheapest pressing they could find. The aim was to produce the record for as little money as possible, to make it accessible to their audience. They were created with wild enthusiasm, as evident in the immediacy of the form.

Some bands saw the act of releasing their own records as the only way to get them to their audience. The Buzzcocks, for example, issued their 'Spiral Scatch' EP in February 1977 on their own New Hormones label. This release increased their audience and helped them to sign with United Artists later that summer. Other bands did not see the act of releasing their own records as a step on the way to signing to an established label. To them, it was the one and only way to release music.

Formed in Dalston, East London, during March 1977, The Desperate Bicycles were one of the first bands to seriously aspire to the DIY recording ethic that punk had begun. They moved beyond punk's initial angry call to action and told bands that they could take full creative and financial control over their own music. Early punk bands, such as The Sex Pistols and The Clash, signed early on to major record labels. Their music raged about independence, but they were controlled by big business. Many musicians and fans wanted the independence that punks were singing about.

The Desperate Bicycles formed the Refill label in May 1977 and released their first single 'Smokescreen Handlebars' – an unusual EP featuring the same tracks on both sides (to cut mastering costs in half), recorded in mono with a breakdown of recording costs on the back. Recorded in just three hours it cost just £153 for five hundred copies. An amount that John Peel said any band could afford if the bass player sold their motorbike and the rest of the band robbed a few telephone boxes. For little more than the price of recording and producing a demo tape, a band could now press a run of five hundred records to produce their own end product. By producing their record as cheaply as possible, with budget recording and pressing plus a home-designed sleeve, they could share their music easily with their audience. The traditional division between artist and audience would be broken down. This was lo-fi, the very act of production and distribution being considered more important than the quality. It was not polished, it was urgent and 'real'.

On the single The Desperate Bicycles chanted, 'It was

easy, it was cheap – go and do it!' This became the rally call of DIY. To help their fans do this, they included contact details of the companies they used to record and press the single. By doing so, they created one of the most useful and subversive record sleeves ever, speeding up the demystification of recording and release processes, and taking some of the power away from the music industry. Their next single's notes read: '"No more time for spectating," they sing and who knows? They may be right. They'd really like to know why you haven't made your single yet... So if you can understand, go and join a band. Now it's your turn...'

They were directly challenging their audience to do-it-themselves, there was no sense of superiority or exclusivity. The Desperate Bicycles wanted others to follow their lead. Firmly rooted in London's independent culture, their 1978 EP, 'New Cross New Cross,' was even named after the South London area close to where they lived. They wanted to work to create a new music scene with a prevailing sense of accessibility.

By 1980, The Desperate Bicycles had released six singles completely independently. They were dismissed by many critics as being shambolic and amateurish but to others it was their approach towards releasing their music that was inspirational, liberating themselves and others from the struggle of the music industry. For them, the importance did not lie in the end product but in the very means of production. Of course they wanted to release a single but they wanted to do it independently, on their own terms. The band did have a great impact on an audience waiting for such inspiration. *Zigzag* magazine's 1978 'Small Labels Catalogue' listed independent labels in operation, including those influenced by punk. This last category jumped to eight hundred labels in 1980 showing just how popular and accessible releasing your own records had become.

One band particularly inspired by The Desperate Bicycles approach to music production was Scritti Politti. After moving from Leeds to a London squat in January 1978, they became involved in the burgeoning independent music scene. The band followed the ideal that you learnt fast, and made sure they were ready to play punk gigs in a matter of weeks. They soon became regular players on London's punk scene. Scritti Politti were highly original; addressing political, personal, national and global issues and creating music with a Jamaican influence. In an interview in *Sounds* magazine a year after they formed (1979), they claimed, 'It was The Desperate Bicycles that gave us the incentive. "If you're thinking of making a tape why not go the whole way and make a record?" they said.'

They soon got to work on their first single, 'Skank Bloc Bologna'. This was made using just £350 borrowed from drummer Tom Morley's brother, and was released in November 1978 on their own label, St. Pancras Records. On their folded-over A4 sized sleeve they printed details of their production costs and contact information for affordable resources – recording studios and manufacturers that would cheaply master and press the vinyl records. The band were proud that they had achieved this release themselves. 'It was self-empowerment through not letting yourself be bamboozled any more,' they explained. 'People exert control through mystification, they like to make you think it's all over your head.' The second single, consisting of a live session they recorded for John Peel's radio show, was released in 1979 jointly by St. Pancras and Rough Trade. The sleeve featured their complaint that the BBC contract prevented them from providing recording costs alongside manufacturing costs.

But Scritti Politti were later seen to lose their DIY ethic, to the disappointment of many of their early fans. Following the release of three singles, which seemed to many to epitomize DIY values, the band returned to recording in 1982 with revised ideas about the value of independent records. Further Scritti Politti releases took a less reverential stance on self-produced records and so were criticized by many of their original fans, fans who objected to their signing to a record label and who felt that the punk scene was beginning to mirror the situation of the mid-70s when early punk bands signed to major labels.

Bands were trying to move away from a reliance on past rock traditions, you didn't have to work to get spotted by a record label, you could run your own record label and work to release your own records. All stages of the music production process were accessible. For many musicians, this realization that they could operate on the independent underground was a truly liberating experience, especially as there were certain people within the established music industry who were keen to support their efforts. There were other bands willing to offer advice, DJs such as John Peel, who were eager to play their records on the radio and an audience looking for an alternative to what the music charts were offering. There was a network and a market for self-produced, home-made vinyl.

Bands began to form their own communities and their own independent scenes. These were not trends spotted by the mainstream, but the result of their own organic networks. Compilation records were released featuring bands from a particular community and various zines supported these efforts, devoting pages to documenting the new bands that were emerging. Cult figures and celebrities were produced on the underground, it didn't matter that the band had only sold two hundred 7" records or never played a gig. The access aesthetic glorified in the zine was now adopted by bands willing to create, record, release and distribute their own music and the zines in turn support these efforts.

In Newcastle, the zine *Fast Connection*, for example would champion lo-fi music from the North, and across the UK. Alongside commentary with a political slant this zine was packed with interviews with bands like Bette Davies and the Balconettes, The Yummy Fur and the founder's own bands Milky Wimpshake and Red Monkey.

It was not always easy and the DIY approach was not without its critics. Some questioned whether the ease by which bands could produce and distribute their own music inevitably meant that the standard of music dropped. If anyone could make their own record then surely many of these would be of a low standard? To those involved, however, this simply did not matter. It was not about the standard of musicianship or the quality of recording, but instead the very fact that they released it themselves.

Independent Labels

The 70s, the era of punk, was an intensely fertile time for the independent record label. The major labels were typically run by middle-aged men, who chose who was signed, whose records were sold in shops and who received radio play. Following the high media profile of The Sex Pistols in 1976, the major labels were eager to sign punk bands. They signed up almost all the most prominent punk bands during 1977, seeing punk as a new youth trend from which to profit. Those musicians who wanted to release their music away from major label control, but without having to make the record themselves, needed an alternative. Independent label pioneers realized that they couldn't compete with the major labels commercially and didn't want to – they had to try something different. This gamble led to a boom period in the history of independent music. The term 'indie', to mean independent, was later adopted to describe these labels, a term which would resonate for decades to come.

Many were certainly vocal in airing their dislike and distrust of the music industry and its major labels, which they saw as exercizing an unfair control over music. Independent labels, on the other hand, developed artists on a grass roots level, supporting their musicians whilst enabling them to retain creative control.

By the late 70s, the relationship between artist and major label was seen to be potentially damaging to the artist, with the label in a position of financial and legal control. Most received an advance instead of a fee for their work, often to pay for all expenses from recording and touring to musical instruments and living expenses. They only began to earn money on record sales once their royalties had 'paid back' the advance. If the artist's royalties didn't match the value of the advance, they in effect owe the record company money. This relationship has always caused friction and resulted in many conflicts within the music industry. A further dispute would often arise concerning the issue of artistic control. Bands were often pressured to record the record that the label wanted to sell rather than the band wanted to make. This passive position that the artist was placed in did not easily fit with the ideals of punk. Punk musicians wanted control of their music. By releasing their music on independent labels with similar views to themselves, punk bands did not have to compromise their ideals. Bands retained a sense of authenticity, which the audience celebrated. Therefore, as the first wave of punk became more established, there developed a strong tendency among some of those that followed to see independence as an end in itself, and not simply as a means to the end of getting a deal.

Small labels were started by fans of music who wanted to help release music by the bands who would otherwise not be heard. By the late 70s, mini labels were being run from bedrooms all around Britain and America. These consisted of one or two people sending master tapes away to be pressed into vinyl, photocopying or screen printing record sleeves, packaging them up and sending them out by mail order or negotiating to get them on the shelves of their local record shop.

Other independent labels took a more professional route, moulding themselves on the major labels – not in terms of their ethics but in the way that they set themselves up and operated.

One of the first of these independent labels began in 1975, during the height of punk. Operating to start with from a couple of market stalls and the trunk of its founder Ted Carrol's battered Peugeot, the label Chiswick invented the British shoe-string independent. Riding the crest of the punk wave, the Chiswick's seven year career produced its fair share of eccentricities and the odd hit. The ecleticism shows in the three most successful acts – rock and roll revivalists, Rocky Sharpe and The Replays, adult rock band Sniff n' The Tears and punk band The Damned.

Stiff Records was formed in September 1976, founded by Jake Riviera and Dave Robinson, who were both involved in London's pub rock circuit. With its sense of enthusiasm and naïvete, it became a model for other independent labels to follow. It introduced the radical idea of releasing records of bands you liked simply because you wanted to and thought that others would like them too.

Other labels soon followed, all with different ideals and agendas. Illegal, Deptford Fun City and Step Forward (all linked via Miles Copeland's Faulty Products umbrella), as well as Fast Products, were all set up specifically as a stepping stone for bands wanting to sign to the major labels. Meanwhile, others, including Cherry Red, had become key players in the independent scene by the early 1980s, as had Mute Records: which was originally a means through which its owner Daniel Miller could release his own single.

Such labels achieved loyalty from their customers who respected their independent ethics. As independent brands, they appealed to those record buyers who did not want to support the mainstream labels.

These labels that sprung up in the late 70s were serious about changing the shape of the British music industry. With their independence, they could afford to be daring when it came to new music. Virtually every independent label in the business of recording contemporary music has come into the business for one reason only: those who start the label sincerely appreciate and love new music, and want to play a role in its promotion. This means that they will typically only release music that they like and not just what they feel is commercially viable. This leads to great new music being released.

Other independent labels, such as Rough Trade, Beggar's Banquet, Small Wonder and Good Vibrations were offshoots of independent record shops. One of the most respected of these was Rough Trade. Located in Ladbroke Grove, West London, the original Rough Trade shop was opened for business in February 1976 and became a magnet for the local bohemian community. 'We had comfy chairs, huge reggae speakers pumping out music incredibly loud, and all the pre-releases,' explained founder Geoff Travis. It was the time of the punk and reggae explosion in London and the shop was very popular with bands themselves. Having begun by distributing independent records and after realizing that his retail perspective helped him judge what was popular with record-buyers, Travis set up the Rough Trade label in 1978.

The first release was the French band Metal Urbain's, 'Paris Maquis' – a band whose import records had proved popular with their customers. It was not until their third release, Cabaret Voltaire's 'Extended Play,' that the label achieved cult recognition as a promoter of underground music. In the 70s, the label released records by The Television Personalities, The Slits, Stiff Little Fingers and Young Marbels Giants. In an interview with Theresa Stern (www.furious.com) in November 1996, Travis explains why punk left such fertile ground for new music. 'It was coming out of a dead decade musically so I think that then the conditions were right. Punk gave everyone on the scene the impetus to do things for themselves. If that hadn't happened, perhaps we wouldn't have started.' Then, in the early 80s, Travis discovered British band The Smiths and signed them to the label. Their phenomenal success meant that Rough Trade changed from being a specialist post-punk label to a more mainstream contender.

Rough Trade bridged the gap between the older hippie culture and punk. The business was run as a co-operative: everyone had equal say and equal pay. They tried to be fair to their artists, contracts were for one record at a time, rather than forcing commitment from their bands, profits were split fifty-fifty between the label and the band after recording, and promotion costs were made back. They wanted to avoid the exploitation that was experienced by many bands in the music industry.

In an interview in 1996, Gina Birch from The Raincoats describes the experience of releasing records through Rough Trade in its early years. 'It was all this thing about democracy. Everybody, if you worked in the shop or in the back packing boxes, you part-owned it, or whatever. Everybody had the same wages and the same input, and the bands would come along to meetings and (starts laughing) it was very funny. Everyone was trying desperately to be "right-on". There were moments when it worked really well, and moments where it was completely farcical and comical.'

As Rough Trade became more established, the label became a key supporter of the British underground scene. In no way elitist, it encouraged others to follow its lead by setting up their own labels. They would even advance them money and provide a base for operations.

Towards the end of the 80s, the label began to suffer financial problems and was sold to One Little Indian. Although its founder continued to release records under the names Trade 2 and Rough Trade Recordings, with the same ethics, neither of these outfits achieved the same success. It was not until the mid-90s, when Travis re-acquired the name and again could release Rough Trade records that the label began to reaffirm it original success and survives today.

Rough Trade Records was not the only label to operate from the Rough Trade shop. It was a fertile ground for other labels, offering support and resources. In 1988, Gary Walker worked part-time at Rough Trade and then ran Wiiija from a back room on the premises, along with colleagues Pete, Nigel and Jude. They were influenced by the innovative new music that was arriving in the shop from America, particularly the post-punk sound of Sonic Youth and the Butthole Surfers. Named after the postcode of the shop's Notting Hill branch (W11 1JA), the label was very much concerned with reflecting the new music being produced in Britain with similar musical influences to themselves. Their first releases were Terminal Cheesecake, Bastard Kestrel and Silverfish.

The label grew and was soon releasing records by Huggy Bear, whose lo-fi recordings had been given to them by the band via the record shop. Records by Cornershop and Jacob's Mouse followed, and 1993 became the year that the label found the bands that would make its name. The list of bands they recorded on the label were the crop of lo-fi bands: Comet Gain, Pussycat Trash, Skinned Teen, Linus, Blood Sausage, the Tindersticks and Cee Bee Beaumont. By 1994, they licensed the debut Bikini Kill album from Kill Rock Stars in America and were joining forces with other American bands and labels, forging links between the underground communities. In 1995, they left the support of the Rough Trade shop for the Beggar's Banquet group – now a powerful force in British underground music. They continued to release records by bands from the British underground, including successes such as Bis and Cornershop.

Of course, for many DIY enthusiasts, it is the smaller labels that are the true pioneers of the cause, and despite advance in technology, many are still flying the flag. Paul Kearney, founder of the Guided Missile label, based in East London, explains the benefits of small label life.

'I started Guided Missile Recordings in 1994 to release records from alternative bands such as The Yummy Fur (featuring Alex Kapranos and Paul Thomson later of Franz Ferdinand), The Karelia (Kapranos pre-Franz again),

Mogwai and The Country Teasers.

At the time, I had just become utterly disinterested in the whole stagnant "indie" scene. It was too serious. I wanted to have some fun producing records with colourful, badly drawn, cheaply packaged sleeves, folded over and inserted into plastic covers; but most importantly, records by by exciting bands with real character.

Donkey, for example, would dress up and jump around while playing quirky Fall-esque disco punk-rock music with blaxploitation samples. As the first Guided Missile release, we pressed five hundred records for them, and bribed someone at *Melody Maker* to put us in the Indie Top 20 for two weeks (Shhh!). From that point on the bands recommended their mates' bands and they in turn recommended their own mates' bands until Guided Missile naturally evolved into its own scene. John Peel was an instant fan and played everything we ever released. God bless John Peel!'[122]

Ten years on since his first release, Paul Kearney remains optimistic, his humour undiminished. As he says, 'These days the label still promotes a host of superb 'quirky Fall-esque' bands like The God-Like Genius Of The Beale and Wetdog...' as well as releasing what he unashamedly describes as 'low budget, shit novelty records'. He says, 'Like I mentioned, when you're doing-it-yourself, the attraction is that you have complete freedom in what you put out and why – this is what keeps you going – but if this sounds ultra serious it needn't be!' Kearney explains, when gaining publicity for example, which can be a problem for minor label releases, extreme measures sometimes have to be taken: 'When the Strokes first broke through over here me and a mate invented a tribute band called "Diff'rent Strokes" and hastily released a four track EP called "This Isn't It" –

recorded on a 4-track with cheap, crap instruments in a Shoreditch bedroom. I conned the *NME* into printing a news story about the release on the basis that it "featured members of some very cool bands", and spread rumours that members of Blur, Pulp and even The Strokes themselves, were behind the release. And the whole lot made it into print, with me and my mate laughing at how ridiculous (and brilliant) the whole industry is. You could never get away with this kind of project at a major label. I am not in it for the money. So I can do whatever the hell I choose. There are no restrictions. Therein lies the joy!'

The Underground Network

A crucial element of the independent scene has always been to radically transform the relations of production. In terms of music, this was to break down the dependence of bands on record labels. This did not just involve establishing new record labels but also distributors, publishers, retailers and promoters – all the established networks through which the labels operated. To sell enough records to be able to support and continue their work, independent labels needed to create the network through which to operate. There needed to be some kind of distribution infrastructure, which was both accessible and away from the corporate values that they were trying to avoid. Many realized that without effective distribution, the do-it-yourself ethos would not get you anywhere. To operate successfully as labels they needed the same networks as the major labels.

Geoff Travis realized the need for an independent distributor through which labels could sell their records. Following the opening of the store and the label, he started work on Rough Trade Distribution in the mid-80s – an independent distribution network in alliance with regional retail label and distribution outfits like Probe, Revolver and Red Rhino. By setting up an independent distribution network, labels like Rough Trade tried to prove that the approach of the major labels was not necessary – that you could operate successfully on the independent music scene.

Rough Trade became known, at the end of the 1970s and during the early 1980s, as an organization that supported bands wanting to maintain this kind of autonomy outside the mainstream record industry. They distributed bands' self-released records, were willing to stock poorly produced lo-fi records and even stocked zines in their shops – further encouraging the different areas of British DIY culture to flourish under their support. With the support of a network of record shops like Rough Trade, airplay from John Peel and coverage in the weekly music press and fanzines, it was possible to release a record for very little money and get it heard. This accessibility, through the channels that others had already forged, allowed the scene to flourish at this stage in the late 70s. This shadow network, operating just below the surface of the music industry, along similar structures but with more ethical ideals, was the underground.

Today, it is far less easy for a band or small label to release its own records. The problem is with the distribution network. Irene Revell, from small British label Irrk points out that, 'In general, in the UK, distributors, even the independent ones, aren't really interested in small DIY labels, or any label that isn't trying to sell a few thousand copies of a release at the least. Not that there's anything wrong with operating on that larger scale, we would love to be selling that many copies of some records, but how do you grow to that scale, its a bit of a catch 22?' She continues to explain a possible solution, ' The thing is to try to create alternative

DIY distribution networks of course, swapping records and selling to small distros around the world, helping each other to learn about local DIY communities that way.' Michal Cupid from the Cardiff label Spazoom said that he always felt if a record or tape was really good you could just trust that people would play it to their friends and word would spread just like that. This seems to be the hope of many of those independently releasing records, that they can bypass traditional distribution routes and reach their audience through an alternative, more organic, network. The indie motivation, the lack of commerciality, brings a more idealistic approach to both music production and distribution.

The Age of the Indies

The 80s and early 90s was the boom time of a new crest of independent record and tape labels in America. Those operating in the post-punk underground started labels to release and distribute the new music. These labels spanned America, with Touch & Go in Chicago, Dischord in Washington DC, and the previously mentioned K Records and Kill Rock Stars in Olympia and Sub Pop in Seattle; each of whom released records by the bands emerging in their own corners of the country. Each city had its own way of working and together they forged a creative underground, enabling bands to tour the country, supported by this network. This was the indie underground: where, much like in the early days of punk, authenticity was important and the DIY concept has endured to this day. The reluctance to 'sell out' or be seen to do so is at base of the DIY moral code that operates here. Bands with such a supportive network should not need to look for the alternative of major labels. Many bands, such as Fugazi, have managed to forge a musical career on this indie underground; creating lo-fi music from a range of eclectic influences, retaining full control over the style and distribution of their music and remaining DIY.

The music industry, in both Britain and America, has changed since the early 1980s. It is now a multi-billion dollar industry. It can be argued that there is little room for independent record labels. It is increasingly difficult for a label to remain completely independent and operate away from the major labels. Now those outfits often called 'independent' labels may in fact be financed by a major label. Many retain control over their output but need to rely on major labels for distribution. For example, Creation, one of the most visible independent labels of the 1990s, is partly owned by Sony but retains control over its output and has independent distribution. (Creation records was started by Alan McGee in 1984 with a bank loan of £1,000. Working independently McGee released records by The Legend, Jesus and Mary Chain, Primal Scream, My Blood Valentine and Oasis; and now runs the label Poptones.) Such developments confuse the issue as to what really counts as independent. The concept now more commonly comes to mean the independent ethic and access aesthetic rather than complete financial independence from the mainstream music industry. The important thing is the motivation and the content.

Choosing Lo-fi over Hi-fi

In the mid-90s, there was a new independent music scene emerging in Britain. Britpop was ruling the mainstream charts and those who had been active during the riot grrrl movement focused their attentions on creating an alternative. There followed a truly lo-fi period in British music. They had become cheaply available and so became the ideal tool for the lo-fi musician, recording from their bedrooms. Bands recording on 4-tracks, releasing cassettes and low-cost vinyl. A rejuvenated network spreading across the country.

Newcastle label Slampt championed the scene, started by Pete and Rachel in 1992, they released records by bands such as Golden Starlet, Kenickie, The Yummy Fur and their own lo-fi bands Red Monkey and Avocado Baby, organised gigs, produced zines and passing on information to others so that they too could do-it-themselves. They were fiercely independent, avoiding working with the music industry at all costs. Seeing the creative possibilities of operating underground, they worked hard to spur a British lo-fi scene into existence, to encourage others to follow their lead.

Similar activities were taking place in Glasgow, with labels starting and bands playing at the 13th Note. The heroes of this scene were pop band Bis, who became the first unsigned band to appear on 'Top of the Pops'. In a glorification of childhood culture, with songs with titles such as 'Kandy Pop' and a celebration of glitter and hair clips, they were very different from Britpop. Their fans followed their lead, starting their own bands, writing their own zines. This was an exciting, post-riot grrrl scene. It raised many questions about DIY ethics, whether a band could survive entirely on the underground scene.

Of course, some had always stuck to lo-fi recording techniques, such as the painter, poet and musician Billy Childish, who prefers the more 'rounded' and integrated sound of analogue recording techniques to digital. Sticking to 4 or 8 track machines. and championing the 'one mic in a room' technique, musicians like Childish re-emphasize the fact that anyone can do this – really. In 1991, American Indie label Simple Machines distributed a booklet called

Introductory Mechanics Guide to explain the whole record-making process in simple terms. Over the eight years it was printed, an astonishing 100,000 copies of this manual were sent out, and in 1999 a new issue was produced, updating the information and explaining how to release CDs as well as vinyl. Available on the internet this empowers thousands of individuals looking to record and release music themselves.

Delia Barnard of bands The A-Lines and The Scha-La-Las agrees that vast sums of money don't necessarily have to be spent when recording, what counts is the music. 'I don't particularly hanker after either lo-fi or hi-fi culture. It's the content that matters. The heart behind it and the ideas. Records recorded for two peanuts and a cup of cold custard can sound as good and often more beautiful than those recorded in a million-pound-a-day studio. I once recorded in a studio which was super-duper high tech with computerized EVERYTHING and masses of space and wizardry everywhere. But it was hot as hell and the people that ran it were absolute arseholes. One of my bands used to record on a battered old tape-recorder. We recorded as we wrote the songs. That's the only band of mine that's ever managed to put out TWO albums! Sometimes the lack of money and technology neccesitates having a better idea and you end up with a great object that pisses all over slickly produced super-experienced product.'[123]

Cassette Culture

In the late 70s, there was a new format rising in popularity in which lo-fi musicians saw potential. The cassette tape seemed perfect for their needs. It offered the opportunity for truly low budget, home-made music. There was no reliance on costly recording or manufacture. Musicians could record their music at home on tape recorder directly onto cassette tapes and did not have to subject their music to the controls of a recording studio or pressing plant.

This format had been used in the mail art movement by artists who were working with sound recordings as well as visual art and adopted the cassette to record their work and then distribute through the postal network they had already created. Musicians soon followed in their tracks, seeing the potential for spreading their music in this way.

With the cassette medium, the creator could retain full control. It also freed musicians from the need for record labels to release their music. Releasing their music themselves, they could cheaply and easily enjoy the freedom from outside control or censorship. They did not need to produce a demo tape with the sole purpose of sending to record companies in the hope of attracting their interest but facing possible rejection. Instead the home recorded tape could be their finished product, one which they could distribute themselves. This meant that musicians could be as experimental as they wanted without the constraint of having to appeal to a mainstream record-buying audience. Subsequently, many independently recorded and distributed cassettes were avant garde sound collages, containing complex looping sequences or using sampling techniques to produce unique sounds.

For many it was an individual operation – a musician creating music in their bedroom, recording and then sharing the outcome with others. Others decided to go one step further and set up their own tape labels. These inexpensive operations were typically run not-for-profit, with cassettes often being traded rather than sold, and so from the start were very different from commercial record labels. Tape labels did not have to work to a rigid release schedule. Cassettes were so inexpensive and easy to record on that they could release almost as many as they wanted. The output of many labels was huge. It was an informal, accessible version of the music industry. Similar in many ways to the live experience, this was an immediate form of music, recorded live and sent out to listeners in two easy stages.

Through this output, an underground cassette culture soon flourished, a network of musicians and music fans who communicated via the cassette tape. In Olympia, The Lost Music Network, part of KAOS community radio, first started publishing Op magazine in 1979 with the aim of reviewing little known music. Music enthusiast Graham Ingels, was intrigued by the cassette format, which began appearing in the early 80s and was asked to begin a column in the magazine to review these, which he called 'Castanets'. This was an acknowledgement that in the underground press these cassette releases were being taken seriously as their reviews appeared alongside reviews for vinyl releases. Such recognition strengthened the cassette community, catching the interest of many more new tape fans. Op ended in 1984, while cassettes were still at their peak of production in America, but by now other publications were writing about the format. Ingel's own fascination with cassettes continued and he set up Cassette Mythos. This was a not-for-profit organization, which involved him making compilations from the tapes he was sent and then sending copies to each contributor, with the contact details of everyone else who had taken part.

A world-wide network connected via the postal service developed. Every genre of music was released but the lo-fi means of recording and distribution meant that their aims were the same. These were people who wanted their music to be heard and who were bypassing the record industry in order to achieve this.

The underground use of cassette format was acknowledged by the mainstream music press for a short time in the early 80s. In Britain, the *NME* and *Sounds* featured columns exploring cassette output. These further spurred readers to do-it-themselves. Despite this interest from the music press, however, mainstream radio would not consider the independently released tape to be a proper release and so would not play these recordings on the airwaves. This kept independent cassette culture as a marginal activity, operating on the fringes of the music culture.

A second boom in independently released cassettes came in the 90s when the indie underground began to use cassettes to distribute lo-fi music. By this time, cassettes – which had always been seen as an inferior format – were also seen as old-fashioned. Adopting them to release music was certainly a pro lo-fi and low-budget statement. It became seen by some as a direct form of anti-capitalist action, rejecting the capitalist values of the major labels.

Michal who ran the British tape label Spazoom in the late 90s believes that the cassette is a perfect example of the concept of lo-fi culture. He explains that, '[lo-fi culture] means using what you've got available to the furthest extent you can. You can release your own music by recording it on a tape recorder and releasing cassettes of it and that's just as legitimate as pressing 10,000 CDs and selling them through HMV. That kind of translates into everything – people writing zines, because that's an immediate way of getting writing out instead of publishing a magazine or a book. It's just as legitimate to express yourself in those ways.' He explains how Spazoom operated, with the same intentions as the first tape labels. 'Most things we released were our own music. It was basically a way of getting our music out. To start with it was because no one else would put it out anyway. Then it started becoming important to us to show people that you could just put out your own tapes. So we had a lot of people writing to us and asking if we could put out their tapes and most of the time we would write back and say you should do it yourself. Mostly we would just say, 'It's easy – you've probably got a tape to tape player as well as us, you can be doing this as well.'[124]

Michal describes the scene during the 90s as a time when others were working similarly. 'It seemed like there were quite a few people doing it but then most of the other tape labels were more kind of noise labels. It seemed like they didn't really share the same kind of political feeling that we had about it. We were doing it because we were trying to show that this is something that anyone can do and there was that kind of feeling with tape labels at the time that anyone could do a tape.'

This was one of the dominant attitudes of the underground cassette network, that it was accessible to anyone. Labels such as Spazoom were operating radically differently to major record companies. They were promoting the idea that anyone can make music and release it themselves, as the technology was cheap and available and it was easy to build networks through which they could reach listeners.

This sense of accessibility, with its potential for the release of poor quality and self-indulgent material, can also explain why tape labels are often not taken as seriously as labels releasing on other formats. Michal explains, 'At the same time, the argument that anyone can do a tape label backfires. There was a lack of quality control. People were releasing music on tape but a lot of the stuff we didn't find that interesting. There wasn't a lot of thought put into it.'

But it is this sense of operating away from the

mainstream music industry, the freedom to release whatever you want, that is the heart of cassette culture. It quickly removed itself from the rigid controls of mainstream music, both in terms of its style and its relationship with money. Michal discusses how Spazoom set out as a non-profit operation. 'When we started Spazoom, our first decision we made was, 'We are not ever going to make money off this.' This was something that we decided to do because we had seen people changing what they were doing – not releasing certain records because they wouldn't sell so well. We kind of knew right from the start that this was going to cost us money.' The low-cost option of cassettes meant that people could work in this way, operating without the restrictions that a need to make money can impose.

Cassette labels are still run by people today, even when faced with other options such as CD-Rs or distributing MP3s on the internet.[125] Affection for the low-tech, low cost option has endured, as has the idea that if you don't like what you hear on the cassette, you can always record over it and start again.

Lo-fi is My-fi: The Way Forward

With the rising powerful control of major record labels over the decades since the peak of the indie label in the 70s, independently produced music has suffered a decline. The rise of the internet in particular, has brought with it a new age in music distribution. If they choose to, bands can bypass both major labels and the option of releasing single themselves, and instead distribute their music online, promoting themselves through their website. This has meant that many bands who would have never otherwise had the opportunity to be heard can be potentially accessed by millions of people around the world. Again it is advances in technology that has allowed bands access to their own means of production. The reduced cost of computers and recording equipment has allowed bands to distribute their own music in this way on a relatively low budget.

Bands can now potentially communicate with their fans directly by email, and make announcements via online mailing lists and message boards. This further breaks down any division between a band and its audience, to an extent that could not have been possible at any time previously.

File Sharing
This is a difficult time for the recording industry who are concerned by the ease at which people can now distribute music. Even music by the artists they've invested money in, paying for recordings, can be distributed illegally via the internet. Sites such as the infamous Napster, started in 1999, allow anyone with a connection to find and download almost any type of music they want.

By enabling users to connect with each other's hard drives this enables individuals to swap tunes. It seems music has moved away from being a consumable physical object, as major record labels and indies once believed it to be. Instead it is now an ethereal product and in being so is more difficult to make money from.

Napster was the most well-known site from which people first experienced the advantages of downloading music. It was developed in 1999 by teenager Shawn Fanning, who had developed revolutionary software which would enable fans to swap songs from their hard drives and find the music they were looking for through a central directory. The numbers of people using the site meant that users could find almost anything – from the current releases by major artists to rare bootlegs. Major record labels were angered by this development as well as smaller labels who were worried that any drop in profits would mean that they wouldn't be able to survive. At its peak Napster attracted millions of users who exchanged music files across the internet. However, before Fanning could begin to negotiate any deal to compensate the artist and songwriters for their songs, legal action followed with the Record Industry Association of America (RIAA), which represents five major record labels, suing Napster in December 1999 for copyright infringement. They were most concerned that the service was allowing users to download files without paying. In February 2001, a judge ruled that Napster had to stop the distribution of copyright material through its network and record labels supplied lists of songs which could not be downloaded. This was soon followed by an order in July 2001 that Napster must block all files infringing copyright.

Many others saw the potential of the technology that Fanning had developed and utilized through Napster. He tried to sell to Bertelsmann, who had invested heavily in the company, in the hope that it would provide a secure commercial file sharing application, but this sale was blocked by a Delaware court in September 2002. With Napster gone, others took the initiative and developed similar sites.

The RIAA continued to target websites fostering file-sharers. In June 2003, it claimed it would use software to seek pirated music in these networks and gather evidence against individuals. In 2002, Napster sold its brand name and patents to CD-burning software firm Roxio, for five million dollars in cash and $300,000 worth of Roxio shares. As part of the deal, Roxio were insulated from any future litigation against Napster of the past. Napster's assets, such as servers, routers and computers, were auctioned to pay their creditors as part of their bankruptcy proceedings. In July 2003, they announced plans for a new version of Napster, remodelled under the old name, selling digitalized music on behalf of record companies. They had to redesign the service, involving complex agreements with record companies but, retaining its original name, this is now the slick, legal version of Napster.

The concept of downloading music from the internet is a difficult one for those who make their money from the music industry. Many are caught between feeling that it is a revolutionary new wave to be embraced and feeling that that deserving musicians and labels will lose out, as people now have access to music without paying. While some bands embrace this new technology, others angrily reject it, often voicing their responses publicly.

Metallica's Lars Ulrich raged against online traders and his band launched a lawsuit against them, whereas British band Chumbawamba publicly support the changes, explaining their belief that it will make music much more accessible. This may mark the biggest change in the music industry, but it remains to be seen exactly how much it alters things.

The music industry has long complained that internet piracy causes a drop in CD sales and predicted that huge profit losses would follow. But a survey by Forrester Research in August 2002 concluded this is simply not true, that those who were downloading music were also buying CDs. They predicted that the money record labels could raise from digital music would be substantial if they worked to encourage fans to download music directly from them.

Napster's new chief executive, Hank Barry, has urged the US Congress to pass a law requiring record labels to make music easily available on the internet, claiming that Napster would be willing to pay royalties to musicians. He believes that licensed music should now be available over the internet as it is over the radio, arguing that such a change is a necessary and important step for the internet that will be good for artists, listeners and businesses. However, major record labels, led by the Recording Industry Association of America (RIAA), claim that Napster is simply a tool for music piracy.

This digital revolution hasn't yet taken over the music industry. Since the original incarnation of Napster, many other sites offering illegal music downloads have appeared on the internet. Many of these face similar legal action. Others, realizing that there is money to be made, have launched official sites and record labels have begun to make music available via the internet for a fee.

The practice of bands offering their own music for download follows long established DIY principles. This is the most immediate form of distribution. Musicians can record a song and then almost immediately make it available for others to listen to. This bypasses the manufacturing stage completely, with music flowing digitally from musician to audience.

The issue of illegal downloading is less straightforward. In many ways, it is similar to the operation of the pirate radio stations, illegally operating to distribute music for the simple reason that they wanted others to have access to it. It moves away from traditional principles of DIY culture, acting on a more rebellious impulse. Instead of working just to make their own music available, they try and liberate music on major labels, making it free for others to listen to. Although this raises complex ethical issues concerning recording rights and royalties, it is an impulse which has long had a place in DIY culture.

Although there is potential in reaching a wider audience, many bands are cautious about the impact the use of the internet in distributing music will have. Lynn Breedlove, from Tribe 8, explains 'Free shit gets into more hands than shit that costs money, but what indie band can afford to record for free? We need to find a way to get some cash to artists. Musicians do love to make music and want everyone to hear what they do, but they gotta eat, pal! So fork it over. Go to shows, buy merch. Support bands you love unless you wanna listen to what the radio feeds you forever.'

It has become easier for bands to release their music via the internet, but for many bands and small scale labels, the aesthetics of music recorded onto a physical object still holds appeal. Even at this time of mass-technology, many are still embracing the 7" record as a enduring emblem of the indie scene. Irene Revell from Irrk Records prefers to release music on this vinyl format but questions why, when other technology is more easily available and cost effective. 'Why we still press vinyl is a question I've often considered. It's supposedly not great for the environment and in any case, you can make CD-R copies and tapes on demand for much much less, and with less initial financial outlay. And yet we still snobbishly cling to it, why?' She continues, 'Beyond it's clear aesthetic superiority, is its almost like the format has been reclaimed by the DIY, punk and experimental scenes. The mainstream record industry has stopped making 7" records because they are apparently not financially viable...but then this makes them even more pertinent products for us.'[126]

Live Music

Live music events have always been an essential part of the DIY experience, with bands and independent promoters organizing gigs and festivals to bring like-minded people together to listen to music and also communicate in person. DIY communities have often relied on zines, radio and records through which to speak to one another, but the live event offers a chance to interact on a more personal level.

Playing in front of an audience is a special experience for bands, bringing them and their audience into close physical proximity; but the experience can be even more memorable for the audience. The March 1972 issue of British independent publication *The International Times* explained this experience. 'At any rock concert, an individual band in fact only plays a small part in the overall event. If a show lasts for five hours, one band will only play for, at most, a little over an hour. The actual environment in which the music is presented prevails for the entire event and has by far the major effect on the audience's energy and enjoyment.'[127] It is this sense of the live music experience which has endured through the different threads of DIY culture. It is the feeling of 'being there' when the music is happening that matters.

Punk bands were not the same as the traditional rock band, just as many were eager to hurriedly release their own records, they were also keen to play live as soon as possible. This was what the whole experience of being in a band was about. No-one wanted to spend long forming their bands, practising and gaining experience, before playing live. They wanted immediate action. As soon as they formed they wanted to be playing in front of an audience. As Andy from Linus says, 'The most astonishing thing is finding yourself on a stage, with no idea how you got there.

You're supposed to be some accomplished musician and performer, but uh-oh, there you are, and you've nothing to rely on but your ideas. That's when you make the joyous discovery that ideas are all you need — at least to begin with. It's not about technique, You can see it in the faces of bands doing their first shows. If they connect, and the audience responds, they just can't believe it. It's like getting drunk for the first time.'[128]

It was this live experience that made punk what it was. The experience of people with similar attitudes gathering together was a vital element of the scene, as was the sense of impatience that drove it — young punks wanted everything to be instant. Bypassing the traditional rock circuit they claimed venues like London's 100 Club and the Roundhouse, or New York's CBGB's for their own.

Club Nights
Even if music venues owners were not aware of particular bands or styles of music, this did not mean that they didn't have a chance to find an audience. Independent music promoters could make use of venues by booking bands to play as part of club nights; either a one-off gig or a regular series of events. For some, such as Alan McGee, of Creation Records who started a club called The Living Room on Tottenham Court Road, it was a good way to meet people. For others, it was a way to promote particular bands or sell records.

Many of those who have started labels have inadvertently become promoters too, through running club nights and gigs to feature bands from their labels. Paul Kearney, who runs Guided Missile Club as an outlet for his label's somewhat unusual taste, discusses the many advantages of doing-it-yourself on the gig and club circuit: 'The reason I take the DIY ethic over to running club nights myself also, is that you get to feature all the obscure acts you've ever liked (like Spinmaster Plantpot, The Rebel and Reverend Pike) along with more mainstream stuff – we've had The Darkness and Franz Ferdinand play at Guided Missile – guaranteeing new acts a bigger audience. Even better, you also get to include more bizarre happenings...At our Xmas gig I dislocated my shoulder by dressing as Santa and riding a Sinclair C5, spraypainted gold, down the stairs of The Buffalo Bar [a London venue]. At the following Easter show I had a posse of dwarves in crudely assembled rabbit costumes handing out creme eggs to the punters. Putting on a show yourself definitely means you get complete creative freedom!'

By organizing events themselves, bands or promoters could bypass the music industry and run their community the way they wanted it to be. In America, there had always been a problem with young people being restricted from the live music experience. Those under 21 can't enter a place where alcohol is being served, and as many venues have bars they are often denied access from seeing bands. To bypass this, all-ages shows are organized with the express purpose of making music available to all. Others go one step further and start their own venues, spaces where truly independent events can take place.

Festivals

The 60s saw a wave of music festivals taking place in both America and Britain. Typically organized by the hippie community, they were a seen as a cultural experience, rather than just a show. Bands would be billed as the main attraction, but many were there for the experience of attending the festival as much to see the bands play. It was a means to bring like-minded people together, to have fun and feel part of a wider network. For those taking part in the underground scene, it was a chance to feel that they were working alongside others who felt the same. For others, it was a crazy few days spent camping with their friends with constant entertainment if they wanted it.

During the 70s, there continued to be festivals, which adopted many of the elements of the earlier 60s festivals and embraced the burgeoning sense of DIY. Whereas the festivals of the 60s were promoted as events celebrating peace, love and community, those of the 70s were more about creating an independent arena to contrast with the mainstream music scene.

One of the most celebrated and best remembered festivals of 1970 was Phun City. It was organized by Mick Farren, Edward Barker and David Goodman, key players in the London freak scene,[129] and backed by Farren's leading underground newspaper, the *International Times*. Anarchist, writer and artist Farren championed the reclamation of public space and a creation of free zones – 'phun cities'. His ideas culminated in the festival, which aimed to bring the best elements of the underground to a festival arena. This three day event was held near Worthing in the UK, and combined music, literature, visual arts and a left-wing political agenda, and featured The MC5, William Burroughs, The Pretty Things and The Pink Fairies.

Phun City was one of the last events that mixed art and politics before they were commercialized by the music industry, repackaged, marketed and then sold back to the audience as an 'authentic' festival experience. The festival was remembered as shambolic but achieved almost legendary status in the underground community. Official bodies did not want this large scale event to go ahead and so an injunction was served ten days prior to the festival, leading to site work being stopped as well as the withdrawal of some financial backing. When the injunction was withdrawn a few days later, the organizers were left with little money and no time to complete all the work. By the time the festival opened three days later, there was much left unfinished. There were still no fences around the site and so no way of taking admission fees. With no tickets being sold, it ended up being the first large scale free festival held in Britain and the bands had to be asked if they would perform for no money. With Hells Angels working as the security force, the organizers lost control. The audience were in charge, with the organizers merely facilitating the event. Through this series of incidents, Phun City accidentally became a true people's festival – a contrast to the mainstream festivals of the time.

Britain's best-known festival has for decades attracted bands and huge audiences to a field in Glastonbury. Though now operating as a commercial venture, it was originally conceived as very much part of the underground community. Its second year, 22nd-26th June 1971, was seen by many as where the legend of the festival really began. It was planned to coincide with the summer solstice – mainly because of the deeply held beliefs of the organizers. Glastonbury showed it was possible for any music festival to break through the conventional barriers that ordinarily regulate behaviour, creating a false environment, one consisting of both entertainment and a break from everyday life. People set up camp for a few days and experienced a new form of communal living. The second Glastonbury festival was only attended by seven thousand people, giving the atmosphere of a small, involved community. The newsletter issued during the festival that year explained the emotional experience of the event: 'People are asking when the Fair ends. It ends like a circle ends. Take it with you, the sounds, the smiles, the lights and the scene. It isn't just an experience is it? It's a...a... (you name it, it was probably IT)'.

Glastonbury festival became a model for others to follow. Not only did corporate promoters take the idea and make it commercially viable, hundreds of independent organizers wanting to recreate this atmosphere have since planned their own festivals. Taking many forms and following different themes, the DIY festival has always tried to be a place where people can physically meet as a community. By creating a physical space, however temporary, they can celebrate their scene and develop it further.

Olympia has become famed for the festivals that its indie community have held. These include The International Pop Underground festival in 1991, celebrating the bands growing around Calvin Johnson's band, Beat Happening, and K Records. In a similar style Yo Yo A Go Go began shortly afterwards. Ladyfest 2000 promoted the achievements of women in independent music and Homoagogo celebrated queer culture. All took place in this small Washington town and the impact of each reverberating around DIY communities across the world.

Ladyfest is another particular festival, which has had wide impact. At the end of the four day festival, the organizers urged attendees to go home and produce their own festivals, taking the name Ladyfest and making it their own. Ladyfests have subsequently sprung up in cities such as San Francisco, New York, Glasgow, London, Amsterdam, Bristol and continue to spread around the world. Each follow a similar model as that of the original Olympian festival, combining music with film, visual and performance art as well as workshops.

Others took the model and developed their own versions of the independent festival. Organizers of Ladyfest Bristol 2003, took what they had learned and created a new form of festival. Taking elements from Ladyfest but combining it with their own ideas, they organised Bringyourselfest in 2004. This festival was a wholly DIY experience, the festival was free to attend, as was a place to sleep. People were asked to contribute something, whether it be organizing a workshop, performing with their band or cooking. This festival took many elements of 60s counterculture events, such as the removal of commerciality, relying on a different form of working together, but mixing this with festival ideas developed in Olympia.

Rave Culture

In Britain in the late 50s, the term 'rave' referred to the wild bohemian parties held by the more outrageous socialites of the time. By the mid-80s it was used to describe the illegal London warehouse party scene. These raves were usually held in derelict warehouses, fields or any building the organizers could find to hold thousands of people and a mass of equipment.

At the rave scene's peak in the late 80s, events could attract tens of thousands of people. Secrecy was of paramount importance as these parties were usually illegal. The venue would often remain secret up until hours before the party was to begin as a way of keeping the police away.

The British rave movement of this era was spurred on by the social conditions of the time. Margaret Thatcher was in charge and whilst the media was often seen to celebrate consumerism and individualism, certain sections of youth culture began to rebel against this. English DJs spending time in Ibiza brought back with them news of its burgeoning rave scene. They brought the influences they had been exposed to back to the British youth and within a year, raves were taking place all over the country. This new rave culture celebrated a sense of community and euphoria rather than the pursuit of money and power. The principles were the same as all the DIY actions – the willingness of people working without payment, the operation of a different set of rules. As they were initially free, there was no other motivation for organizing these events other than witnessing other people's fun and developing a mass community.

Throughout the 80s, free festivals, squat culture, the traveller 'new age' movement and later acid house parties (playing a particular kind of dance music) became the dominant force in underground British culture. An obvious progression from acid house parties was to link up with the mobile sound systems of the free festival circuit that had toured Britain since the 60s. This free rave DIY movement became an outlet for people dissatisfied with a restrictive modern society. They began to realize that if they worked together they could achieve a brand new cultural experience. These mirrored many of the previous DIY cultures, which have grown up in Britain over the decades, though this time it focused on dance music.

The summer of 1992 was the peak of the scene with an event held at Castlemorton[130] at the end of May. The party was huge with estimates of the numbers present vary from 25,000 to 40,000. The media depiction, however, was of a threatening chaos. Newspapers wrote about a dangerous new youth culture, which was getting out of control. As well as being about enjoyment, this DIY scene was political. Those involved in these free parties were often also involved in political actions, campaigning against injustices and protesting against road building for example.

By the early 90s, the Conservative government, the police, the tabloid press and middle England had all had enough of rave culture. In an attempt to combat the development of the scene, the government passed the Criminal Justice and Public Order Act (1994). This served to prevent all manner of public gatherings, particularly the rave, which they defined as, 'a gathering of one hundred plus people, at which amplified music is played which is likely to cause serious distress to the local community, in the open air and at night'.

Some sound systems found a more co-operative response from foreign authorities and the free party scene spread to many parts of the world – from Goa to the San Francisco Bay Area. In post CJA Britain, parties were increasingly difficult to organize. Many people, outraged by the draconian governmental powers that were working to prevent parties, become determined to create bigger and better events. The political impetus behind the scene developed fast. It was now as much about challenging the law as it was about dancing.

Gail, who organizes illegal parties with the DIY collective called 'Justice?' in Brighton explained that the passing of the CJA made organizers even more determined to have better parties. Justice? was born out of a desire to raise public awareness about the Criminal Justice Act. One of their first high profile initiatives was to squat in a disused courthouse and turn it into a thriving community centre. Once the inevitable eviction came, they moved their community centre to another derelict building and started again.

Another group organizing illegal raves in the early 90s was 'Exodus', which was the name for the activity of a large number of people moving from one lifestyle to another. On New Year's Eve 1992 Exodus held its largest party, with

10,000 people present. Two weeks later it supported the squatted occupation of a derelict building, Haz Manor, and started channelling money from collections at raves for renovation costs. Aiming to provide a space for homeless people and start a community farm – Exodus's Long Meadow Community Farm – this was a genuine DIY project. Organizers were not just trying to provide entertainment in the form of large scale parties but were also working to help others and build a community.

With the Criminal Justice Act in place, authorities had begun to exercize their new powers of prevention over such parties. However, as an increasing amount of violent incidents were recorded, many were of the opinion that policing methods were just too harsh. The police launched a series of operations to close down Exodus's community projects as well as the raves. Criminal charges such as drug possession followed, many of which were considered to include false allegations.

The passing of the Criminal Justice Act was seen as a means for the government to control this form of DIY youth culture. The development of free community space had the potential to threaten social stability, as these were events operated along DIY lines and following a sense of morality not prevalent at the time in British society. The Act did succeed in preventing many of the organizers from continuing such large scale parties, through many remained involved in the dance music scene today.

As one regular DJ on the free party circuit known as 'Dead Man Walking' explains, the bill has not destroyed the scene – far from it. 'DIY culture is very much alive and well in the UK, the CJA did put an end to the massive festivals such as Castlemorton but things are still happening on a smaller scale. Every weekend you can find a squat, barn or field where people will gather with soundsystems and provide themselves with entertainment that no town centre could provide. The problem is if you don't pay for your entertainment the authorities will clamp down on you, someone somewhere has to be making a buck for the authorities to allow it, look at Glastonbury now taken over by Mean Fiddler, sponsored by Orange TM with sky high ticket prices. The difference with free parties, raves or whatever you want to call them is that people are putting these events on because they enjoy it, just for the love of it if you like.

I think people are fed up of being spoon fed the latest X-factor hit, they know what they like and it isn't corporate. People nowadays are aware that music is an industry and that, as with any industry, the focus is profit orientated, so anyone with half a brain will look for alternatives. Governments know that they are in the hands of the industry so they legislate against things that damage it – for example the laws on illegal music downloads. With more laws being implemented people just have to look further afield where they can choose what they want to hear rather than just listen to what is being pumped out by the mainstream. Unfortunately with the expansion of Europe even places where the scene is relatively new, like the Czech Republic are conforming to the Western attitude that: "If there isn't money in it we won't allow it". This just makes those of us who aren't willing to be spoon-fed more angry, though, and more determined than ever to keep free parties that play decent tunes going.'[131]

Guerilla Gigging
London's live music scene was reinvigorated in 2003 with the development of guerrilla gigging. Just when it was

thought that every form of underground event had already been attempted decades before, here came a new DIY movement. Inspired by the practice of flash mobbing, the gathering of masses in public spaces in an unexpected takeover, bands have begun to call their audiences to them to participate in almost spontaneous gigs.

The origins of guerilla gigging lay in the band Jane's Addiction's decision to flash notices of London performances to fans using text messages. Soon English rockers, The Libertines, realized that this was an ingenious way of announcing their own gigs and started to use an online forum to make last minute announcements for their gigs, a way to reach their fans instantaneously.

The Others are amongst the better known instigators of this new live experience and have played guerrilla gigs in unexpected venues such as in flats and parks, on a London bus and in the Radio One foyer with a megaphone as a microphone. Martin Oldham, drummer in The Others, admits that the strangest place the band have played so far was on the London underground, 'Sitting on a tube has never been the same since after witnessing crowd surfing on the Hammersmith and City line!'[132]

Technology plays an integral part in the plans. Cryptic messages are posted on The Others' website about where the next gig will be, information can be found at the end of a mobile phone number and fans relay information via text messages. Crowds of a couple of hundred people can be summoned quickly.

Is this a publicity stunt or an innovative new live experience? Such techniques have previously been used by major record labels, who set up free concerts and public appearances that are seemingly spontaneous though meticulously planned. By organizing such events themselves and by having access to the technological means to do so, bands can bypass the marketing departments of major labels and the usual route of sending demos to promoters who run club nights, and build their own fanbases themselves. The internet has played a crucial role in this change. Bands can now easily build their own websites and through these sites distribute MP3s of their music, interacting directly with their fans via messageboards and email. It is this sense of community and personal interaction between band and audience that for many is the attraction of the guerrilla gig. 'The strength of this movement is in its community,' said Imran Ahmed of the *NME*. 'Gigs can be organized in a matter of hours. The venue, time and possible fee will be communicated via message board, text or blog; the community then congregates at a place beforehand and then all head down to the guerrilla gig together.' The band and their audience are seen by both as equals, the boundaries of consumer and creator broken down. Oldham explains this relationship between The Others and their fans, 'As a community we see no barriers between the band and the audience, the only difference between us is that we are the ones playing the songs. The community that has been built around us is very special and will probably be there for a long time to come.' To him, this sense of community is vitally important, particularly with their infamous group of fans, the 853 Kamikaze Stage Diving Division. Oldham says, ' We have a very strong relationship with our fans, and can't understand why other bands wouldn't have. Our numbers are available on the internet and our website forums are being used hourly by our fans as a centre for the community.'

They break the traditional formula of the live experience. Oldham describes his view of them as 'fraught and risqué and very close to the edge of madness, but in some ways that makes for the best performances and spectacles.'

With a guerrilla gig, no one knows quite what will happen. It is the unpredictability that attracts so many people. They are accessible, free events with the thrill of the illegal. As Sarah Bacon, of bands The Rocks and Wetdog says: 'The London gig scene has definitely changed quite a bit over the last year or so. I think people got genuinely bored of the whole Camden circuit and just decided to look for new things. I remember The Rocks did a gig with Special Needs last year at their singer's bedroom in Acton – it was bloody hilarious and not having to deal with po-faced soundmen was a definite bonus! Of course bands like The Libertines with their numerous "Albion Rooms" gigs and The Others hijacking the Hammersmith and City Line, have been in the music press a lot and there's a certain trend for gigs in squats and "guerrilla gigging" emerging.

I think this is great and definitely goes some way to perpetuate the whole punk aesthetic of breaking down the band/audience divide – I mean, I'd say most of the kids who go to Pete Doherty's gigs are probably on speaking terms with him, a far cry from the notion of the unobtainable popstar. Whether or not this has lead to more kids getting into music and forming bands I don't know, but it's exciting to see people getting involved in a way which was previously not possible. It's also nice to see some South London bands getting some attention, though I have to say that the whole New Cross scene must really be a figment of some bored journalist's imagination – as far as I'm aware the only people involved who actually live in New Cross are a few of Art Brut and perhaps Bloc Party and James from The Rocks!'[133]

Oldham views this guerilla gigging as a distinct, and new,

form of DIY culture, 'We "Did-It-Ourselves" because we had to, and we were pioneers of a new movement for this country, but our motives were based around our fans and not personal gains...we did it to create memories for the people that came to see them, it's all more crazy than your average gig at the Bull and Gate.'

Of course, the concept behind the guerrilla gig is not exactly new, its essence has existed in DIY communities for decades. It contains elements of happenings of the 50s and 60s, early punk gigs of the 70s and raves of the 80s, as well as all the other recognizably lo-fi activities which have brought audience closer to performer and operated away from the cultural mainstream. The audience is probably similar to the disenfranchised youth who has been attracted to the DIY community and its revolutionary potential.

The Future

Do-It-Yourself culture will continue to develop, following new routes, inspired by new ideas and fuelled by new participants. Examining the ideas that have been carried across the 20th century and into the 21st, it is clear that despite being influenced by previous developments in the DIY ethos, each movement adds its individual mark. With the arrival of the the internet, MP3s and digital recording, following previous advances such as photocopiers, four-track recorders and vinyl records, far more people are able to take part. *Anyone* can be a musician, a writer, a journalist, a publisher or a producer. DIY culture has always promoted the maxims of anti-elitism and, with new technology, they are truer than ever.

Of course there are flaws in the DIY approach. Some argue that without a knowledge of available alternatives many cannot even begin to take part. However, if the problem of accessibility can be overcome, if everyone who is interested can be invited to join in, the potential of this alternative culture is far reaching. This is an exciting phase in the history of the do-it-yourself approach, with new mediums emerging alongside older ideals. Music and words are of course just one aspect of this history, but by illustrating developments in these areas we can begin to chart the rise of this passionate and rebellious vision of independent culture – spreading the word to anyone who has had enough of being fed mediocre products via the mainstream media. There has never been a greater need, or a better time, to enjoy independent culture, boycott the mainstream industries and produce something more exciting yourself.

Endnotes and References

PART I

1. Wertham, Fredric, *The World of Fanzines: A Special Form of Communication*, (Carbondale: Southern Illinois University Press, 1974).

2. Romenesko, Jim, 'Fanzines Explained' (*American Journalism Review* 1993).

3. Duncombe, Stephen, *Notes from the Underground: Zines and the Politics of Alternative Culture*, (New York, Verso, 1997).

4. Vale, V, *Zines!* Vol.II (V/Search, 1997).

5. From an interview with Chip Rowe for this book (2005) (and all quotes hereafter).

6. Gunderloy, Mike and Cari Goldberg Janice, *The World of Zines: A Guide to the Independent Magazine Revolution* (London, Penguin, 1992).

7. Friedman, R Seth, *Factsheet Five Reader: Dispatches from the Edge of the Zine Revolution* (New York, Three Rivers Press, 1997).

8. From an interview with Stephen Duncombe for this book (2005).

9. From an interview with Ericka Bailie for this book (2005) (and all quotes hereafter).

10. From an interview with Elke Zobl for this book (2005) (and all quotes hereafter).

11. Teixeira, Rob, Punk-lad Love, 'Dyke-core and the Evolution of Queerculture in Canada,' *Broken Pencil 9*.

12. From an interview with Bruce La Bruce for this book (2003).

13. From an interview with Larry Bob for this book (2003).

14. From an interview with Erica Smith by Charlotte Cooper entitled 'Erica Smith Can Do Anything,' (2003).

15. From an interview with China Martens for this book (2005) (and all quotes hereafter).

16. From an interview with Betsy Greer for this book (2005) (and all quotes hereafter).

17. Railla, Jean, *Hip Home Ec: the Getcrafty Book!* (New York, Broadway Books, 2004).

18. From an interview with Amy Prior for this book (2004) (and all quotes hereafter).

19. Marr, John, 'Zines are Dead,' (*Bad Subjects,* Issue 46, December 1999).

20. From an interview with Jean Encoule for this book (2005) (and all quotes hereafter).

21. From an interview with Stephen Duncombe for this book (2005).

PART II

22. Hugo Gernsback (1884-1967). Born in Luxembourg and moved to America in 1905. He is credited as starting the modern genre of science fiction. He also wrote fiction, including the novel *Ralph 124C 41+.*

23. Edgar Rice Burroughs (1875-1950). An American author writing science-fiction and fantasy stories, probably best known for his creation of the jungle hero Tarzan.

24. Fitch, Don, 'Some Comments, History and Opinionations Concerning Fanzines and 'Zines,' (http://www.zinebook.com).

25. Louis Russell (Russ) Chauvenet (1920-2003). As an early member of Boston's 'Stranger Club', he was one of the founders of science fiction fandom and is credited with coining the term 'fanzine'.

26. Mort Weisinger (1915-1978). After this early interest in science fiction fandom, he became a magazine and comic book editor. He is most well known for being an editor of DC Comics' *Superman.*

27. Jerome (Jerry) Siegel (1914-1996). He became active in science fiction fandom during its early stages and in 1939 produced *Cosmic Stories*, an early sci-fi zine. He was co-creator of Superman.

28. Joe Shuster (1914-1992). At the age of eighteen he began to produce a science fiction magazine with his friend, Jerome Siegel. Later became famed for his co-creation of Superman.

29. From an interview with Andy Sawyer for this book (2003) (and all quotes hereafter).

30. From an interview with Ilona Jasiewicz for this book (2004).

31. From an interview with Steve Clay for this book (2005).

32. Clay, Steve and Rodney Phillips, *A Secret Location on the Lower East Side: Adventures in Writing, 1960-1980: A Sourcebook of Information* (New York, Granary Books, 1998).

33. From an interview with Steve Clay for this book (2005).

34. Jones' writing explored the experience of African-Americans and he also worked on many black civil rights projects. His most notable work was poem *Preface to a Twenty-Volume Suicide Note* (1961).

35. Hettie Cohen was a writer herself and later wrote children's books dealing with black and Native American themes.

36. Di Prima was born in 1934 in New York and now lives in San Francisco.

37. Timothy Leary (1930-1996). American writer, psychologist and radical drug campaigner. He particularly saw medical and spiritual benefits in LSD. He coined the phrase: 'Tune on, tune in, drop out'.

38. Hayward, Michael, 'Unspeakable Visions: The Beat Generation and The Bohemian Dialetic,' (1991).

39. Herbert Marshall McLuhan. (1911-1980). Influential communications theorist, interested in popular culture, advertizing and observations of everyday life.

40. Clay, Steve and Rodney Phillips, *A Secret Location on the Lower East Side: Adventures in Writing, 1960-1980: A Sourcebook of Information* (New York, Granary Books, 1998).

41. Hayward, Michael, 'Unspeakable Visions: The Beat Generation and The Bohemian Dialetic,' (August 1991).

42. Audre Lorde (1934-1992). Writer and activist, particularly famed for her poetic works.

43. From an interview with Nazmia Jamal for this book (2005).

44. Wright, Fred, 'The History and Characteristics of Zines,' (http://www.zinebook.com/resource/wright1.html).

45. The pseudonym of Sami Rosenstock (1896-1963). Born in Romania but spent most of his life in France. Credited as being a founder of the dadaist movement, producing numerous texts and manifestos. He later became involved in the surrealist movement and attempted to link marxism and surrealism, in line with his political ideals.

46. French dadaist and surrealist painter (1879-1953).

47. Wright, Fred, 'The History and Characteristics of Zines,' (http://www.zinebook.com/resource/wright1.html).

48. Held Jr, John, 'Dada to DIY: The Rise of Alternative Cultures in the 20th Century,' (http://www.mailart.com/johnheldjr/DadatoDiY.html).

49. Monte Cazazza was a performance artist from San Francisco renowned for unusual and shocking art projects. He is credited for coining the phrase 'Industrial

Music for Industrial People,' which later encapsulated sound of the Sheffield record label IndustrialRecords – noise collages and experimental sounds.

50. La Monte Young (born 1935) has been one of the most influential underground composers of the 20th century. He has pioneered extended time duration in contemporary music, contributing to the development of the minimalist style.

51. Yoko Ono entered the avant-garde art world in the early 1960s. Like many of her peers, she challenged the traditional forms of art and was an active participant in the early fluxus movement in New York.

52. Korean-born American video artist (born 1932).

53. German-born Swiss mixed media artist (1930-1998).

54. Emmett Williams (born 1925).

55. Michael, Crane and Mary Stofflet (eds), *Correspondence Art* (San Francisco, Contemporary Arts Press, 1984).

56. Toby Speiselman was one of Ray Johnson's closest friends, working for many years as the 'acting secretary' of the Correspondance School.

57. Bloch, Mark, *Ray Johnson 1927-1995: 'The Most Famous Unknown Artist in the World'* (1995).

58. Language experiments of Russian Futurist poets such as Velimir Khlebnikov and Aleksei Kruchenykh. Named in 1913, by joining the Russian prefix '*za-*' (beyond, behind) to the noun '*um*' (the mind).

59. Originally a literary movement created by Filippo Tommaso Marinetti in 1909 with the manifesto *Le Futurisme*, calling for an artistic revolution where Italians would create a new art for themselves. It became an avant-garde movement inspired by technology and war as they developed a unique art and political ideology.

60. A a small Japanese silkscreen printer, which enables the user to easily and economically print designs from a template often used in DIY craft projects.

61. Streitmatter, Rodger, *Voices of Revolution: The Dissident Press in America* (New York, Columbia University, 2001).

62. Neier, Aryeh, 'Surveillance as Censorship', Geoffrey Rips (ed), *Unamerican Activities: The Campaign Against the Underground Press* (San Francisco, City Lights Books, 1981).

63. Streitmatter, Rodger, *Voices of Revolution: The Dissident Press in America* (New York, Columbia University, 2001).

64. Rips, Geoffrey (ed), *Unamerican Activities: The Campaign Against the Underground Press* (City Lights Books: San Francisco, 1981).

65. Neier, Aryeh, 'Surveillance as Censorship', Geoffrey Rips (ed), *Unamerican Activities: The Campaign Against the Underground Press* (San Francisco, City Lights Books, 1981).

66. Wolf, Daniel and Edwin Francher, *The Village Voice Reader* (New York, Grove Press, 1963).

67. Brackman, Jacob, 'The Underground Press,' (*Playboy* August 1967).

68. From an interview with Art Kunkin for this book (2005) (and all quotes hereafter).

69. http://www.cridder.com/glue/4-22-98/editorial.html

70. Streitmatter, Rodger, *Voices of Revolution: The Dissident Press in America* (New York, Columbia University, 2001).

71. Chester Anderson (1933-1991) founded news service The Communications Company in 1967. A literary figure of the beat era, he wrote a work of science fiction entitled *The Butterfly Kid* and *Fox & Hore*, a novel set in Greenwich Village.

72. Running 1967-1981, The Liberation News Service was co-founded by Ray Mungo, Marshall Bloom and Verandah Porche, after Mungo and Bloom had left College Press Service following a dispute. LNS established links world-wide and sent twice-weekly packages of news and photographs to all member underground papers.

73. From an interview with John Lennon and Yoko Ono by Robin Blackburn and Tariq Ali for *Red Mole*, Thursday 21st January 1971 (http://homepage.ntlworld.com/carousel/pob12.html).

74. Forcade, Thomas King, *Obscenity, Who Really Cares?* (Countdown, 1971).

75. Rips, Geoffrey (ed), *Unamerican Activities: The Campaign Against the Underground Press* (San Francisco, City Lights Books, 1981).

76. From an interview with Richard Reynolds for this book (2005) (and all quotes hereafter).

77. Gross, David M, 'Zine But Not Heard,' (*Time* Magazine, 5th September, 1994).

78. Sewell, John, 'Zine Pool,' (Citypaper Online, 21st February 2001 http://www.citypaper.com/arts/story.asp?id=4143).

79. From an interview with John Holmstrom for this book (2003) (and all quotes hereafter).

80. Legs McNeil quote from various sources.

81. From an interview for this book with Jon Savage (2005) (and all quotes hereafter).

82. From an interview with Lemmy Caution from Black Time for this book (2005).

83. From an interview with Stephen Duncombe for this book (2005).

84. Duncombe, Stephen, *Notes from the Underground: Zines and the Politics of Alternative Culture* (Verso, 1997).

PART III

86. Ken Colyer (1928-1988) was Britain's leading New Orleans styled trumpeter. Chris Barber (born 1930) started up his own bands in 1948 and went on to become an influential figure, helping the careers of musicians such as Lonnie Donegan.

87. Chas McDevitt (born 1934). Along with Lonnie Donegan, The Chas McDevitt Skiffle Group were the only British skiffle players to achieve success in America.

88. From an interview with Chas McDevitt for this book (2005) (and all quotes hereafter).

89. From an interview by Jon Savage in *England's Dreaming: The Sex Pistols and Punk Rock* (Faber and Faber, 2001).

90. The band, formed in 1964, in Texas, are credited with being one of the first of the punk bands which began to emerge in America during the 60s.

91. Formed in Michigan in 1962, The Mysterians were fronted by Question Mark, who mysteriously always wore sunglasses and later legally changed his name to '?'.

92. Formed in Texas, The 13th Floor Elevators are one of the earliest psychedelic rock bands of the 60s.

93. An experimental San Francisco band of the 60s who styled themselves after the British Mods.

94. From an interview with Richard Hell for this book (2005) (and all quotes hereafter).

95. From an interview with Jon Savage for this book (2005).

96. From an interview with Jamie Reid by Jonty Adderley in 'From Punk To J18 – Jamie Reid on Protests, Art and Shamanarchy,' (www.jamiereid.uk.net).

97. A youth culture emerged in Britain during the early 50s, influenced by American rock and roll. Male youth popularizing a style of modified Edwardian style of clothes were known as 'Teddy Boys' (Teddy being a shortened form of Edward).

98. From an interview in 1981 reprinted in *The Wicked Ways of Malcolm McLaren* by Craig Bromberg (New York, Omnibus Press, 1991).

99. From an interview by Jonty Adderley in 'From Punk To J18 – Jamie Reid on Protests, Art and Shamanarchy,' (www.jamiereid.uk.net).

100. Sabin, Roger, *Punk Rock: So What?: The Cultural Legacy of Punk* (Routledge, 1999).

101. From an interview with Geoff Travis by Theresa Stern (www.furious.com/perfect/rt.html, November 1996) (and all quotes thereafter).

102. From 'The Jolt' by Lucy Toothpaste.

www.punk77.co.uk/groups/womeninpunjkoltarticle.htm

103. From an interview with John Holmstrom for this book (2003).

104. Pseudonym of Jeremy John Ratter, a drummer, writer, poet, activist and former member of Crass.

105. Unterberger, Richie, *Unknown Legends of Rock n Roll* (Miller Freeman, 1998)

106. A term coined by the British music press to describe a music scene of the early 70s, with bands such as Tangerine Dream and Faust, mixing electronic instrumentation and rock music styles.

107. Reynolds, Simon, 'Independents Day Post-Punk 1979-1981', *Uncut*, (December 2001).

108. Azerrad, Michael, *Our Band Could Be Your Life* (Little, Brown and Company, 2001) (and all quotes hereafter).

109. All quotes from Huggy Bear members taken from an interview by Fabian Ironside, for *Libeller's Almanac*.

110. Reed College located in Portland, Oregon.

111. From an interview with Jody Bleyle by Gina Arnold in *Kiss This: Punk in the Present Tense* (St Martin's Griffin, 1997).

112. From an interview with Lynn Breedlove for this book (2003).

113. From an interview with Ponyboy for this book (2005).

114. From an interview with Charlotte Cooper for this book (2005).

115. From an interview with Mike Weyld for this book (2003) (and all quotes hereafter).

116. From an interview with Matt Wobensmith for this book (2003) (and all quotes hereafter).

117. From an interview with Gina Birch by Richie Unterberger. (www.richieunterberger.com, 1996).

118. Young, Amanda, *Riot Grrrls To Spice Girls: The Commercialisation of a Phrase Meant to Instil a Sense of Individuality*, (The Burr 1998).

119. From an interview with a John Peel fan for this book (2005).

120. From an interview with Susan Carpenter for this book (2005)(and all quotes hereafter).

121. Unterberger, Richie, *Unknown Legends of Rock n Roll*, (Miller Freeman, 1998)

122. From an interview with Paul Kearney for this book (2005) (and all quotes hereafter).

123. From an interview with Delia Barnard for this book (2005).

124. From an interview with Michal Cupid of Spazoom for this book (2004).

125. A CD-R (CD-Recordable) is a writable CD on which you can save files from your computer (including music files.) This technology has been utilized by musicians recording their music straight from their computers on to CDs ready to distribute. An MP3 is a digital audio file capable of reducing the amount of data required to reproduce good quality sound. It has become a popular file to distribute via the internet, as music can be stored and played on your computer and downloaded onto MP3 players.

126. From an interview with Irene Revell for this book (2005).

127. First published in *The International Times,* March 1972.

128. From an interview with Andy from Linus for this book (2005).

129. A post-hippie, pre-punk scene, revolving around British festivals and gatherings. It contained many elements of both hippie and punk culture and included a rejection of sexism and homophobia, embracing the term 'freak'.

130. A small town in the Malvern Hills, which became the unexpected site of Britain's biggest illegal rave when 40,000 people turned up for a party organized by dance collective Spiral Tribe in May 1992.

131. From an interview with DJ Alisdair McGibbon aka 'Dead Man Walking' for this book (2005).

132. From an interview with Martin Oldham for this book (2005).

133. From an interview with Sarah Bacon for this book (2005).

Further Resources

The Zine Revolution

Personal Zines

Cometbus, Aaron, *Despite Everything: A Cometbus Omnibus* (Last Gasp, 2002).

Hoff, A L, *Thrift Score: The Stuff, The Method, The Madness* (Perennial, 1997).

Wertham, Fredric, *The World of Fanzines: A Special Form of Communication* (Southern Illinois University Press, 1974).

Duplex Planet www.duplexplanet.com

Community

Block, Francesca Lia and Hillary Carlip, *Zine Scene: The Do It Yourself Guide to Zines* (Girl Press, 1998).

Brent, Bill, *Make a Zine!* (Black Books, 1997).

Daly, Steven and Nathaniel Wice, *Alt.Culture: An A-to-Z Guide to the 90s Underground, Online and Over-the Counter* (Fourth State 1995).

Duncombe, Stephen, *Notes from Underground: Zines and the Politics of Alternative Culture* (Verso, 1997).

Farrelly, Liz, *Zines* (Booth Clibborn, 2001).

Friedman, R. Seth: *The Factsheet Five Zine Reader: Dispatches from the Edge of the Zine Revolution* (Three Rivers Press, 1997).

Gunderloy, Mike and Carl Goldberg Janice: *The World of Zines. A Guide to the Independent Magazine Revolution* (Penguin Books, 1992).

Rowe, Chip, *Book of Zines. Readings from the Fringe* (Henry Holt and Co, 1997).

Sabin, Roger and Teal Triggs, *Below Critical Radar: Fanzines and Alternative Comics From 1976 to Now* (Codex Books, 2002).

Vale, V, *Zines! Vol.1 and 2* (V/Search, 1996).

Clamor Magazine (home of the Zine Yearbook) www.clamormagazine.org

Riot Grrrl and Feminist Zines

Karp, Marcelle and Debbie Stoller, *The BUST guide to the New Girl Order* (Penguin Books, 1999).

Mitchell, Allyson, Lisa Bryn Rundle and Lara Karaian: *Turbo Chicks: Talking Young Feminisms* (Sumach Press, 2001).

Robbins, Trina. *From Girls to Grrrlz: A History of Women's Comics From Teens to Zines* (Chronicle, 1999).

Smith, Erica, *The Girl Frenzy Millennial* (Slab-O-Concrete Publications, 1998).

Taormio, Tristan and Karen Green, *Girls Guide to Taking Over the World: Writings From The Girl Zine Revolution* (St. Martin's Griffin, 1997).

Mama Zines

Arnoldi, Katherine, *The Amazing True Story of a Teenage Single Mom* (Hyperion Books, 1998).

Gore, Ariel, *The Essential Hip Mama: Writing from the Cutting Edge of Parenting,* (Seal Press, 2004).

Craft

Railla, Jean, *Get Crafty: Hip Home Ec.* (Broadway Books, 2004).

www.craftivism.com, www.craftster.com and www.getcrafty.com

The History of Self-Publishing

Beat Generation

Michael Rumaker, *Black Mountain Days* (Black Mountain Press, 2003).

Harris, Mary Emma, *The Arts at Black Mountain* (MIT Press, 2002).

City Lights www.citylights.com

Fiction Zines

Clay, Steve and Rodney Phillips, *A Secret Location on the Lower East Side: Adventures in Writing, 1960-1980; A Sourcebook of Information* (Granary Books, 1998).

Kennedy, Pagan, *Zine: How I Spent Six Years of My Life in the Underground and Finally...Found Myself...I Think* (St Martin's Press, 1995).

Rose, Joel and Catherine Texier, *Between C and D: New Writing from the Lower East Side Fiction Magazine* (Penguin, 1988).

Artists and the Zine

De Salvo, Donna and Catherine Gudis, *Ray Johnson: Correspondences,* (Flammarion, 1999).

Held Jr, John, *Mail Art: An Annotated Bibliography,* (Scarecrow Press, 1991).

Johnson, Ray, *Ray Johnson: How Sad Am I Today* (University of British Columbia Press, 2001).

The Radicals

Leamer, Laurence, *The Paper Revolutionaries: The Rise of the Underground Press* (Simon and Schuster, 1972).

Makepeace, Jo, "*Schnews at Ten*": *Ten Years of Party and Protest in Britain* (Justice, 2004).

McAuliffe, Kevin, *The Great American Newspaper: The Rise and Fall of the Village Voice* (Scriber, 1978).

Rips, Geoffrey, *Unamerican Activities: The Campaign Against the Underground Press* (City Lights, 1981).

Seeger, Arthur, *The Berkeley Barb: Social Control of an Underground Newsroom* (Irvington Publishers, 1983).

Schnews, *Schnewsround: The Inside Story from the Direct Action Frontline* (Justice, 1996).

Stokes, Geoffrey, *The Village Voice Anthology (1956-1980): Twenty-five Years of Writing From The Village Voice* (William Morrow and Company, 1982).

Streitmatter, Rodger, *Voices of Revolution: The Dissident Press in America* (Columbia University, 2001).

Wolf, Daniel and Edwin Francher, *The Village Voice Reader* (Grove Press, 1963).

Guerilla Newsreporting

Adbusters www.adbusters.org

Alternative Press Center (APC) www.altpress.org

Guerilla News www.guerillanews.com

Independent News Collective (INK) www.ink.uk.com

Independent Media Center www.indymedia.org

Schnews www.schnews.org.uk

Music Zines

Holmstrom, John, *Punk: The Original: A Collection of Material from the First, Best, and Greatest Punk Zine of All Time* (High Times Press, 1998).

Perry, Mark, *Sniffin' Glue: The Essential Punk Accessory* (Sanctuary Press, 2000) and *Action Time Vision: The Story of Sniffin' Glue, Alternative TV and Punk Rock* (Helter Skelter, 2004).

Sinker, Daniel, *Punk Planet: The Collected Interviews* (Akashic Books, 2001).

Vale, V, *Search and Destroy: Authoritative Guide to Punk Culture* (V/Search, 1996).

Maximumrocknroll. www.maximrocknroll.com

The Rise of Lo-fi Music

Skiffle

Dewe, Mike, *The Skiffle Craze* (Planet, 1998).

McDevitt, Chas, *Skiffle: The Roots of UK Rock* (Robson Books, 1998).

Punk

Bockris, Victor, Beat Punks, (Da Capo Press, 1988).

Boot, Adrian and Chris Salewicz, *Punk: the Illustrated History of a Music Revolution* (Penguin Studio, 1996).

Savage, Jon, *England's Dreaming: Sex Pistols and Punk Rock* (Faber & Faber, 1991)

Punk Planet www.punkplanet.com

Post-punk

Azerrad, Michael, *Our Band Could Be Your Life: Scenes from the American Indie Underground 1981-1991* (Little Brown, 2002).

Blush, Steven, *American Hardcore: A Tribal History* (Feral House, 2001).

Coon, Caroline. *1988: The New Wave Punk Rock Explosion* (Omnibus Press, c1977, 1982).

Marcus, Greil, *Lipstick Traces, A Secret History of the 20th Century* (Harvard University Press, 1989).

O'Brien, Lucy, *She Bop: the Definitive History of Women in Rock, Pop and Soul* (Penguin 1995).

and *She Bop II* (Continuum International Publishing Group, 2003).

McNeil, Legs and Gilian McCain, *Please Kill Me: The Uncensored Oral History of Punk* (Penguin, 1997)

Women in Punk and Riot Grrrl

Baumgardner, Jennifer and Amy Richards, *Manifesta: Young Women, Feminism, and the Future* (Farrar, Straus and Giroux, 2000)

Findlen, Barbara, *Listen Up: Voices From the Next Feminist Generation* (Seal Press, 1995.

Gaar, Gillian G. *She's A Rebel: The History Of Women In Rock & Roll* (Seal Press, 1992).

Juno, Andrea, *Angry Women in Rock* (Re/Search Publications, 1991).

Raphael, Amy, *Grrrls: Women Rewrite Rock* (St. Martin's Griffin, 1994) and *Never Mind the Bollocks: Women Rewrite Rock* (Virago, 1995).

Whiteley, Shelia, *Sexing the Groove: Popular Music and Gender* (Routledge, 1007).

Rave

McKay, George, *DIY Culture: Party and Protest in 90s Britain* (London, Verso, 1998).

Pirate Radio

Braga, Newton C, *Pirate Radio and Video: Experimental Transmitter Projects* (Newnes, 2000).

Carpenter, Sue, *40 Watts from Nowhere: A Journey Into Pirate Radio* (Scribner Book Company, (2004).

Chapman, Robert, *Selling the Sixties: Pirates and Pop Music Radio* (Routledge, 1992).

Teflon, Zeke, *The Complete Manual of Pirate Radio* (Sharp Press, 1994).

Yoder, Andrew R, *Pirate Radio Stations: Tuning in to Underground Broadcasts* (McGraw-Hill Education, 1988).

Internet

Alderman, John, *Sonic Boom: Napster, MP3 and the New Pioneers of Music,* (Fourth Estate, 2001).